T0143392

Agile Model-Based Development Using UML-RSDS

Agile Model-Based Development Using UML-RSDS

Kevin Lano
Department of Informatics
King's College London, London
United Kingdom

CRC Press
Taylor & Francis Group
Boca Raton   London   New York

CRC Press is an imprint of the
Taylor & Francis Group, an **informa** business

A SCIENCE PUBLISHERS BOOK

CRC Press
Taylor & Francis Group
6000 Broken Sound Parkway NW, Suite 300
Boca Raton, FL 33487-2742

© 2017 by Taylor & Francis Group, LLC
CRC Press is an imprint of Taylor & Francis Group, an Informa business

No claim to original U.S. Government works

Printed on acid-free paper
Version Date: 20160701

International Standard Book Number-13: 978-1-4987-5222-0 (Hardback)

Visit the Taylor & Francis Web site at
http://www.taylorandfrancis.com

and the CRC Press Web site at
http://www.crcpress.com

Preface

Model-based development is moving into the mainstream of software engineering, and it is an approach that all software developers should know about as one option to use in solving software problems. In this book we give a practical introduction to model-based development, model transformations and agile development, using a UML and Java-based toolset, UML-RSDS. Guidance on applying model-based development in a range of domains is provided, and many examples are given to illustrate the UML-RSDS process and techniques. The book is suitable both for professional software engineers and for postgraduate and undergraduate teaching.

I would like to acknowledge the contributions of my research team members and colleagues who have helped in the development of the UML-RSDS tools and method: Kelly Androutsopoulos, Pauline Kan, Shekoufeh Kolahdouz-Rahimi, Sobhan Yassipour-Tehrani, Hessa Alfraihi, David Clark, Howard Haughton, Tom Maibaum, Iman Poernomo, Jeffery Terrell and Steffen Zschaler. The support of Imperial College London, King's College London and the EPSRC is also acknowledged.

I dedicate this book to my wife, Olga.

Contents

Chapter 1

Introduction

In this chapter we introduce model-based development and UML-RSDS, and discuss the context of software development which motivates the use of such methods and tools.

1.1 Model-based development using UML-RSDS

Model-based development (MBD) is an approach which aims to improve the practice of software development by (i) enabling systems to be defined in terms closer to their requirements, abstracted from and independent of particular implementation platforms, and (ii) by automating development steps, including the writing of executable code.

A large number of MBD approaches, tools and case studies now exist, but industrial uptake of MBD has been restricted by the complexity and imprecision of modelling languages such as UML, and by the apparent resource overheads without benefit of many existing MBD methods and tools [3, 5, 6, 7, 8].

UML-RSDS[1] has been designed as a lightweight and agile MBD approach which can be applied across a wide range of application areas. We have taken account of criticisms of existing MBD approaches and tools, and given emphasis on the aspects needed to support practical use such as:

- *Lightweight method and tools*: usable as an aid for rapidly developing parts of a software system, to the degree which developers

---

[1] 'Rigorous Specification, Design and Synthesis', although 'Rapid Specification, Design and Synthesis' would also be appropriate.

find useful. It does not require a radical change in practice or the adoption of a new complete development process, or the use of MBD for all aspects of a system.

■ *Independent* of other MBD methods or environments, such as Eclipse/EMF.

■ *Non-specialist*: UML-RSDS uses only a core subset of UML class diagram and use case notations, which are the most widely-known parts of UML.

■ *Agile*: incremental changes to systems can be made rapidly via their specifications, and the changes propagated to code.

■ *Precise*: specifications in UML-RSDS have a precise semantics, which enables reliable code production in multiple languages.

The benefits of our MBD approach are:

■ Reduction in coding cost and time.

■ The ability to model an application domain, to define a DSL (domain specific language) for a domain, and to define custom code generators for the domain.

■ Reducing the gap between specification and code, so that the consequences of requirements and specification choices can be identified at an early development stage.

■ The ability to optimize systems at the platform-independent modelling level, to avoiding divergence between code and models caused by manual optimization of generated code.

■ The ability to formally analyse DSLs and systems at the specification stage.

These capabilities potentially reduce direct software development costs, and costs caused by errors during development and errors persisting in delivered products. Both time-to-market and product quality are potentially improved.

Figure 1.1 shows the software production process which is followed using UML-RSDS: specifications are defined using UML class diagrams and use cases, these can be analysed for their internal quality and correctness, and then platform-independent designs are synthesised (these use a pseudocode notation for a subset of UML Activity diagram notation). From these designs executable code in a particular object-oriented programming language (currently, Java, C# or C++) can then be automatically synthesised.

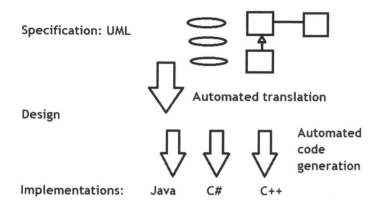

Figure 1.1: UML-RSDS software production process

Unlike many other MBD approaches, which involve the management of multiple models of a system, UML-RSDS specifies systems using a single integrated Use Case and Class Diagram model. This simplifies the specification and design processes and aligns the approach to Agile development practices which are also based on maintaining a single system model (usually the executable code).

Some typical uses of UML-RSDS could be:

■ Modelling the business logic of an application and automatically generating the code for this, in Java, C# or C++.

■ Modelling and code generation of a component within a larger system, the remainder of which could be developed using traditional methods.

■ Defining a model transformation, such as a migration, refinement, model analysis, model comparison, integration or refactoring, including the definition of custom code generators.

UML-RSDS is also useful for teaching UML, OCL, and MBD and agile development principles and techniques, and has been used on undergraduate and Masters courses for several years. In this book we include guidance on the use of the tools to support such courses. An important property of MBD tools is that the code they produce should be *correct*, *reliable* and *efficient*: the code should accurately implement the specification, and should contain no unintended functionality or behaviour. To meet this requirement, the UML-RSDS code generators have been developed to use a proven code-generation strategy which both ensures correctness and efficiency.

In the following chapters, we illustrate development in UML-RSDS using a range of examples (Chapter 2), describe in detail the UML notations used (Chapters 3, 4 and 5) and the process of design synthesis adopted (Chapter 6). Chapter 7 describes how model transformations can be expressed in UML-RSDS. An illustrative example of UML-RSDS development is given in Chapter 8.

Chapter 9 describes design patterns and refactorings that are supported by UML-RSDS. Chapter 10 explains how UML-RSDS systems can be composed. Chapters 11, 12 and 13 describe how migration, refinement and refactoring transformations can be defined in UML-RSDS. Chapters 14 and 15 describe how bidirectional, incremental and exploratory transformations can be defined in UML-RSDS. Chapters 16, 17 and 18 describe in detail the development process in UML-RSDS, following an agile MBD approach. The development of specialised forms of system is covered in Chapters 19 (reactive systems) and 20 (enterprise information systems).

Chapter 21 describes how the tools can be used to support UML, MBD and agile development courses, and gives examples of case studies and problems that can be used in teaching.

The Appendix gives technical details of the UML-RSDS notations and tool architecture.

1.2   The 'software crisis'

The worldwide demand for software applications has been growing at an increasing pace as computer and information technology is used pervasively in more and more areas: in mobile devices, apps, embedded systems in vehicles, cloud computing, health informatics, finance, enterprise information systems, web services and web applications, and so forth. Both the pace of change, driven by new technologies, and the complexity of systems are increasing. However, the production of software remains a primarily manual process, depending upon the programming skills of individual developers and the effectiveness of development teams. This labour-intensive process is becoming too slow and inefficient to provide the software required by the wide range of organisations which utilize information systems as a central part of their business and operations. The quality standards for software are also becoming higher as more and more business-critical and safety-critical functionalities are taken on by software applications.

These issues have become increasingly evident because of high-profile and highly expensive software project failures, such as the multi-billion pound costs of the integrated NHS IT project in the UK [4].

New practices such as agile development and model-based development have been introduced into the software industry in an attempt to improve productivity and quality. Agile development tries to optimize the manual production of software by using short cycles of development, and by improving the organization of development teams and their interaction with customers. This approach remains dependent on developer skills, and subject to the limits which hand-crafting of software systems places on the rate of software production. Considerable time and resources are also consumed by the extensive testing and verification used in agile development.

Model-based development, and especially model-driven development (MDD) attempts to automate as much of the software development process as possible, and to raise the level of abstraction of development so that manually-intensive activities are focussed upon the construction and analysis of *models*, free from implementation details, instead of upon executable code. *Model transformations* are an essential part of MBD and MDD, providing automated refactoring of models and automated production of code from models, and many other operations on models. Transformations introduce the possibility of producing, semi-automatically, many different platform-specific versions of a system from a single platform-independent high-level specification of a system.

MBD certainly has considerable potential for industrializing software development. However, problems remain with most of the current MBD approaches:

- The development process may be heavyweight and inflexible, involving multiple models – such as the several varieties of behaviour models in UML – which need to be correlated and maintained together.

- Support tools may be highly complex and not be interoperable with each other, requiring transformation 'bridges' from tool to tool, which increases the workload and possibilities for introducing errors into development.

- The model-based viewpoint conflicts with the code-centered focus of traditional development and of traditional computer science education.

For these reasons we have aimed to make UML-RSDS a lightweight and agile MBD approach which requires minimum development machinery, and which provides simple tool support for MBD, interoperable with external tools for analysis and verification. We have also endeavoured to make the tools compatible with traditional practices, so that developers can use UML-RSDS in combination with conventional coding. We report on experiences of use of UML-RSDS for education and in industry in Chapter 21.

1.3   Model-based development concepts

MBD is founded, naturally enough, on the concept of *models*. The dictionary definition of a model is:

> Something that represents another thing, either as a physical object that is usually smaller than the real object, or as a simple description that can be used in calculations. (Cambridge Advanced Dictionary, 2015)

Models are representations of actual artifacts (cars, bridges, buildings, executable software systems, and even living organisms [1]) which are used to analyse, simulate and document the artifacts. The representations can be physical scale models or prototypes, diagrams or mathematical models, or computer simulations.

In this book we are concerned with models of real-world data and entities, and with models of processing on these data and entities, to be implemented in software. The models will be either visual representations in a subset of the Unified Modelling Language (UML) [2] or textual representations (in pseudocode). These models can be used in discussions between the stakeholders of a software system (customers, users, clients) and developers, to agree on the scope and functionality of the system, and to precisely express the system requirements. Models can also be checked for validity (that they are internally consistent and satisfy other properties). In UML-RSDS, models serve as a description of the system design and can be used to generate the design and executable implementations of the system in multiple programming languages, with minimal human intervention.

A key principle of UML-RSDS is that *"The specification is the system"*, and that development work should be focussed upon defining a correct specification, instead of upon low-level coding.

For example, Fig. 1.2 shows part of a UML class diagram model for the data typically found in a university teaching administration system: such a system will record what are the courses on offer, who teaches the courses, and which students are attending which courses. This could be an initial model of the data of the system, and should be enriched with further attributes (such as the year of a student, and the level of a course) and classes (such as a representation of degree programmes). Even in this outline form it already conveys some information about the data, for example, that each course has a single lecturer and that each student belongs to a single department, whilst a department has sets *students* of *Students*, *courses* of *Courses* and *staff* of *Lecturers*. The UML-RSDS tools can check that this model is a valid class diagram, and generate outline Java, C# and C++ code from the diagram.

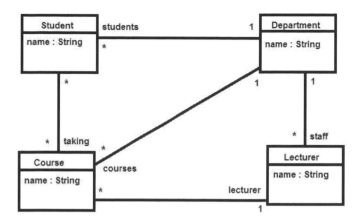

Figure 1.2: Class diagram example

The generated Java code for the Course class is:

```
class Course
{ private String name = "";
  private Lecturer lecturer;

  public Course(Lecturer lecturerx)
  { lecturer = lecturerx; }

  public String getname()
  { return name; }

  public void setname(String namex)
  { name = namex; }

  ... other update and query operations ...
}
```

The model abstracts from code details (for example, the visibilities *private* and *public* of Java instance variables and operations) and presents a logical view of the data manipulated and stored by the system. Thus it is potentially easier for stakeholders to understand than the code. The model also has a precise mathematical semantics (as we discuss in Chapter 18), enabling formal verification and analysis of the system if required.

Model-based Development is a term for those software development approaches where models are an essential part of the development process. UML-RSDS could be termed a *Model-driven Development* (MDD) approach, which are those MBD approaches where models are the primary artifact used in development, and code production is mainly automated. Another, closely related, MDD approach is the Model-driven Architecture (MDA), an OMG standard (www.omg.org/mda) for MBD using the UML. MDA is based on the idea of separating Platform Independent Models (PIMs) from Platform-specific Models (PSMs) of a system: a developer should express the logical business data and rules in a platform-independent manner using UML notations such as class diagrams, then, for the required implementation platforms, map these PIMs to PSMs for the specific platforms. From the PSMs code can be generated automatically (Fig. 1.3).

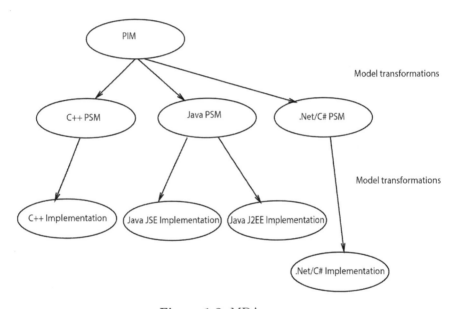

Figure 1.3: MDA process

Compared to UML-RSDS, MDA is broader in scope: the UML-RSDS specification in Fig. 1.1 is only independent of platform across the range of Java-like languages: a single PSM representation (the design) is used for all these languages. The PIM to PSM step in MDA may only be semi-automated, whilst the specification to design step in UML-RSDS is highly automated, and developers do not need to manually construct a PSM.

Summary

In this chapter we have introduced the concepts of model-based development and agile development. We have described UML-RSDS, and we gave the motivation for the UML-RSDS approach.

References

[1] OpenWorm project, www.artificialbrains.com/openworm, 2015.

[2] M. Fowler and K. Scott, *UML Distilled: Applying the Standard Object Modeling Language*, Addison-Wesley, 2003.

[3] J. Hutchinson, J. Whittle, M. Rouncefield and S. Kristoffersen, *Empirical Assessment of MDE in Industry*, ICSE 11, ACM, 2011.

[4] The Independent, *NHS pulls the plug on its £11bn IT system*, 3 August 2011.

[5] M. Petre, *"No shit" or "Oh, shit!": responses to observations on the use of UML in professional practice*, Softw Syst Model, 13: 1225–1235, 2014.

[6] B. Selic, *What will it take? A view on adoption of model-based methods in practice*, Software systems modeling, 11: 513–526, 2012.

[7] A. Vallecillo, *On the Industrial Adoption of Model Driven Engineering*, International Journal of Information Systems and Software Engineering for Big Companies, Vol. 1, No. 1, pp. 52–68, 2014.

[8] J. Whittle, J. Hutchinson and M. Roucefield, *The state of practice in Model-driven Engineering*, IEEE Software, pp. 79–85, May/June 2014.

Chapter 2

Overview of Development Using UML-RSDS

In this chapter we give an overview of the UML-RSDS development approach by means of some simple examples illustrating the different ways in which it can be used in software development: to develop components in a larger system, to develop self-contained applications, or to define model transformations.

2.1 Component development: statistical correlation calculator

As part of a system development it may be necessary to create some utility components which provide services to other parts of the system, but which are otherwise independent of the system. These components could therefore be reused in other systems.

In this section we describe such a component which carries out a numerical computation of the *Pearson correlation coefficient* between two sets of values: a measure of how linearly dependent one set of values is on the other. This computation could be used in a wide range of data analysis applications. Figure 2.1 shows the class diagram of this component.

This diagram means that each *CorrelationCalculator* has an associated sequence *datapoints* of *DataPoint* objects, each of which has an x and y coordinate in a graph (for example, as in Fig. 2.2). The x coordinate values of the data points represents one set of values, to be compared with another set, represented by the y coordinate values.

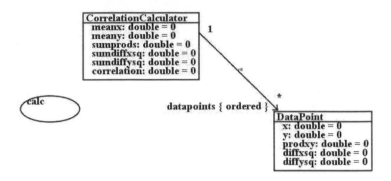

Figure 2.1: Correlation calculator class diagram

There are other auxiliary data items which are used to store properties of the dataset as a whole, such as the mean values *meanx* and *meany* of the x and y coordinates of data points. The Pearson correlation of the x and y values in this example is 0.91, indicating that there is a strong positive linear correlation between the values.

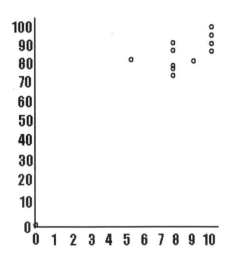

Figure 2.2: Correlation example

The calculator component has (initially at least) just one use case, *calc*, which can be described informally as:

Compute the Pearson correlation coefficient

$$P = \frac{\Sigma_d(x_d - \overline{x})(y_d - \overline{y})}{\sqrt{(\Sigma_d(x_d - \overline{x})^2 \Sigma_d(y_d - \overline{y})^2)}}$$

of a non-empty (at least 2 points) series of real-valued data points (x_d, y_d), where at least 2 points have different x_d values, and at least 2 have different y_d values.

Use cases express the functional capabilities or services which a system/component provides. This informal use case can be specified by a UML use case *calc*, represented as an oval in Fig. 2.1. In UML-RSDS use cases are shown together with the class diagram of the data that they operate upon,[1] and the relations between the use cases and classes can also be displayed on the diagram.

UML-RSDS use cases can be given a *precondition* or assumption: a logical condition that should be satisfied before the use case can be invoked. For the correlation calculator, the precondition is the constraint that there are two or more data points, not all of which are vertically aligned or horizontally aligned:

$datapoints.size > 1$ &
$datapoints \rightarrow exists(d1 \mid datapoints \rightarrow exists(d2 \mid d1.x \neq d2.x))$ &
$datapoints \rightarrow exists(d1 \mid datapoints \rightarrow exists(d2 \mid d1.y \neq d2.y))$

on *CorrelationCalculator*.

The functionality of a use case is defined by a series of *postcondition* constraints, which describe the logical processing steps that the use case should carry out in order to achieve its complete functionality. The conjunction of these postconditions also defines the final state achieved at termination of the use case. For *calc* we can define the following series (1), (2), (3), (4) of postcondition constraints on *CorrelationCalculator*. (1) is:

$meanx = datapoints.x \rightarrow sum()/datapoints.size$ &
$meany = datapoints.y \rightarrow sum()/datapoints.size$

This first constraint computes the mean x and y values, $\bar{x}$ and $\bar{y}$.

(2) :
$\quad d : datapoints \Rightarrow$
$\qquad d.prodxy = (d.x - meanx) * (d.y - meany)$ &
$\qquad d.diffxsq = (d.x - meanx) * (d.x - meanx)$ &
$\qquad d.diffysq = (d.y - meany) * (d.y - meany)$

This constraint computes, for each datapoint d, the values of $(x_d - \bar{x})(y_d - \bar{y})$, $(x_d - \bar{x})^2$ and $(y_d - \bar{y})^2$. A constraint $P \Rightarrow Q$ has the intuitive meaning "if P is true, Q should also be true". P is called the *antecedent* or *condition* of the constraint, Q is its *succedent*. d here is an additional

---

[1] In standard UML they are shown in separate diagrams.

quantified variable – the constraint is applied for each possible value of d in *datapoints*, for each *CorrelationCalculator*.

(3) :
$$sumprods = datapoints.prodxy \rightarrow sum() \ \&$$
$$sumdiffxsq = datapoints.diffxsq \rightarrow sum() \ \&$$
$$sumdiffysq = datapoints.diffysq \rightarrow sum()$$

This constraint computes the main terms of the correlation calculation.

(4) :
$$sumdiffxsq > 0 \ \& \ sumdiffysq > 0 \ \Rightarrow$$
$$correlation = sumprods/(sumdiffxsq * sumdiffysq) \rightarrow sqrt()$$

This constraint computes the final correlation result, if it is well-defined.

The postcondition constraints define the successive steps of the correlation calculation, computing the data averages and standard deviations. The final result is placed in the *correlation* attribute. At termination of the use case, *all of the postconditions are true*, so that *correlation* expresses the correct correlation value according to the original formula.

This example illustrates a key principle of UML-RSDS:

A postcondition constraint P means "Make P true" when interpreted as a specification of system behaviour.

The implementation of *calc* must make all the postconditions true, and hence solve the problem. The order of the postconditions is not logically significant, but provides a guide to the design synthesis and code generation process. The ordering of the postconditions will normally result in synthesised code which sequentially executes the corresponding code fragments. The constraints should be ordered so that data is defined before it is used – as with attributes such as *meanx* and *prodxy* in the above example.

The precondition of the *calc* use case can be derived from the *definedness* conditions of its postcondition constraints (Chapter 18), in this case that both *sumdiffxsq* and *sumdiffysq* are positive. In turn, this means that at least one *d.diffxsq* and at least one *d.diffysq* term are non-zero, which is ensured by the formalised use case precondition.

From this specification, a platform-independent design can be generated using the Generate Design option on the UML-RSDS Synthesis menu (Fig. 2.3). Language-specific code can then be synthesised in Java, C# or C++ for incorporation of this component in a number of different systems: an API to the component is provided by the Controller class in the generated code.

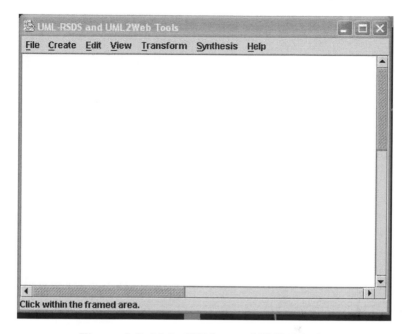

Figure 2.3: Main GUI frame of UML-RSDS

Table 2.1 shows the efficiency of the calculator on different input sizes, using the Java 4, Java 6 and C# generated code. Since the constraints can each be implemented by a bounded loop (Chapter 6), a linear increase in execution time with input size is expected, and this is observed. The Java 6 implementation seems generally to be the most efficient.

Table 2.1: Test results for correlation calculator

Input size	Java 4	Java 6	C#
1000 data points	16ms	16ms	5ms
10,000 data points	47ms	26ms	21ms
50,000 data points	78ms	51ms	59ms
100,000 data points	141ms	63ms	105ms

2.2 Application development: Sudoku solver

This system tries to solve a partially completed Sudoku puzzle, and identifies if the puzzle is unsolvable. For simplicity, we consider 4-by-4 puzzles, but the approach should work (in principle) for any size of puzzles. The board is divided into four columns, four rows and four 2-by-2 corner subparts, each column, row and subpart must be completely filled with the numbers 1, 2, 3, 4, without duplicates, to solve the puzzle. The following shows a partially completed board, where 0 is used to mark an unfilled square.

```
2 1 0 0
0 0 0 0
0 0 0 0
0 0 0 3
```

The following strategies could be used to fill in the blank squares:

■ (R1): if a blank square is restricted by the Sudoku rules to only have one possible value *val*, then set its value to *val*.

■ (R2): if there is a choice of two or more values for a blank square, make a random choice amongst these and put on the square.

■ (R3): if there is no possible value that can be used for a blank square, abandon the solution attempt.

R1 should be applied as many times as possible before applying R2. This is an effective strategy in many cases, although it does not provide any facility for backtracking and undoing choices made by R2. We will consider a backtracking approach in Chapter 15.

The data of a Sudoku puzzle can be formalised as a class diagram (Fig. 2.4), and the above informal rules expressed as postconditions of use cases *solve* (for R1 and R2) and *check* (for R3) operating on this class diagram.

A query operation of *Square* is defined to return the set of possible values for the square:

```
Square::
query possibleValues() : Set(int)
post:
  result = Integer.subrange(1,4) - parts.elements.value
```

Integer.subrange(a,b) is the sequence Sequence{a, ..., b} of integers from a up to b, inclusive. The result of *possibleValues* is the set of values in 1..4 which are not already on some square in the board parts

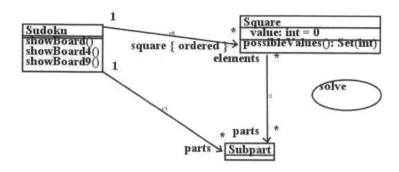

Figure 2.4: Sudoku class diagram

in which the square itself occurs (there are always three such parts: one row, one column and one of the four 2-by-2 corner regions).

An operation *showBoard* of the *Sudoku* class displays the board state:

```
Sudoku::
showBoard()
pre: true
post:
  ( square[1].value + " " + square[2].value + " " +
    square[3].value + " " + square[4].value )->display() &
  ( square[5].value + " " + square[6].value + " " +
    square[7].value + " " + square[8].value )->display() &
  ( square[9].value + " " + square[10].value + " " +
    square[11].value + " " + square[12].value )->display() &
  ( square[13].value + " " + square[14].value + " " +
    square[15].value + " " + square[16].value )->display() &
  ""->display()
```

R1 can then be formalised by a constraint (C1) iterating over the *Sudoku* class:

```
sq : square & sq.value = 0 &
v = sq.possibleValues() & v.size = 1  =>
                sq.value = v->min() & self.showBoard()
```

This can be read as "for all squares sq on the board, if the square is blank, and the set v of possible values has a single element, set the square value to that value". v here is a *Let-variable*, a read-only identifier which holds the value of its defining expression, *sq.possibleValues()*, so that this expression only needs to be evaluated once in the constraint. The board is also displayed to the console after the update.

$R2$ can be formalised as constraint $C2$:

```
sq : square & sq.value = 0 &
v = sq.possibleValues() & v.size > 0  =>
                    sq.value = v->min() & self.showBoard()
```

This is very similar to $C1$, but handles the case where there is more than one possible value for sq.

Finally, $R3$ is formalised by $C3$:

```
sq : square & sq.value = 0 &
v = sq.possibleValues() & v.size = 0  =>
    ("No possible value for square: " + sq)->display()
    & self.showBoard()
```

$C1$ is our first example of a constraint which both reads and writes the same data (the values of squares) and which therefore requires a *fixed-point iteration* implementation: while the assumption

```
sq : square & sq.value = 0 & v = sq.possibleValues() &
v.size = 1
```

remains true for some $sq : square$, the conclusion

```
    sq.value = v->min() & self.showBoard()
```

is performed. At termination of $C1$, the assumption is false for all squares, and so no square has a unique possible value, i.e.:

```
sq : square & sq.value = 0 & v = sq.possibleValues()  =>
v.size /= 1
```

for all sq.

This example also illustrates the key principle:

> *A postcondition constraint P means "Make P true" when interpreted as a specification of system behaviour.*

In this case, the principle means that the implementation of a constraint such as $C1$ must continue to apply the constraint to elements of the model (Sudoku squares) until it is true for all elements: while there is any square with a unique possible value, the constraint implementation will continue to execute, to try to make the conclusion of $C1$ true for such squares. At termination, the constraint $C1$ is therefore established for all squares, because there is no square for which the antecedent/condition of $C1$ is true.

Logically, the succedent of $C1$ contradicts the antecedent (because $value = 0$ in the antecedent, but is set to a non-zero value in the succedent). So the constraint has the form

$$\forall\, x : S \cdot (P \Rightarrow not(P))$$

The only way to establish $P \Rightarrow not(P)$ is to establish $not(P)$. Thus a specification using a constraint such as $C1$ does have a precise meaning, even though it may seem contradictory at first sight.

Such constraints are pervasively used for refactoring transformations and active systems such as game-playing programs, problem solvers and other software 'agents' because they directly express requirements of the form "If there is an unwanted situation s, then make changes to remove or correct s":

Unwanted situation s $\quad\Rightarrow\quad$ *Make changes to remove/correct s*

Here, the unwanted situation is a blank square on the board.

$C2$ is very similar to $C1$. Because $C2$ writes data which $C1$ reads, they are inter-dependent (a choice made by $C2$ will typically enable some new applications of $C1$) and so (if they are defined in the same use case) they will be grouped together into a single fixed-point iteration with the behaviour $(C1*;\ C2)*$, i.e.: "Apply $C1$ repeatedly as many times as possible, then apply $C2$, and repeat this process as many times as possible". This behaviour only terminates when no square satisfies either the assumption of $C1$ or $C2$, this means that either all squares are filled, or that some blank square has no possible value. $C3$ will show which squares, if any, satisfy the latter case. $C3$ itself does not update any data that it reads (or indeed any data at all), so can be given a bounded (for loop) iteration, as with the constraints of the correlation calculator. All of these design choices are performed automatically by the "Generate Design" option of the tools. More details on this process are given in Chapter 6.

An example execution of this system is shown below:

```
2 1 0 4    <- applied C1 to choose 4
0 0 0 0
0 0 0 0
0 0 0 3

2 1 3 4    <- applied C1 to choose 3
0 0 0 0
0 0 0 0
0 0 0 3
```

```
2 1 3 4
3 4 0 0    <- applied C2 to choose 3; C1 to choose 4
0 0 0 0
0 0 0 3

2 1 3 4
3 4 0 0
0 0 0 0
0 2 0 3    <- applied C1 to choose 2

2 1 3 4
3 4 0 0
0 3 0 0    <- applied C1 to choose 3
0 2 0 3

2 1 3 4
3 4 1 2    <- applied C2 to choose 1; C1 to choose 2
0 3 0 0
0 2 0 3

2 1 3 4
3 4 1 2
0 3 0 1    <- applied C1 to choose 1
0 2 0 3

2 1 3 4
3 4 1 2
4 3 0 1    <- applied C1 to choose 4
0 2 0 3

2 1 3 4
3 4 1 2
4 3 2 1    <- applied C1 to choose 2
0 2 0 3

2 1 3 4
3 4 1 2
4 3 2 1
1 2 0 3    <- applied C1 to choose 1

2 1 3 4
3 4 1 2
4 3 2 1
1 2 4 3    <- applied C1 to choose 4
```

The start of the second row with 3 is an application of C2, as is the choice of 1 in the third position of this row. Otherwise, square fillings are the result of C1.

An initial formalisation of R1 as a constraint could have been (C0):

```
sq : square & sq.value=0 & sq.possibleValues()->size()=1 =>
          sq.value = sq.possibleValues()->min() &
          self.showBoard()
```

Here the function *possibleValues*() is evaluated twice, which is a waste of computational effort, and could slow the solver significantly for larger versions of Sudoku. Instead, we can avoid the duplicated computation by introducing the new variable v, setting this to *sq.possibleValues*() and then using v in place of the operation call in the two places in C0 where the operation result is read.

This illustrates a further important UML-RSDS principle:

> *Improve the efficiency of a system at the specification level where possible, whilst keeping a clear and platform-independent specification style.*

In the above case the use of the let-variable v slightly increases the syntactic complexity of the constraint, but may improve its clarity because it makes explicit that the same value is being used throughout the constraint. This is an application of the Remove Duplicated Expression Evaluations optimization pattern, we give more details of relevant design patterns in Chapter 9.

2.3 Transformation development: class diagram refactoring

This is an example of an *update-in-place* model transformation, which carries out a *refactoring* of a class diagram to improve its quality. The aim of the transformation is to remove situations of apparently duplicated attributes in different classes from the diagram, for example, if all subclasses (more than 1) of a given class all have an attribute with identical name and type, then these copies can be replaced by a single attribute in the superclass. Figure 2.5 shows the metamodel for the source and target language of the transformation. This is a small subset of the UML 2.0 class diagram language. It will be assumed that in the initial model to be refactored:

- No two classes have the same name.

- No two types have the same name.

- The owned attributes of each class have distinct names within the class, and do not have common names with the attributes of any superclass.

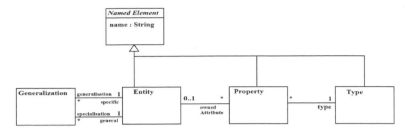

Figure 2.5: Basic class diagram metamodel

■ There is no multiple inheritance, i.e., the multiplicity of *generalisation* is restricted to 0..1.

These properties must also be preserved by the transformation.

The informal transformation steps are the following:

(1) Pull up common attributes of direct subclasses: If the set of all direct subclasses $g = c.specialisation.specific$ of a class c has two or more elements, and all classes in g have an owned attribute with the same name n and type t, add an attribute of this name and type to c, and remove the copies from each element of g. (Fig. 2.6). This is the "Pull up attribute" refactoring of [2].

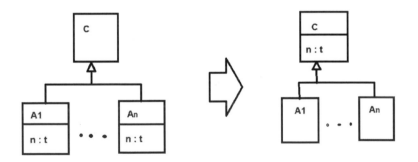

Figure 2.6: Rule 1

(2) Create subclass for duplicated attributes: If a class c has two or more direct subclasses g, $g = c.specialisation.specific$, and there is a subset $g1$ of g, of size at least 2, all the elements of $g1$ have an owned attribute with the same name n and type t, but there are elements of $g-g1$ without such an attribute, introduce a new class $c1$ as a subclass of c. $c1$ should also be set as a direct superclass of all those classes in g which own a copy of the cloned attribute. (In order to minimise the number of new classes introduced, the *largest* set of subclasses of c which all contain a copy of the same attribute should be chosen). Add an attribute of name n and type t to $c1$ and remove the copies from each of its direct subclasses. (Fig. 2.7).

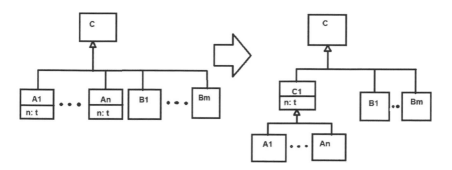

Figure 2.7: Rule 2

This is the "Extract superclass" refactoring of [2].

(3) Create root class for duplicated attributes: If there are two or more root classes all of which have an owned attribute with the same name n and type t, create a new root class c. Make c the direct superclass of all root classes with such an attribute, and add an attribute of name n and type t to c and remove the copies from each of the direct subclasses. (Fig. 2.8).

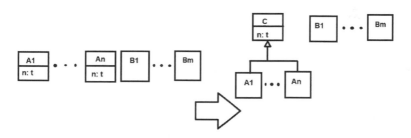

Figure 2.8: Rule 3

We will just consider the first scenario here, for simplicity. In common with most refactorings, this can be viewed as a logical assertion:

Unwanted situation s in model ⇒ *Modify model to remove s*

In this case the unwanted situation is that there is a duplicated attribute in every subclass of a class, and the modification is to promote one attribute copy to the superclass and to delete all the other copies.

A possible transformation rule that formally expresses scenario 1 is then:

$(C1)$:
$a : specialisation.specific.ownedAttribute$ &
$specialisation.size > 1$ &
$specialisation.specific \rightarrow forAll($
$\qquad ownedAttribute \rightarrow exists(b \mid b.name = a.name$ & $b.type = a.type)) \quad \Rightarrow$
$\qquad\qquad a : ownedAttribute$ &
$\qquad\qquad specialisation.specific.ownedAttribute \rightarrow select($
$\qquad\qquad\qquad\qquad name = a.name) \rightarrow isDeleted()$

This rule operates on instances of *Entity*. An instance (*self*) of *Entity*, and instance a of *Property* match the constraint test if: (i) a is in the set of attributes of all direct subclasses of *self*, (ii) there is more than one direct subclass of *self*, and (iii) every direct subclass of *self* has an attribute with the same name and type as a.

The conclusion of the constraint specifies that (i) the property a is moved up to the superclass *self* (by adding it to *self.ownedAttribute* we implicitly remove a from its current class, because an attribute can belong to at most one class according to Fig. 2.5), (ii) all other attributes with name $a.name$ are deleted from all direct subclasses of *self*.

$s \rightarrow isDeleted()$ is a built-in operator of UML-RSDS, which deletes the object or set of objects s from their model, removing them from all the entity types and association ends in which they occur.

As with the Sudoku solver, applying the constraint $(C1)$ to particular elements in a model may change the application of the constraint to other elements – for example, promoting the attribute $x : T$ from subclasses C and D of class B in Fig. 2.9 up to B will enable a further application of the constraint to B and its sibling class E. This means that the rule has to be applied repeatedly until no further change takes

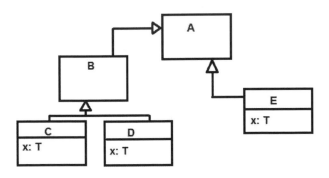

Figure 2.9: Rule 1 example

place – which means until the rule cannot be applied, and in that case no situation in the diagram matches the rule condition. This also means that all cases of the quality problem (duplicated attributes in sibling classes) have been removed from the diagram. The specification is very concise, and corresponds quite closely with the informal requirement for the rule. However, several questions should be asked about the correctness of such fixed-point rules:

- Does the execution terminate?

- Does the rule application preserve any necessary invariant properties of the model – such as single inheritance in our case?

- Does it preserve the semantic meaning of the model?

For this example it is possible to show that these properties are true: the transformation process terminates because each rule application reduces the number of *Property* instances by at least one – so there can only be finitely many rule applications. The rule does not create classes, types or generalisations, and does not change class nor type names, so the invariants concerning class name uniqueness, type name uniqueness and single inheritance are clearly preserved. Attributes cannot have names in common with any ancestor class attribute, so promoting an attribute to a superclass cannot create a name clash in the superclass, and the rule maintains the name uniqueness property (since copies of the attribute in the subclasses are deleted). Finally, regarding the semantic meaning of the class diagram, this can be considered to consist of the possible objects that could be instantiated from the concrete (leaf) classes of the diagram, characterised by their class name and attribute names and types. The collection of such object templates is preserved by the transformation, which simply relocates the place at which attributes are declared.

2.4 Integrating UML-RSDS applications with external applications

The scope of UML-RSDS application development for general software applications is primarily the business tier or business-logic tier within a three- or more-tier architecture (Fig. 2.10).

This tier contains the core business functionality of the application, and additionally contains object-oriented code representations of the business data. There should be no technology-specific code for particular UI or data storage technologies, instead such functionalities should be invoked via interface components. In UML-RSDS such components can be declared as classes with the stereotype *external* or *externalApp*

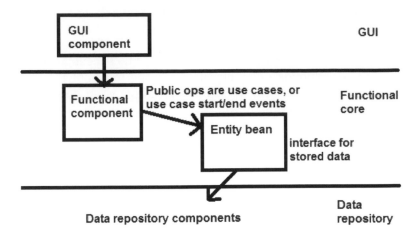

Figure 2.10: UML-RSDS systems architecture

(Chapter 10). The operations offered by these components should be listed in the class (only the operations needed by the current system need to be listed). The operations should have parameter types that are valid in UML-RSDS (boolean, int, long, double, String, class type names). The actual code of the components would be given externally, e.g., by hand-written Java classes or by separate UML-RSDS developments. For example, in the case of the correlation calculator, it may be required to read the datapoints from a spreadsheet CSV file, with one datapoint on each row of the spreadsheet. Such input could be the responsibility of an interface component *SpreadsheetReader* which has operations *getFirstRow*() : *Sequence*(*String*) and *getNextRow*() : *Sequence*(*String*). For each row a datapoint would be created, for use by the main *calc* use case.

For model transformations, on the other hand, the simple file input and output facilities provided within synthesised transformations, and the simple synthesised GUI, may be sufficient, without the need for additional external software (Chapter 7).

2.5   What is different about UML-RSDS?

Most MBD tools and methods have originated from academic research, and often are highly specialised and sophisticated. The Xmodeller tool from Xactium [1] was an example of this type of product. Such tools give many advanced capabilities for software development – to those developers and organisations who are able to use them. The barriers to their use include the cost of training, and the inability to combine the tools with existing development practice, in particular with manual coding practices. Tool costs, and dependence upon small research-based companies for tool support and upgrades, are other negative factors which have discouraged potential users from adopting them.

We attempt to overcome some of these problems with UML-RSDS by keeping the notations needed and the development steps as simple as possible: only (subsets of) UML class diagram, use case and OCL notations are needed. Apart from various checks on specifications, the main process is design and code generation. Rather than having separated UML diagrams and multiple system models, which then need to be correlated and maintained consistently, we combine use case and class diagrams together in a single diagram. This combined model is adequate for the specification of the data and behaviour of many software systems, and it gives a clear representation of the purpose of the class diagram in terms of the required services of the system. The generated code can be easily used by and integrated with manually-produced code. In contrast to sophisticated MBD tools, we have found that even second year undergraduate students are able to learn and apply UML-RSDS successfully within a short time. UML-RSDS can be used as part of component-based development (CBD) or service-oriented architecture (SOA) approaches, and with either an agile or plan-based development process.

Another agile MBD approach is Executable UML (xUML) [6]. This differs from UML-RSDS in several ways:

- xUML models systems using class diagrams, use case diagrams, domains, sequence diagrams, class collaboration diagrams, state machines and an action language.

- Developers must model the properties of the implementation platform.

- A concurrent execution model is assumed.

The approach is a relatively 'heavyweight' model-based development method, involving the construction of multiple inter-related models. In contrast, UML-RSDS uses only class diagrams, OCL and use cases, in a single integrated model. It does not require implementation platform modelling, and it has a sequential execution model.

Use cases are the main unit of incremental development in agile methods such as Scrum and eXtreme Programming (XP): the product backlog and iteration backlog are both expressed as prioritised lists of use cases (or "stories" as they are termed in Scrum). Therefore it seems appropriate to make use cases a central part of the specification models. Use cases can represent services in a SOA, or the operations of a component in CBD. The functionality of use cases is in turn defined using the data and operations of classes in the class diagram. State machines can be used in UML-RSDS to model the intended life histories of objects, and detailed behaviour of operations, but are optional. UML-RSDS has a higher level of abstraction than xUML: use case functionality is defined by a series of logical constraints, rather than actions in an action language (a design level of description). Alternative designs can be generated from the same specifications. Some other agile MBD approaches also use xUML-style action languages [4] and suffer from the costs of too-detailed low-level coding which these languages require, and which seems to negate the benefits (apart from platform-independence) of MBD. On the other hand, UML-RSDS is more restrictive than xUML, since the implementation platforms supported are restricted to C++, Java (two variants) and C#, whilst xUML supports a wider range of platforms. New code generators for UML-RSDS (e.g., to ANSI C) can be developed using UML-RSDS itself, but this involves a significant amount of work (Section 12.2 illustrates this procedure).

Summary

In this chapter we have illustrated the use of UML-RSDS on a range of examples, and we described the general UML-RSDS development process and compared UML-RSDS to other MBD approaches.

References

[1] T. Clark and P.-A. Muller, *Exploiting model driven technology: a tale of two startups*, Software Systems Modelling, 11: 481–493, 2012.

[2] M. Fowler, K. Beck, J. Brant, W. Opdyke and D. Roberts, *Refactoring: Improving the Design of Existing Code*, Addison-Wesley, 1999.

[3] S. Kolahdouz-Rahimi, K. Lano, S. Pillay, J. Troya and P. Van Gorp, *Evaluation of Model Transformation Approaches for Model Refactoring*, Science of Computer Programming, 2013, http://dx.doi.org/10.1016/j.scico.2013.07.013.

[4] I. Lazar, B. Parv, S. Monogna, I.-G. Czibula and C.-L. Lazar, *An Agile MDA Approach for Executable UML Structured Activities*, Studia Univ. Babes-Bolyai, Informatica, Vol. LII, No. 2, 2007.

[5] R. Matinnejad, *Agile Model Driven Development: an intelligent compromise*, 9th International Conference on Software Engineering Research, Management and Applications, pp. 197–202, 2011.

[6] S. Mellor and M. Balcer, *Executable UML: A Foundation for Model-driven Architectures*, Addison-Wesley, Boston, 2002.

[7] M.B. Nakicenovic, *An Agile Driven Architecture Modernization to a Model-Driven Development Solution*, International Journal on Advances in Software, Vol. 5, Nos. 3, 4, pp. 308–322, 2012.

Chapter 3

Class Diagrams

Class diagrams are the central specification notation of UML and of UML-RSDS. This chapter describes how class diagrams can be defined in UML-RSDS and used to specify system data.

3.1 Class diagram concepts

A class diagram specifies the data of a system (and possibly data external to a system which it needs to be aware of). The diagram is a graphical representation of:

Classes or *entity types* – such as *Student* or *Lecturer* in Fig. 3.1. These denote the collection of all student or lecturer instances currently existing in the system (perhaps stored as objects in a Java executable, or as rows in a database table, for example). *Abstract* classes do not have instances of their own, instead their instances actually belong to the *concrete* subclasses of the class, at the leaves of the inheritance hierarchy beneath it.

Attributes of classes denote the features of instances of the class, and the type of the value of these features. For example, in Fig. 3.1, every student has a name, which is a string.

Operations of a class represent computed properties of instances of the class (in the case of *query, instance scope* operations), or computed properties independent of particular instances (*query, static* operations), or represent updates to the state of instances. Query operations must have return types, an example is *possibleValues*() : *Set*(*Integer*) in Fig. 2.4.

31

Associations between classes (or between a class and itself) denote the links which exist between instances of one class and another. For example, in Fig. 3.1, each department has an associated set of students (the students registered in the department).

Inheritances between classes, representing that one class (at the source of the inheritance arrow) is a specialisation of another (at the target of the arrow). For example, the inheritance of *NamedElement* by *Entity* in Fig. 2.5. In UML-RSDS it is a rule that superclasses must be abstract. Classes may have multiple subclasses, but at most one superclass (single inheritance).

Class diagrams define the structure and inter-relationships of data managed by the system, and hence underpin the definition of the functionality of the system.

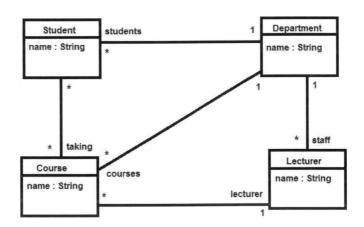

Figure 3.1: Class diagram example

3.2 Class diagram notations

The following class diagram notations are taken directly from UML 2.0:

- Classes, shown as rectangles, with a centered name, usually with an initial capital letter. Abstract classes are shown with italic font names, otherwise standard font is used.

- Enumerated types, shown as rectangles, with a centered name, and with the individual elements (values) of the enumeration listed in the second compartment of the enumeration box. An example is *Status* in Fig. 15.4. The name of the enumerated type can then be used as a type for attributes (in Java, C# and C++

enumeration type elements are typically implemented as small unsigned integers).

- Attributes of primitive (int, long, double, boolean, or enumeration) type or of String type. These are shown in the next compartment of the class box. Static (class scope) attributes are shown underlined. Attributes cannot be abstract. If an attribute is a primary key/identity attribute for the class (distinct objects must have different values for the attribute), this is indicated by the constraint {*identity*} beside the attribute. Initial values are also shown after the declaration.

- Operations, with optional input parameters and return types, are shown in the next compartment of the class box, beneath the attributes. Italic font denotes an abstract operation, underlining denotes a static operation. The declaration

```
op(x : T) : RT
```

denotes an operation with input parameter x of type T, and with result of type RT. A query (non-updating) operation has the constraint {*query*} written beside it in UML class diagrams. Query operations must have a return type.

- Associations, denoted by lines between classes (including between a class and itself, in the case of a *reflexive* association). Each end of the line can have a rolename, and both ends should have a multiplicity. In UML-RSDS the default is a unidirectional association (navigated from the source class – at the end without the rolename – to the target class – the end with the rolename), but bidirectional associations with rolenames at both ends can be defined. Multiplicities have the standard meanings (Table 3.1). Other multiplicities can be expressed by using constraints on the size of the collection denoted by the rolename. An association end of * or 0..1 multiplicity can be ordered, this is denoted by the constraint {*ordered*} at the end.

- Inheritance is shown by an arrow with a triangle head, pointing to the superclass.

Table 3.1: Multiplicity symbols in UML

Multiplicity	Meaning
*	Any finite number (including 0) of objects at this end of the association can be associated with one object at the other end
1	Exactly one object at this end of the association is associated with any object at the other end
0..1	At most one object at this end of the association is associated with any object at the other end

Some less common but still possible modelling elements are:

- Association classes: denoted by an association line with a dashed line to a class box.

- Qualified associations: denoted with a small box at the end with the qualifier index variable, and the variable is written in the box. In UML-RSDS we assume that the index is always String-valued.

- Interfaces: denoted as classes but with the stereotype ≪ *interface* ≫ written at the top.

- Interface inheritance: inheritance of an interface by another interface or by a class.

- Aggregation: an association with a whole-part meaning, the association end at the 'whole' class end is marked with a filled diamond.

To illustrate the construction of class diagrams, the following simple example system will be modelled:

- There is data on the courses, students and lecturers within each department of a college.

- Students are registered for a set of courses, and each lecturer teaches a set of courses.

- Each student, course, department and lecturer has a name, which is a string.

Figure 3.1 shows the class diagram which models this data.

3.2.1 The class diagram editor

The class diagram editor is the main panel of the UML-RSDS tools. The menu options are, in brief:

File menu: options *Set name* to set the package name of the class diagram model, *Recent* to load a recent class diagram (in the file *output/mm.txt*), *Load data* to load a class diagram in text format, *Load Ecore* to load a class diagram *output/mm.ecore* in Ecore XML format, *Save* to save the current model in text format (into *output/mm.txt*), *Save as*, to save the class diagram in a number of formats, including *Save data* to save in text format, *Save Ecore* to save as an Ecore metamodel definition (in *output/My.ecore*) and *Save model* to save as an instance model (in *output/model.txt*) of the UML-RSDS metamodel. *Print* and *Exit* options are also on the *File* menu. A *Convert* menu allows XMI data in XML files (by default, *output/xsi.txt*) to be converted to model data format (in *output/model.txt*).

Create menu: options

> **Class** – create an entity type, including interfaces and abstract classes
>
> **Type** – create an enumerated type
>
> **Association** – create an association between two classes or between a class and itself
>
> **Inheritance** – draw an inheritance arrow from the subclass to the superclass (the superclass must be an abstract class or an interface)
>
> **Association Class** – create an association class
>
> **Invariant** – introduce a constraint for a class or for the system.

Edit menu – options to *Move*, *Delete* and *Modify* visual elements. *Modify* is the default action and clicking on a class, use case or association (at the association label, usually in the centre of the association line) invokes this option.

View menu – options to view the invariants, types, operations, etc., of the system.

Transform menu – options to apply refactoring, refinement or design pattern transformations to a class diagram or system.

It is possible to load a class diagram in parts: if a class (with the same name) is defined both in the current displayed model and in a loaded file, then the union of the features and stereotypes of the two definitions is taken.

3.2.2 Drawing a class diagram

To create our example system, we create the four classes *Student*, *Course*, *Lecturer*, *Department*. Classes are created by selecting the *Create Class* option, entering the name, and clicking on the location for the class. Figure 3.2 shows the class definition dialog. Options in the *stereotypes* field include *abstract* for abstract classes, and *interface* for interfaces. *leaf* denotes that the class cannot have subclasses. *persistent* denotes that the class represents persistent data (e.g., data repository data in an enterprise information system). In this example the default *none* option is used.

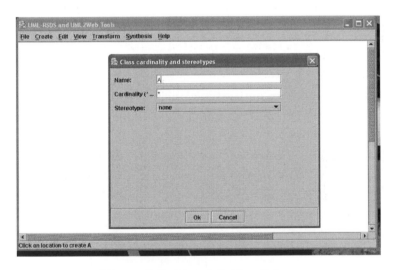

Figure 3.2: Class definition dialog

Class names (by convention) should begin with a capital letter, they can then consist of any further letters or digits. The classes are then edited by clicking on them or by using the *Edit* menu *Modify* option to add attributes *name* : *String* to each entity. The attribute dialog (Fig. 3.3) is used to define attributes. Only the name and type fields are mandatory. Attributes cannot be of an entity type or of a collection type: associations should be used to model data in these cases. The Scope field indicates if the attribute is static (class scope) or not (instance scope). The Uniqueness field indicates if the attribute is a primary key/identity attribute or not.

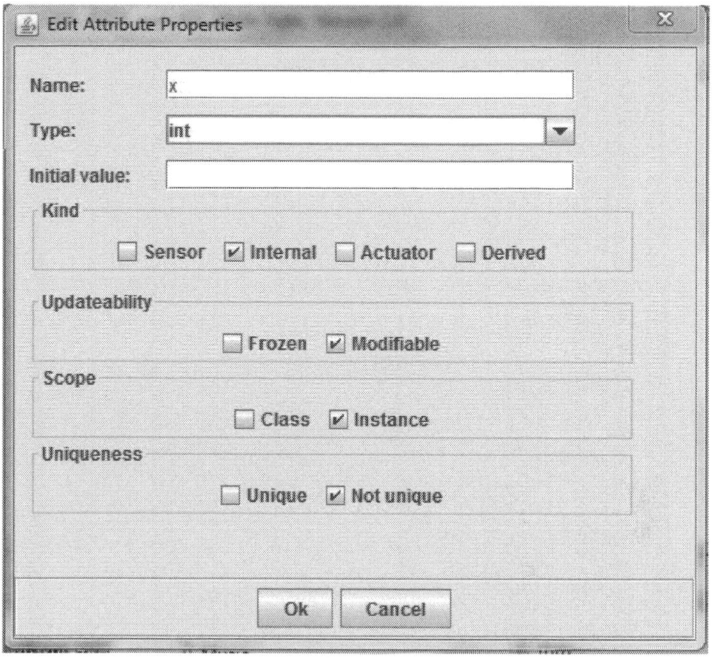

Figure 3.3: Attribute definition dialog

Associations are defined using the dialog of Fig. 3.4. Associations are created by selecting *Create Association* and dragging the mouse from the source class to the target class. Waypoints can be created by pressing the space key at the point (provided the class diagram editor panel has focus – click on the editor panel to ensure this). The *Role*2 field must be filled in – this is the end to which the association is directed. *Role*2 will become a feature of the source class. *Role*1 may be left blank, it is filled in for bidirectional associations, and then it will become a feature of the target class.

Association stereotypes include *implicit* (for associations calculated on demand using a predicate, rather than being stored), *source* (for associations belonging to the source metamodel of a model transformation), etc. The default *none* can be used in most cases. The construction process for our example should produce the class diagram of Fig. 3.1.

3.2.3 Operations

Operations can be added to classes using the *Modify* option (or by clicking on the class in the editor), and the edit class dialog (Fig. 3.5) and the operation definition dialog (Fig. 3.6).

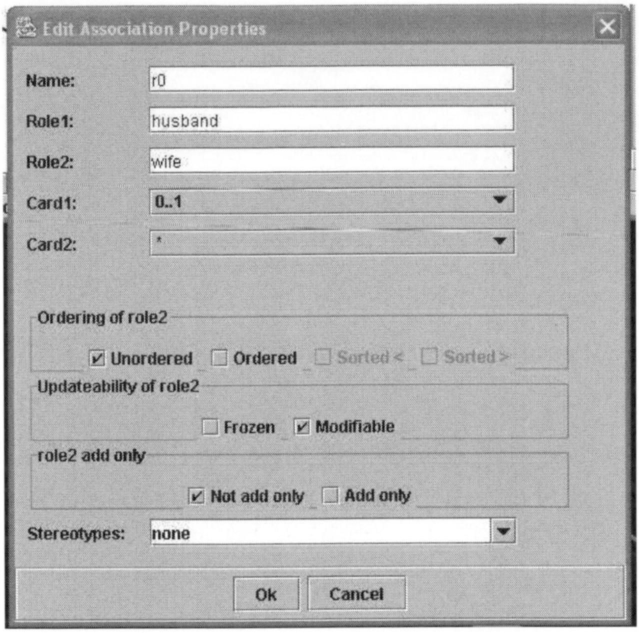

Figure 3.4: Association definition dialog

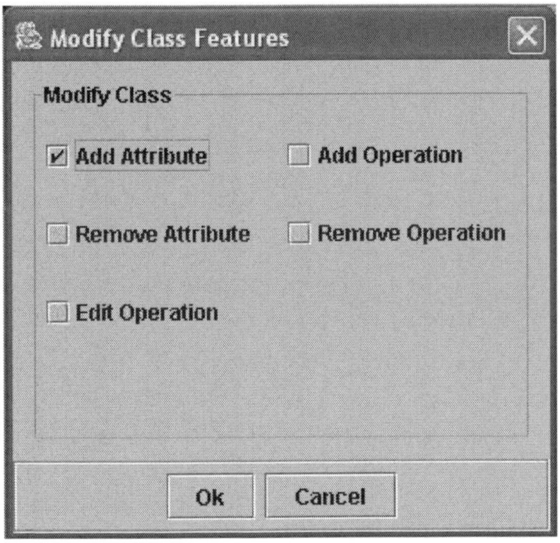

Figure 3.5: Edit class dialog

In the operation dialog both the precondition and postcondition predicate should be entered, `"true"` can be entered to denote no constraint.

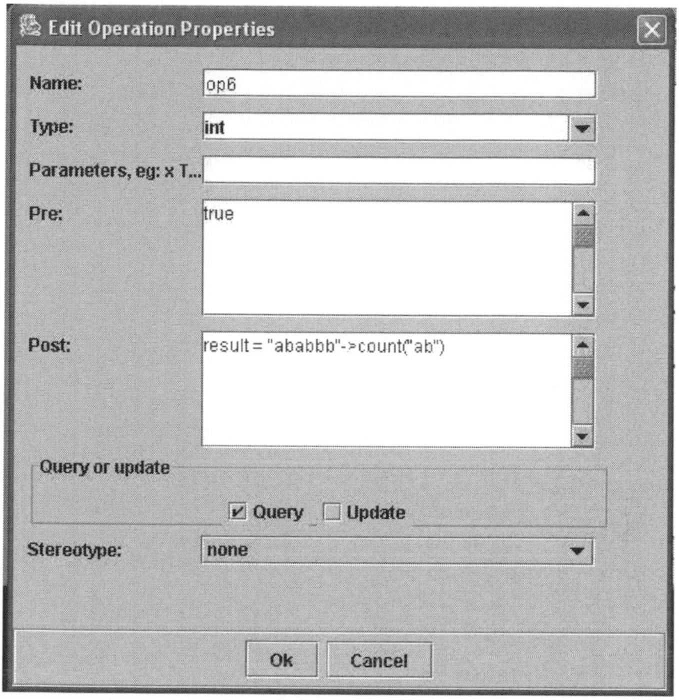

Figure 3.6: Operation definition dialog

Query operations must have a result type, and some equation *result* = *e* as the last conjunct in each conditional case in their post-condition (as in Fig. 3.6 and the factorial example below). Update operations normally have no return type, but this is possible. Input parameters and their types are entered in a list, for example:

```
x int y int
```

for an operation with two integer input parameters.

Operations can be defined recursively, for example:

```
static query factorial(i : int) : int
pre: i >= 0
post:
  (i <= 1  =>  result = 1) &
  (i > 1  =>  result = i*factorial(i-1))
```

Operations can be called by the notation *obj.op*(*params*) as usual. Such calls are expressions, in the case of query operations, and statements in the case of update operations. If *op* is a query operation then this expression can be used within other expressions as a value of its declared return type. Update operations should not be used as values or in contexts (such as conditional tests or constraint antecedents) where a pure value expression is expected. Static query operations with at least one parameter, or instance scope query operations with no parameter, can be stereotyped as *cached*, which means that caching is used for their implementation: the results of operation applications are stored in order to avoid recomputation of results. This can make a substantial difference to efficiency in the case of recursive operations. Only operations owned by a class (not an interface or use case) can be cached. For example, for the function defined as:

```
static query f(x : int) : int
pre: x >= 0
post:
  ( x = 0  =>  result = 1 ) &
  ( x = 1  =>  result = 2 ) &
  ( x > 1  =>  result = f(x-1) + f(x-2) )
```

there are 331,160,281 calls to f when evaluating $f(40)$ without caching, and an execution time of 7.5s. With caching there are only 41 calls, and an execution time of 10ms. However, the user should ensure that cached behaviour is really what is intended – if the operation result could legitimately change if the operation is invoked at different times with the same argument values then this stereotype should not be used.

3.2.4   Rules and restrictions

UML-RSDS class diagrams are valid UML 2.0 class diagrams, but there are the following additional language rules in UML-RSDS:

Single inheritance: a class can have at most one direct superclass. However, it may inherit directly from multiple interfaces.

No concrete superclasses: All superclasses must be abstract, and all leaf classes must be concrete, in a completed system specification.

These restrictions are intended to improve the quality of the models and the quality of generated code. Both multiple inheritance and concrete superclasses introduce ambiguous semantics into models and should be avoided by modellers.

The following UML class diagram features are not supported, again because of their complex semantics, which may lead developers into producing erroneous models:

■ n-ary associations for $n > 2$

■ nested classes

■ visibility annotations

- subset relationships between associations

- constraints such as disjointness on families of inheritances.

3.2.5 Code synthesis from class diagrams

Outline code in Java, C# or C++ can be produced from UML-RSDS class diagrams, by the Generate X options on the Synthesis menu. The architecture of the implemented system has a standard structure (Fig. 3.7): a simple user interface component (GUI.java in a Java implementation) invokes operations of a Singleton class (Controller) which has operations corresponding to the use cases of the system, and which acts as a single point of access to the system functionality. There are also classes corresponding to each class of the class diagram, and their operations are invoked by the controller class.

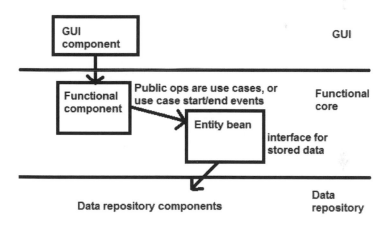

Figure 3.7: UML-RSDS systems architecture

Java code can be generated from a class diagram model by the option Generate Java on the Synthesis menu. There are two options: Java 4 and Java 6. The main difference is that the Java 6 code uses HashSet to represent unordered association ends, and ArrayList to represent ordered association ends, whilst the Java 4 code uses Vector for both. The Java 6 version can be more efficient for systems involving unidirectional unordered associations.

For our example model, the generated code consists of Java classes for each class of Fig. 3.1, in a file *Controller.java*, together with the main class, *Controller*, of the system. A file *SystemTypes.java* contains an interface with utility operations (for computing OCL expressions), and *ControllerInterface.java* contains an interface for *Controller*. These files are in the same Java package *pack* if this is specified as the system name. A file *GUI.java* defines a simple user interface for the system, with buttons for each use case (an example is shown in Fig. 3.13). The file *Controller.java* is also displayed to the user (Fig. 3.8).

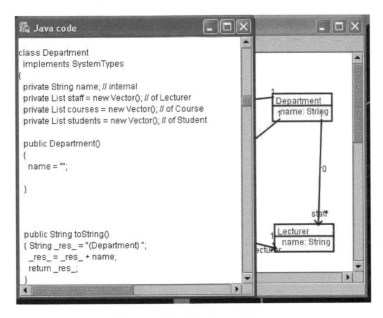

Figure 3.8: Display of Java

The Java code can be used directly in other applications, a standard interface of operations is provided for each class *C*. In the case of the Java 4 generated code, this is:

- A no-argument constructor $C()$ which sets attributes and roles to the default values of their types.

- A constructor $C(T\ attx, ..., D\ rolex)$ which takes input values for each *final* or *frozen* instance attribute and for each 1-multiplicity role.

- An operation $setatt(T\ attx)$ for each modifiable instance attribute $att : T$

- An operation $setrole(D\ rolex)$ for each modifiable instance role $role : D$.

- An operation $setAllf(List\ objs, T\ val)$ to set $ob.f$ to val for each $ob : objs$ for each modifiable feature $f : T$.

For sequence-valued roles f there is an operation

$setAllf(List\ objs, int\ ind, D\ fx)$ to set $ob.f[ind]$ to fx for $ob : objs$.

■ Operations $setrole(List\ rolex)$, $addrole(D\ rolexx)$, $removerole$ $(D\ rolexx)$, $addAllrole(List\ objs, D\ rolexx)$, $removeAllrole(List\ objs,$ $D\ rolexx)$ for each modifiable many-valued role $role : Set(D)$ or $role : Sequence(D)$. The $removerole$ and $removeAllrole$ operations are omitted if the role is $addOnly$. An operation $setrole(int\ i, D\ rolex)$ is included for sequence-valued roles, to set the i-th element of $role$ to $rolex$.

■ An operation $getrole() : D$ for a 1-multiplicity role $role : D$.

■ An operation $getatt() : T$ for an attribute $att : T$.

■ An operation $getrole() : List$ for a many-valued role $role$.

■ A static operation $getAllf(List\ objs) : List$ which returns the set (i.e., with duplicate values removed) of all $ob.f$ values for $ob : objs$, for any data feature f of the class.

■ A static operation $getAllOrderedf(List\ objs) : List$ which returns the sequence/bag of all $ob.f$ values for $ob : objs$, for any data feature f of the class (with duplicate values preserved). This corresponds to OCL $objs \rightarrow collectNested(f)$.

■ For interfaces I, the above static operations are instead placed in an inner class $IOps$ of I.

■ There are also specialised operations for manipulating elements of qualified associations using qualifier index values.

Both sets and sequences are represented by the Java List type, and are implemented as Vectors. The Java 6 code instead uses Collection as a general Collection type, and HashSet and ArrayList for sets and sequences, respectively. One limitation compared to standard UML is that multiple inheritance is not fully supported (except for implementation in C++). Only multiple interfaces can be inherited by a single class, not multiple classes. However, unlike Java, such interfaces can contain instance features, which can be inherited by multiple classes. If this is used to simulate multiple inheritance, then before synthesising Java, the Refactoring transformation *Push down abstract features* should be used to copy such features down to all subclasses, thus achieving the effect of multiple class inheritance.

Controller.java contains a public set of operations to modify the objects of a system:

- An operation *setatt*(E *ex*, T *attx*) for each modifiable instance attribute *att* : T of class E.

- An operation *setrole*(E *ex*, D *rolex*) for each modifiable instance role *role* : D of E.

- Operations *op*(E *ex*, *pardec*) and *AllEop*(*List exs*, *pardec*) for each update operation *op*(*pardec*) of class E.

- Operations *List AllEop*(*List exs*, *pardec*) for each query operation *rT op*(*pardec*) of class E.

- Operations *addrole*(E *ex*, D *rolexx*), *removerole*(E *ex*, D *rolexx*) for each modifiable many-valued role *role* : $Set(D)$ or *role* : $Sequence(D)$ of class E. *removerole* is omitted if the role is *addOnly*.

- Operations *killE*(E *ex*) and *killE*(*List exs*) to remove E instances *ex* and collections *exs* of E instances from the model.

- An operation *public rT uc*(*pardec*) for each general use case *uc* of the system.

Note that *objs*.*op*(e) for a collection *objs* and query operation *op* is interpreted by the Controller operation *AllEop*(*objs*, e), and always returns a sequence-typed result (representing a bag of values) even if *objs* is set-valued. Generation of C# follows the same structure as for Java, with classes E.cs for each UML class E, Controller.cs and System-Types.cs being produced. C# ArrayList is used in place of Java List. If a system name is specified, this name is used as the C# namespace name of the generated code. For C++, class declarations are placed in a file Controller.h, and class code is placed in Controller.cpp. The template class *set* is used to represent UML-RSDS sets, and *vector* is used to represent UML-RSDS sequences.

3.2.6 Bi-directional associations

Associations with an inverse can be specified by filling in the 'Role 1' field in the association creation dialog (as in Fig. 3.4). If the association is drawn from class E1 to class E2, then an inverse association from E2 to E1 will be created also. The inverse association is treated as a feature of E2. The generated Java code will automatically maintain the two associations as mutual inverses: updates to the forward association will generally cause updates to the inverse association also, and vice-versa. This maintenance code is in the Controller operations such as addrole2(E1 e1x, E2 e2x) and killE2(E2 e2x).

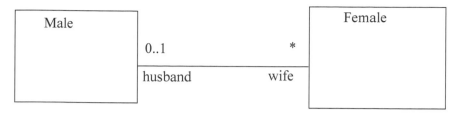

Figure 3.9: Bidirectional association example

In Fig. 3.9, adding a $w : Female$ instance to $m.wife$ also implicitly adds m to $w.husband$, and so is only permitted if the resulting size of $w.husband$ is no more than 1. Likewise, removal of an object from one end of a bidirectional association implies removal of an object at the other end also. Table 3.2 gives details of the updates which are automatically provided in generated code by UML-RSDS, where there is an association between distinct classes A and B, with unordered roles ar and br at these ends of the association. These updates aim to maintain the invariant

$$A \rightarrow forAll(a \mid B \rightarrow forAll(b \mid$$
$$(b : a.br \Rightarrow a : b.ar) \& (a : b.ar \Rightarrow b : a.br)))$$

for a many-many bidirectional association, or

$$A \rightarrow forAll(a \mid B \rightarrow forAll(b \mid$$
$$(b = a.br \Rightarrow a : b.ar) \& (a : b.ar \Rightarrow b = a.br)))$$

for a many-one bidirectional association.

The simplest case is many-many associations, particularly *—*. However, setting the br end of this association to a set bs: $ax.br = bs$ needs the opposite end ar to be updated to (i) remove ax from $bx.ar$ if bx was previously linked to ax and will be unlinked by the assignment because $bx \notin bs$; (ii) add ax to $bx.ar$ if bx was previously unlinked to ax and will be linked by the assignment because $bx \in bs$. Assignments to many-multiplicity ends of bidirectional associations may therefore be computationally expensive. Null values may arise in the case of bidirectional 1—* associations modified by $\notin$ or $=$ at the many end, and in the case of 1—1 associations, and this may cause a failure of semantic correctness unless care is taken to also assign valid objects in place of the null links.

In some cases, the existence of an inverse association may enable more efficient code to be produced. However, it also closely semantically links the classes A and B, so that these must be contained in the same code module. In general, bidirectional associations should only be introduced if they are necessary for the system being developed,

Table 3.2: Derived association updates

ar end	br end	br update	ar update
* or 0..1	* or 0..1	$bx : ax.br$ $bx \notin ax.br$ $ax.br = bs$	$ax : bx.ar$ $ax \notin bx.ar$ $(ax.br@\text{pre}-bs) \rightarrow forAll(bx \mid ax \notin bx.ar)$ $(bs - ax.br@\text{pre}) \rightarrow forAll(bx \mid ax : bx.ar)$
* or 0..1	1	$ax.br = bx$ $bx \neq ax.br@\text{pre}$	$ax \notin ax.br@\text{pre}.ar$ $ax : bx.ar$
1	* or 0..1	$bx : ax.br$ $bx \notin ax.br$ $ax.br = bs$	$bx \notin bx.ar@\text{pre}.br$ $bx.ar = ax$ $bx.ar = null$ $bx.ar = null$ for $bx : ax.br@\text{pre}-bs$ $bx.ar = ax$ and $bx \notin bx.ar@\text{pre}.br$ for $bx : bs - ax.br@\text{pre}$
1	1	$ax.br = bx$	$ax.br@\text{pre}.ar = null$ $bx.ar@\text{pre}.br = null$ $bx.ar = ax$

i.e., navigation in both directions along the association is required for the functionality of the system. If one end of a bidirectional association is {*addOnly*}, then the other end is also implicitly {*addOnly*} (for a many-valued opposite end), or {*frozen*}, for a single-valued opposite end (because a change to the opposite end of object x requires removal of x from any existing forward role sets).

3.2.7 Qualified associations

A qualified association *br* from class A to class B represents a String-indexed map from each A object to individual B objects or to sets of B objects (depending on if the multiplicity at the B end is 1 or not). The multiplicity at the A end is assumed always to be *, and this end is un-named. Qualified associations cannot be static. Figure 3.10 shows an example of a qualified association, which represents a situation where the students of a department are uniquely identifiable by an id value. The qualified association aims to provide efficient lookup of objects by the index (in Java, the Map type directly supports qualified associations, as does the map template type in C++).

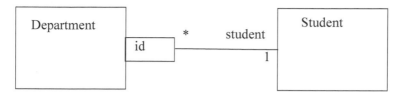

Figure 3.10: Qualified association example

For a qualified association from class A to class B, the Java code generated for A will represent br as a Java Map, and include operations to modify and read br, based on the index values. For many-valued br, the operations are:

■ An operation $setbr(String\ ind, List\ rolex)$ to set $br[ind]$ to a set $rolex$ of B objects.

■ Operations $addbr(String\ ind, B\ rolexx)$, $removebr(String\ ind, B\ rolexx)$, to add/remove $rolexx$ from $br[ind]$.

■ An operation $getbr(String\ ind) : B$ to return $br[ind]$.

Corresponding operations are also defined in the Controller class. Analogous representations are used in C# (the Hashtable class) and C++ (the map template class). Qualified associations should not be used in source or target languages for model transformations, because their values cannot be stored in/read from model data text files. However, they can be used as auxiliary data to support transformation processing.

3.2.8 Association classes

An association class is a class C which is also an association between classes A and B (normally a many-many association). Objects of C are also links $a \mapsto b$ of pairs of related A and B objects, and their attribute values define property values specific to individual links. For example, a salary specific to an employment link between a company and an employee (Fig. 3.11).

In translation to Java, C#, C++ or B AMN, association classes are represented by the two implicit many-one associations $a : C \to A$ and $b : C \to B$. UML does not permit C to be the same class as A or B, we additionally require A and B to be distinct, and unrelated to each other or to C by inheritance. Instances of C should not be created directly, but only as a result of linking an A object to a B object by the association. Likewise, deleting C objects is a consequence of unlinking

A and *B* objects. The set of *C* objects linked to a particular *ax* : *A* is
C→*select*(*a* = *ax*), likewise for the *C*'s linked to some *B* object. The
values of association classes cannot be stored in/read from model data
text files.

Figure 3.11 shows an example of an association class, which represents a situation where there are companies and employees, linked
by employments. Each employee may have several employments, each
with an individual salary. An employee's total salary would then be
expressed as:

$$Employment {\rightarrow} select(employee = e) {\rightarrow} collect(salary) {\rightarrow} sum()$$

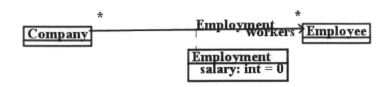

Figure 3.11: Association class example

3.2.9 Aggregation

An aggregation is a specific kind of association which has the informal
meaning of a whole-part relation. For example, a Sudoku board has a
whole-part relation to the board squares (Fig. 3.12). The parts cannot
exist without the whole, nor be shared between two wholes.

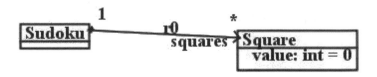

Figure 3.12: Aggregation example

The form of aggregation we use in UML-RSDS is the strong concept of the parts being owned by the whole, known as *composition*. An
aggregation should have 1 or 0..1 multiplicity at the 'whole' end (the
end with the black diamond), and * multiplicity at the 'part' end. The
semantics of aggregations is the same as for associations except that
aggregations cause *deletion propagation* from the whole to the parts:
when a whole object is deleted, so are all its attached parts, in the
same execution step. If there is an aggregation *br* from class *A* to class

B, then any call of $ax{\rightarrow}isDeleted()$ for an instance $ax : A$ also results in a call $ax.br{\rightarrow}isDeleted()$, even if the association is optional at the A end.

Aggregation, qualified associations and association classes are specialised modelling mechanisms, which should only be used if needed in a particular application.

3.3 Models and metamodels

Model-based development is centered on the use of application models, such as class diagrams of a system, instead of on the direct use of application code. As we have seen in this chapter, a class diagram such as Fig. 3.1 can be used to generate all the structural and book-keeping code of a system. Only the application-specific functionalities are missing – these can be specified as use cases in UML-RSDS, as described in Chapter 5. Models are not necessarily represented as diagrams, but could consist of text, and be stored as text files in a specific format (such as XML). UML-RSDS class diagrams are stored in text format in a file *mm.txt* in the */output* subdirectory: the *Save* option on the *File* menu saves the diagram to this file, and the *Recent* option loads the model in *mm.txt* into the class diagram editor. It is possible to edit the class diagram data in *mm.txt* using a text editor, although care must be taken to use the same format for the data.

Class diagrams have *instances*, or *instance models*, in the same way that classes have individual objects as their instances. An instance model m for a class diagram L consists of finite collections of objects (instances of E) for each class (entity type) E of L (the collections may be empty, but all objects of m must belong to some concrete class of L). An object *obj* in m should have an attribute value for each declared attribute of its class in L (including inherited attributes). Links between objects are recorded in m, and represent the instances of associations in L. An instance model corresponds to a possible set of program objects and object feature values that may exist at some time point during the execution of a program that implements the class diagram. The programs synthesised by UML-RSDS from class diagrams can be initialised with a particular instance model (stored in *output/in.txt*) by means of the option *loadModel* of the generated GUI (for Java4 generated code). They can also store the current program state in *output/out.txt* using the option *saveModel*. Figure 3.13 shows an example of the generated GUI.

The text format for instance models in UML-RSDS is very simple, consisting of lines of text of three possible forms:

e : T

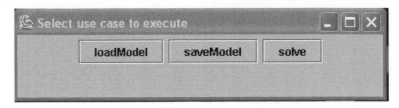

Figure 3.13: GUI example

declaring that the identifier e is an instance of concrete class T,

```
e.f = v
```

declaring that the attribute or 1-multiplicity role f of e has value v, and

```
obj : e.role
```

declaring that *obj* is a member of the many-valued (0..1 or *-multiplicity) role *role* of e. For sequence-valued roles, the order in which these membership assertions occur in the file is the order of elements in *role*. Spaces must be present around the = and : symbols in the lines of the file.

For example, we could have the example instance model

```
d1 : Department
d1.name = "Mathematics"
l1 : Lecturer
l1.name = "David"
l1 : d1.staff
c1 : Course
c1.name = "Algebra1"
c1 : d1.courses
c1.lecturer = l1
```

for the Department class diagram of Fig. 3.1. Here there is a single instance of the *Department* class, a single instance of *Lecturer*, and a single link between these instances. There is an instance of *Course*, linked to the department and lecturer instances. The declaration of an object (such as $d1 : Department$) must precede any other line that uses the object.

Class diagrams have two separate but related roles in MBD: (i) they can describe the data and structure of particular *applications*, as (executable) specifications of these applications – Fig. 3.1 is an example of such a class diagram; (ii) they can describe *languages* (such as English, Russian, Java or a modelling language such as UML) – Fig. 2.5 is an example of such a class diagram. A class diagram at the language level is often called a *metamodel* because its classes (or *entity types*) have instances at the (application) model level. In turn, an application model has instances at the instance model (program execution) level. Figure 3.14 shows the relationships between the different model levels. Both the language level and application level models can be represented using class diagram notation, and are stored in file mm.txt by the UML-RSDS tools. Instance-level models are represented as text files (in model.txt, in.txt, out.txt, etc.).

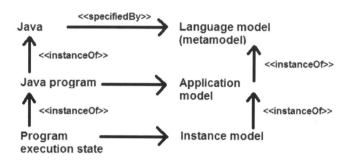

Figure 3.14: Modelling levels

Our application-level class diagram (Fig. 3.1) can be partly represented as an instance of the language-level class diagram (Fig. 2.5) as follows:

```
e1 : Entity
e1.name = "Student"
e2 : Entity
e2.name = "Department"
e3 : Entity
e3.name = "Course"
e4 : Entity
e4.name = "Lecturer"
p1 : Property
p1.name = "name"
p2 : Property
p2.name = "name"
p3 : Property
p3.name = "name"
p4 : Property
p4.name = "name"
p1 : e1.ownedAttribute
p2 : e2.ownedAttribute
p3 : e3.ownedAttribute
p4 : e4.ownedAttribute
t1 : Type
t1.name = "String"
```

```
p1.type = t1
p2.type = t1
p3.type = t1
p4.type = t1
```

The full UML-RSDS class diagram language is given in Fig. B.2.

The ability to represent application models as instances of metamodels enables a developer to apply transformations (such as class diagram refactoring, Section 2.3) to the application models: such transformations can operate on application models in the same way that conventional programs can operate on instance models. In the case of the department application model, the restructuring rule 3 can be applied to rationalise the class diagram structure: the *name* : *String* attribute declared in the four separate root classes *Department*, *Student*, *Lecturer*, *Course*, can be replaced by a single attribute in a new superclass of these classes.

As far as development in UML-RSDS is concerned, there is no practical difference between specifications concerning application models or languages: in both cases the specifications are expressed in terms of the entity types and features of the model, and the model itself is visually represented as a class diagram. In the case of application-level specifications, the implementation of the UML-RSDS specification operates on instance models (in text format), which represent instances of the application model. In the case of language-level specifications, the implementation operates on instance models which represent application models that are instances of the language (as in the above example of the teaching class diagram as an instance of UML).

3.4   Domain-specific languages

A domain-specific language (DSL) is a notation (graphical, textual or a mix of the two), together with a formal language definition, intended to represent the concepts and individual elements within particular application domains.

For example, a notation to describe distributed systems consisting of physical computing devices, connections between devices, and software running on the devices, could be used to draw diagrams such as that in Fig. 3.15. This visual notation is referred to as the *concrete syntax* of the DSL, in the same way that the textual forms of Java statements and declarations is the concrete syntax of Java.

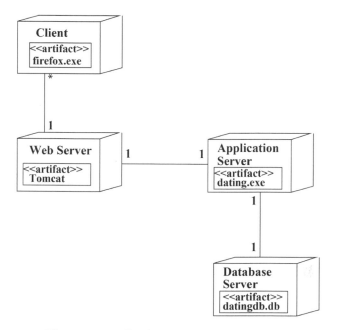

Figure 3.15: Deployment diagram example

The visual representation of a computational device is a 3D box. Connections are shown as lines, and artifacts (software applications and platforms) are written as rectangles and text inside the devices that host them.

A DSL has the following elements:

- An identified application domain where it will be used.

- Representations that are appropriate, visually and conceptually, for modellers in the domain, and for stakeholders who need to review such models.

- A precise abstract grammar, defining the way DSL elements can be combined (e.g., that communication links can connect any two different devices, but not a device to itself). This is known as the *abstract syntax* of the DSL.

- A precise way, usually by means of a model transformation, to map the DSL models to implementations.

In this book, and in UML-RSDS, a DSL is defined by a class diagram that gives the abstract syntax of the DSL as a metamodel. Figure 3.16 shows a possible metamodel for the distributed systems DSL used in Fig. 3.15.

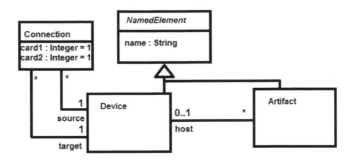

Figure 3.16: Deployment notation DSL

Using such a metamodel, particular DSL models can be specified in a notation such as XML, or in the UML-RSDS textual format for models described in the previous section. For example, the model of Fig. 3.15 could be described by the following textual model in terms of the DSL concepts:

```
pc : Device
pc.name = "Client"
ws : Device
ws.name = "Web Server"
appserv : Device
appserv.name = "Application Server"
dbserv : Device
dbserv.name = "Database Server"
c1 : Connection
c1.source = pc
c1.target = ws
c1.card1 = -1
c1.card2 = 1
c2 : Connection
c2.source = ws
c2.target = appserv
c3 : Connection
c3.source = appserv
c3.target = dbserv
browser : Artifact
browser.name = "firefox.exe"
pc : browser.host
tomcat : Artifact
tomcat.name = "Tomcat"
ws : tomcat.host
app : Artifact
app.name = "dating.exe"
appserv : app.host
db : Artifact
db.name = "datingdb.db"
dbserv : db.host
```

This is an instance model of Fig. 3.16. Notice that default attribute values do not need to be written in the model text file. A transformation (defined in UML-RSDS) can then process such models to generate any necessary configuration files, interfaces for remote invocations, etc., based on the particular network.

A DSL may use the terminology of particular design patterns for a domain. For example, a DSL for enterprise information systems could contain entity types such as *Controller*, *View*, *Model* from the MVC pattern (Chapter 9).

3.5 Generalised application models

For some application domains a DSL may not be necessary, instead a generalised application model may be defined, which defines the common entity types and typical structures of applications in the domain. Such a model can provide systematic and reusable specifications and designs for a number of different developments within the same domain. For example, in the domain of programs for board games (noughts-and-crosses, Sudoku, chess, Scrabble, etc.) there are common concepts (Game, Board, Location, Piece, Move, Score, Player, etc.) and common class diagram structures (a board consists of a fixed aggregation of locations; a game has a number of players, who may make moves using pieces, etc.). This similarity helps a developer to write the general structure and elements of a class diagram, using such concepts, and also helps to make the class diagram comprehensible to stakeholders. Similarly a generalised application model for financial domains could be defined, with concepts such as Option, Market, Share, YieldCurve, etc.

Summary

In this chapter we have described the UML class diagram notations that are used in UML-RSDS, and we have outlined how class diagrams are implemented in code by the UML-RSDS tools. We have also described the concepts of metamodels, domain-specific models and generalised application models.

Chapter 4

Constraints

Logical constraints are used within UML-RSDS to provide more detailed semantics for a class diagram, and to precisely define the functionality of operations and of use cases. Constraints can be translated into formal languages (such as B AMN) to support verification. A subset of the UML Object Constraint Language (OCL) is used as the UML-RSDS constraint language.

The BNF grammar of UML-RSDS OCL expressions, and the abstract syntax of expressions, are given in Appendix A. All expressions have a mathematical semantics ([1]). A significant difference to standard OCL is that we simplify the OCL semantics to use classical 2-valued logic: there are no *undefined* or *null* values in UML-RSDS OCL. In addition, collections are either sequences or sets.

4.1 Constraints in UML-RSDS

OCL and abbreviated OCL constraints can be used in many places in a UML-RSDS specification:

1. Class invariants

2. Global constraints of a class diagram

3. Operation pre and postconditions

4. Use case pre- and post-conditions and invariants

5. State machine state invariants and transition guards.

Constraints are a central facility of UML-RSDS, and enable UML-RSDS specifications to be used both for informal analysis and communication, formal mathematical analysis, and (via code generators) as executable implementations. The key principle of UML-RSDS is:

> *A logical constraint P can be interpreted both as a specification of system behaviour, and as a description of how P will be established in the system implementation.*

Thus an operation post-condition in:

```
static query factorial(i : int) : int
pre: i >= 0
post:
  (i <= 1  =>  result = 1) &
  (i > 1  =>  result = i*factorial(i-1))
```

gives both a declarative and precise description of the factorial function, in a recursive style, and instructs the UML-RSDS code generators to produce recursive implementations based on the postcondition expressions, in Java, C# or C++.

An alternative description could be:

```
static query factorial(i : int) : int
pre: i >= 0
post:
  (i <= 1  =>  result = 1) &
  (i > 1  =>  result = Integer.Prd(2,i,k,k))
```

where Integer.Prd(2,i,k,k) is the product $\Pi_{k=2}^{i}k$ of integers between 2 and i, inclusive. This second description is more efficient, and is of similar clarity to the recursive version.

Figure 4.1 shows the dialog for entering constraints.

A constraint $P \Rightarrow Q$ on entity E is entered by writing E in the first text area, P in the second and Q in the third. We will also write this in text as

$$E ::$$
$$P \Rightarrow Q$$

This has the logical meaning

$$E {\rightarrow} forAll(P \Rightarrow Q)$$

"for all instances of E, if P holds, then Q holds". Operationally, it means "for all instances of E, if P holds, then make Q hold true, if possible".

The default options on the dialog (system requirement, non-critical, update code, unordered) can be chosen in most cases. E is called the *context* or *scope* of the constraint. Local invariants of class C are specified by naming C in the first field of this dialog. Global constraints forAll-quantified over C also need C to be entered here. Use case constraints based on class C should have the class name entered as context (for the options Add Postcondition, Add Precondition or Add Invariant on the edit use case dialog).

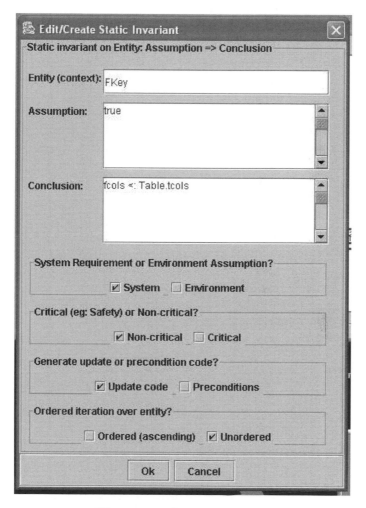

Figure 4.1: Constraint dialog

If the constraint is a local invariant of a class C, or it is a use case constraint based on C, then features of C can be written simply by their names in P or Q. Navigation expressions starting from features of C can also be written. Additional variables x can be introduced by a formula $x : e$ in the constraint antecedent: x must not be the name of a feature of the context class, and it is implicitly universally quantified over the elements of *e*, which may be an entity type name or other collection-valued expression.

For example:

```
c : courses
```

could be defined as a constraint antecedent *P* and

```
c.lecturer : staff
```

as a succedent *Q*. This could be an invariant of class *Department* in our example (Fig. 3.1), expressing that all courses of the department have their lecturer also within the department. *c* is a quantified variable, whose type is inferred as being *Course*. The same logical constraint can be alternatively expressed without *c* by writing

```
true
```

as the antecedent *P* and

```
courses.lecturer <: staff
```

as *Q*. "The lecturers of all courses are members of staff". *Q* could also be written in conventional OCL notation as `staff->includesAll(courses.lecturer)`.

Another form of variable that may be introduced in constraint antecedents is the *let* variable, which assigns a constant value of an expression *e* to the variable to avoid repeated evaluations of that expression:

$$v = e \;\Rightarrow\; P$$

The identifier *v* may then be used in place of the (possibly complex) expression *e* in *P*.

A common simple form of constraint is one that derives the value of an attribute of a class from other features of the class. For example, if we add an integer attribute *numberOfStudents* to *Department* in Fig. 3.1, we can define its value by the invariant constraint

$$numberOfStudents = students.size$$

or

$$numberOfStudents = students{\rightarrow}size()$$

on *Department*.

A constraint has scope or context the entities to which it implicitly applies (features of such entities can be written without object references in the constraint, or with the reference *self*). The most local context is termed the *primary scope* of the expression, and feature references are interpreted as features of this entity by default. Other entities in the scope are termed the *secondary scope*. A local invariant of a class E has primary scope E, as do pre and postconditions of E's instance operations, and state invariants and guards in the entity state machine of E or in its instance operation state machines. A use case constraint with owner entity E also has primary scope E. A predicate P in the body of a select, reject or collect expression without a variable: $e \rightarrow select(P)$, $e \rightarrow reject(P)$, $e \rightarrow collect(P)$, has primary scope the element type of e, if this is an entity type, and secondary scope the scope of the selection expression. Likewise for quantifier expressions without variables: $e \rightarrow forAll(P)$, $e \rightarrow exists(P)$, $e \rightarrow exists1(P)$.

Constraints not only have a declarative meaning at the specification level, defining what conditions should be maintained by a system, but also they may have a procedural meaning, defining code fragments whose execution enforces the conditions. For example, the constraint defining *numberOfStudents* will be used by the UML-RSDS tools to produce code that modifies this attribute in response to any operation *setstudents*, *addstudents* or *removestudents* which affects *students*. For example:

```
public void addstudents(Student studentsxx)
{ students.add(studentsxx);
  numberOfStudents = students.size();
}
```

4.1.1 Basic expressions

Table 4.1 defines the basic expressions which may be used in constraints, and their meanings. *self* corresponds to *this* in programming languages (Java, C# and C++). The notation for attributes, roles and operations is standard. A specific form of basic expression which is used extensively in UML-RSDS is the *object lookup* expression $E[v]$ where E is a class name and v is a string value or a collection of strings. E must have a primary key/identity attribute *att* : *String*, or an attribute *att* : *String* satisfying $E \rightarrow isUnique(att)$. Thus instances of E are uniquely identified by string values: for a string value s there is either 1 or 0 instance x of E at any time that satisfies $x.att = s$. If there is such an instance, it is returned as the value of $E[s]$ (if there is no instance, then $E[s]$ is undefined). This lookup applies for the first (in order of the declarations within the class) attribute that satisfies the primary key/uniqueness property, termed the *principal primary key*. The expression should evaluate in constant time complexity – as with qualified associations, programming language map data structures can be used to ensure this. The returned object can be used in the same way as any other instance of E, in feature application expressions $E[s].f$ or as a parameter value to operations. The expression $E[s]$ could be written as

$$E.allInstances() \rightarrow any(att = s)$$

in standard OCL.

The second variant of the object lookup expression has a collection vs of string values as its argument, and returns the collection of E instances whose att value is in vs:

$$E.allInstances() \rightarrow select(vs \rightarrow includes(att))$$

This is always well-defined. It is a sequence if vs is a sequence, otherwise a set.

Table 4.1: Basic expressions

Expression	Meaning as query or update
self	The current object of class E: for constraints with a single scope E
f $op(e1, ..., en)$	Attribute/role f of class E, for constraints with scope E Invocation of operation op of E, for constraints with scope E
$f[ind]$ $E[v]$ v single value $E[v]$ v collection	ind element of ordered or qualified role f of current scope E The instance of E with (principal) primary key value v The instances of E with (principal) primary key value in v Sequence-valued if v is
$obj.f$ $objs.f$	Data feature f of single object obj Collection (set or sequence) of values $o.f$ for $o \in objs$, collection $objs$. This is a set if $objs$ is a set or if f is set-valued
$obj.op(e1, ..., en)$ $objs.op(e1, ..., en)$	Apply op to single object obj Apply op to each $o \in objs$, collection $objs$ Result value is bag/sequence of individual result values $o.op(e1, ..., en)$ if op has a result
value	Value of enumerated type, numeric value, string value "string", or boolean true, false

Unlike most programming languages, features may be applied directly to collections of objects: $objs.att$ or $objs.f(p)$. These expressions permit concise specification of the collections formed or effects produced by applying the feature on each instance in the collection $objs$.

4.1.2 Logical expressions

Table 4.2 shows the logical operators that can be used in constraints, and their declarative and procedural meanings. The procedural interpretation of a formula P is formally defined as a statement in the activity language (Chapter 6) denoted by $stat(P)$. This is defined in Table 6.2.

Table 4.2: Logical operators

Expression	Meaning as query	Meaning as update
A => B	If A is true, so is B	If A holds, make B true
A & B	A and B are both true	Carry out A, then B
A or B	A holds, or B holds	
E->exists(P) entity E e->exists(P) expression e	An existing instance of E satisfies P An existing element in e satisfies P	
E->forAll(P) entity E e->forAll(P) expression e	All existing instances of E satisfy P All elements of e satisfy P	
E->exists1(P) entity E e->exists1(P) expression e	Exactly one existing instance of E satisfies P Exactly one element of e satisfies P	
E->exists(x | P) concrete entity E e->exists(x | P) other expression e	An existing instance x of E satisfies P An existing element x in e satisfies P	Create $x : E$ and make P true for x Select an element of e and apply P to it
E->forAll(x | P) entity E e->forAll(x | P) expression e	All existing instances x of E satisfy P All elements x of e satisfy P	For all existing $x : E$, make P true for x Make P true for all $x : e$
E->exists1(x | P) concrete entity E e->exists1(x | P) other expression e	Exactly one existing instance x of E satisfies P Exactly one element x of e satisfies P	If no instance of E satisfies P, create $x : E$ and make P true for x If no $x : e$ satisfies P, select some $x : e$ and apply P to it

There should not be a space between the $-$ and $>$ symbols, or between the $>$ and the operator name in the $\rightarrow op$ operators.

There are some special cases in the operational use of the *exists* and *exists1* quantifiers:

■ In the case of $E \rightarrow exists1(x \mid x.id = v \ \& \ P)$ or $E \rightarrow exists(x \mid x.id = v \ \& \ P)$ where id is the principal primary key of concrete entity E, a lookup for $E[v]$ is performed first, if this object exists then (i) the update effect of P is applied to it (unless P already holds for it). Otherwise, (ii) a new instance of E is created and the formula $x.id = v \ \& \ P$ is applied to it.

■ If E is abstract, or of the form F@pre for an entity F, then only the lookup and part (i) of this functionality is performed. Likewise for general expressions e in place of E.

Although checking for existence of an x with $x.id = v$ does affect the efficiency of the implementation, it is necessary to ensure correctness: it would be invalid to create two or more objects with the same id value.

Note that it is invalid to attempt to quantify over infinite sets: $Integer{\rightarrow}forAll(P)$ is not a valid OCL expression. Only entity type names and other expressions denoting finite collections of objects or values may be used as the first argument of a quantifier expression.

4.1.3 Comparitor, numeric and string expressions

Table 4.3 lists the comparitor operators and their meanings.

Table 4.3: Comparitor operators

Expression	Meaning as query	Meaning as update
$x : E$ E entity type	x is an existing instance of E	Create x as a new instance of E (for concrete E)
$x : s$ s collection	x is an element of s	Add x to s
`s->includes(x)` s collection	Same as $x : s$	Same as $x : s$
$x \ / : E$ E entity type	x is not an existing instance of E	
$x \ / : s$ s collection	x is not an element of s	Remove x from s
`s->excludes(x)` s collection	Same as $x \ / : s$	Same as $x \ / : s$
$x = y$	x's value equals y's value	Assign y's value to x
$x < y$ x, y both numbers, or both strings	x's value is less than y's. Likewise for $>$, $<=$, $>=$, $/ =$, $! =$ (not equal)	
$s <: t$ s, t collections	All elements of s are also elements of t	Add every element of s to t
`t->includesAll(s)`	Same as $s <: t$	Same as $s <: t$
$s \ / <: t$ collections s, t	s is not a subset of t	Remove all elements of s from t
`t->excludesAll(s)` collections s, t	No element of s is in t	Remove all elements of s from t

As a query expression, $x : E$ for an entity type (classifier) E corresponds to $x.oclIsKindOf(E)$ in OCL [2] and to x *instanceof* E in Java and to x *is* E in C#. The comparitors $<$, $>$, $<=$ and $>=$ can also be used to compare objects of the same class E, provided that E has a public operation

```
query compareTo(obj : E) : int
```

$obj1 < obj2$ is then evaluated as $obj1.compareTo(obj2) < 0$.

Numeric operators for integers and real numbers are shown in Table 4.4. Instead of OCL Integer and Real, we use types `int` (32 bit signed integers) and `double` (signed double precision floating point numbers) which correspond to the types with these names in Java, C++ and C#. `long` may also be used (64 bit signed integers) for code generation. All operators take double values as arguments except as noted. Three operators: ceil, round, floor, take a double value and return an int.

Table 4.4: Numeric operators

Expression	*Meaning as query*
-x	Unary subtraction
x + y	Numeric addition, or string concatenation (if one of x, y is a string)
x - y	Numeric subtraction
x * y	Numeric multiplication
x / y	Integer division (div) if both x, y are integers, otherwise arithmetic division
x mod y	Integer x modulo integer y
x.sqr	Square of x
x.sqrt	Positive square root of x
x.floor	Floor integer of x
x.round	Rounded integer of x
x.ceil	Ceiling integer of x
x.abs	Absolute value of x
x.exp	e to power x
x.log	e-logarithm of x
x.pow(y)	y-th power of x
x.sin	Sine of x (given in radians)
x.cos	Cosine of x (given in radians)
x.tan	Tangent of x (given in radians)
Integer.subrange(st,en)	Sequence of integers starting at st and ending at en, in order

Other math operators in common between Java, C# and C++ are: log10, cbrt, tanh, cosh, sinh, asin, acos, atan. These are double-valued functions of double-valued arguments. Some functions may not be available in old versions of Java (log10, cbrt, tanh, cosh, sinh). The math operators may also be written in the style $e{\rightarrow}op()$ in cases where e is a bracketed expression or other complex expression. For example: $(x + y){\rightarrow}pow(3)$.

Some examples of constraints using numeric operators are:

```
1000->sqrt()->display() & 1728->cbrt()->display() &
0.5->exp()->display() & 3->pow(10)->display()

0->sin()->display() & 0->cos()->display() &
0.5->log()->display() & 1000->log10()->display()

3.45->floor()->display() & 3.45->ceil()->display() &
3.45->round()->display() & -3.45->abs()->display()
```

These produce the following results:

```
31.622776601683793
1.6487212707001282
59049.0

0.0
1.0
-0.6931471805599453

3
4
3
3.45
```

(not including cbrt and log10, which are not available on old Java implementations).

String operators are shown in Table 4.5. Notice that since strings are sequences of characters (single-character substrings), all sequence operations should be expected to be applicable also to strings.

String positions in OCL are numbered starting at 1, as are sequence positions. Some examples of string expressions are given in the following constraints:

```
"faster"->tail()->display() & "faster"->front()->display() &
"faster"->first()->display() & "faster"->last()->display()

"faster"->indexOf("s")->display() & "faster".insertAt(2,"s")->
display() &
"faster"->reverse()->display()
```

These give the results:

```
aster
faste
f
r

3
fsaster
retsaf
```

Table 4.5: String operators

Expression	Meaning as query
x + y	String concatenation
x->size()	Length of x
x->first()	First character of x
x->front()	Substring of x omitting last character
x->last()	Last character of x
x->tail()	Substring of x omitting first character
x.subrange(i,j)	Substring of x starting at i-th position, ending at j-th
x->toLowerCase()	Copy of x with all characters in lower case
x->toUpperCase()	Copy of x with all characters in upper case
s->indexOf(x)	Index (starting from 1) of s at which the first subsequence of characters of s equal to string x occurs. Default is 0
s->hasPrefix(x)	String x is a prefix of s
s->hasSuffix(x)	String x is a suffix of s
s->characters()	Sequence of all single character substrings of s in same order as in s
s.insertAt(i,s1)	Copy of s with string s1 inserted at position i
s->count(s1)	Number of distinct occurrences of s1 as a substring of s
s->reverse()	Reversed form of s
e->display()	Displays expression e as string on standard output
s1 - s2	String s1 with all occurrences of characters in s2 removed
e->isInteger()	true if e represents an int value
e->isReal()	true if e represents a double value
e->toInteger()	Returns the value if e represents an int value
e->toReal()	Returns the value if e represents a double value

4.1.4 Pre-state expressions

A pre-state expression $f@pre$ for feature f can be used in operation post-conditions and use case post-condition constraints, but not elsewhere. In an operation post-condition, $f@pre$ refers to the value of f at the start of the operation, i.e., the same value as denoted by f in the operation precondition. Occurrences of f without $@pre$ in the post-condition refer to the value of f at the end of the operation. So, for example:

```
op()
pre: b > a
post: b = b@pre - a@pre
```

decrements b by a. Since a itself is not updated by the operation, there is no need to use *pre* with a, and the operation should be written as:

```
op()
pre: b > a
post: b = b@pre - a
```

In use case postconditions, f@pre denotes the value of f at the start of application of the implementation of the postcondition. Pre-state expressions are used to distinguish between this value and any new value for f which is set by the postcondition. Pre-state expressions should not depend upon additional quantified variables or upon let variables. For example, an expression $E@pre[v]$, where v is a quantified variable, is not valid. The variables of quantifiers or of select/reject/collection expressions should not occur in pre-state expressions. The reason for these restrictions is that pre-forms are evaluated at the start of the application of a constraint, and hence can only involve data which is defined at this point. Internal variables of the constraint are not defined at the initiation of constraint execution.

4.1.5 Collection expressions

There are two kinds of collection in UML-RSDS: sets and sequences. Sets are unordered collections with unique membership (duplicate elements are not permitted), sequences are ordered collections with possibly duplicated elements. If br is an unordered * role of class A, then $ax.br$ is a set for each $ax : A$. If br is an ordered * role of class A, then $ax.br$ is a sequence for each $ax : A$. The further two OCL collection types, ordered sets and bags, can be defined in terms of sequences. Table 4.6 shows the values and operators that apply to sets and sequences.

For sequences s, $s^\frown t$ should be used instead of $s \backslash/ t$, which produces the set union of two sets, and $s \rightarrow append(x)$ should be used in preference to $s \rightarrow including(x)$. The implementation of $s \rightarrow including(x)$ for sequence s is to add x to the end of s, and the implementation of $s \rightarrow union(c)$ for sequences s and c is to concatenate c after s. $s \rightarrow at(i)$ for a sequence s is denoted by $s[i]$ in our notation.

Table 4.6: Collection operators

Expression	Meaning as query
$Set\{\}$	Empty set
$Sequence\{\}$	Empty sequence
$Set\{x1, x2, ..., xn\}$	Set with elements $x1$ to xn
$Sequence\{x1, x2, ..., xn\}$	Sequence with elements $x1$ to xn
s->including(x)	s with element x added
s->excluding(x)	s with all occurrences of x removed
s - t	s with all occurrences of elements
	of t removed
s->prepend(x)	Sequence s with x prepended as first element
s->append(x)	Sequence s with x appended as last element
s->count(x)	Number of occurrences of x in sequence s
s->indexOf(x)	Position of first occurrence of x in s
$x\backslash/y$	Set union of x and y
$x/\backslash y$	Set intersection of x and y
$x \frown y$	Sequence concatenation of x and y
x->union(y)	Same as $x\backslash/y$
x->intersection(y)	Same as $x/\backslash y$
x->unionAll(e)	Union of y.e for y : x
x->intersectAll(e)	Intersection of y.e for y : x
x->symmetricDifference(y)	Symmetric difference of sets x, y
x->any()	Arbitrary element of non-empty
	collection x
x->subcollections()	Set of subcollections of collection x
x->reverse()	Reversed form of sequence x
x->front()	Front subsequence of non-empty sequence x
x->tail()	Tail subsequence of non-empty sequence x
x->first()	First element of non-empty sequence x
x->last()	Last element of non-empty sequence x
x->sort()	Sorted (ascending) form of sequence x
x->sortedBy(e)	x sorted in ascending
	order of y.e values (numerics or strings)
	for objects y : x
x->sum()	Sum of elements of collection x
x->prd()	Product of elements of collection x
Integer.Sum(a,b,x,e)	Integer.subrange(a,b)->collect(x | e)->sum()
Integer.Prd(a,b,x,e)	Integer.subrange(a,b)->collect(x | e)->prd()
x->max()	Maximum element of non-empty collection x
x->min()	Minimum element of non-empty collection x
x->asSet()	Set of distinct elements in collection x
x->asSequence()	Collection x as a sequence
s->isUnique(e)	The collection of values of x.e for x : s has no duplicates
x->isDeleted()	Destroys all elements of object collection x
	Can also be used on individual objects x

Some examples of set and sequence operators are given in the following constraints:

```
s = Set{"a", "h", "bed", "aa"} & t = Set{"bed", "h", "uu", "kl"}  =>
    ( s - t )->display() & s->symmetricDifference(t)->display()

s1 = Set{"a", "h", "bed", "aa"} & t1 = Set{"bed", "h", "uu", "kl"}  =>
    ( s1->intersection(t1) )->display() & ( s1->union(t1) )->display()

p = Set{1,3,5,7,2,9}  =>
    p->any()->display() & p->min()->display() &
    p->max()->display() & p->sum()->display() & p->prd()->display()

p1 = Sequence{1,3,5,7,2,9}  =>
    p1->first()->display() & p1->last()->display() &
    (p1[3])->display() & p1->tail()->display() & p1->front()->display()
```

These produce the following results:

```
["a", "aa"]
["a", "aa", "uu", "kl"]

["h", "bed"]
["a", "h", "bed", "aa", "uu", "kl"]

1
1
9
27
1890

1
9
5
[3,5,7,2,9]
[1,3,5,7,2]
```

$st = sq$ for set st and sequence sq is always false, even if both st and sq are empty. Two sets are equal iff they contain exactly the same elements, two sequences are equal iff they contain exactly the same elements in the same order.

Of particular significance are collection operators which construct new collections consisting of all elements of a given collection which satisfy a certain property, or which derive collections from other collections (Table 4.7).

Any order in the original collection is preserved by the *select* and *reject* operators, i.e., if they are applied to a sequence the result is also a sequence. In the operators *select*, *reject* and *collect* without variables, an element of the first argument, s, can be referred to as *self* (where s contains objects, not primitive values).

Some example constraints using these operators are:

```
Set{1, 5, 2, 3, 7, 0}->sort()->display() &
Set{"a", "g", "ga", "b0", "b"}->sort()->display()

Integer.subrange(1,5)->collect( x | x*x*x )->display()

Set{"a", "aa", "hh", "kle", "o", "kk"}->select( x | x.size >
1 )->display()
```

These produce the output:

```
[0, 1, 2, 3, 5, 7]
[a, b, b0, g, ga]

[1, 8, 27, 64, 125]

[aa, hh, kle, kk]
```

Table 4.7: Selection and collection operators

Expression	*Meaning as query*
s->select(P)	Collection of s elements satisfying P
s->select(x | P)	Collection of s elements x satisfying P
s->reject(P)	Collection of s elements not satisfying P
s->reject(x | P)	Collection of s elements x not satisfying P
s->collect(e)	Collection of elements x.e for x : s
s->collect(x | e)	Collection of elements x.e for x : s
s->selectMaximals(e)	Collection of s elements x which have maximal x.e values
s->selectMinimals(e)	Collection of s elements x which have minimal x.e values

As with quantifiers, infinite collections cannot be referred to in OCL collection expressions: $String \rightarrow collect(e)$ and other such expressions are not valid.

4.1.6 Navigation expressions

Navigation expressions are applications of features to objects or to object collections, for example $d.courses.lecturer$ in the department data example, where $d : Department$. They can be read backwards, e.g., as "the lecturers of the courses of d". They will denote single objects or values, or collections of values/objects, according to the rules of Table 4.8.

Table 4.8: Navigation expressions

e	feature f	$e.f$
single object	attribute	single value
	1-multiplicity role	single object
	set-valued role	set of objects
	sequence-valued role	sequence of objects
set of objects	attribute	set of values
	1-multiplicity role	set of objects
	set-valued role	set of objects
	sequence-valued role	set of objects
sequence of objects	attribute	sequence of values
	1-multiplicity role	sequence of objects
	set-valued role	set of objects
	sequence-valued role	sequence of objects

Note that long chains of navigation through a model should be avoided in specifications, as these are both difficult to understand, and expensive to compute.

4.1.7 Object deletion

An object or set of objects x of class E can be deleted by using an expression $x \rightarrow isDeleted()$ as an update. This deletion means that the objects are no longer valid elements of E, and leads to several further possible effects:

1. x is removed from any association which has E as an end class.

2. x is removed from any superclass of E.

3. If an association $r : F \rightarrow E$ has multiplicity 1 at the E end, then any F object linked to x by r is also deleted (since each existing F object must have exactly one valid associated E object).

4. If an association $r : E \rightarrow F$ or $r : E \rightarrow Collection(F)$ is an aggregation (composition association) at the E end, then any F objects linked to x by r will also be deleted: this is the 'deletion propagation' semantics of aggregation.

The generated Java carries out this succession of deletion actions via operations $killE$, $killF$, etc., of the *Controller* class. If cascaded deletions in cases 3 and 4 are not intended, then the F objects should be unlinked from x before the deletion of x. If an association end is $\{addOnly\}$, then objects of the class at this end can only be deleted if they do not occur in any role set of this association.

4.1.8 Additional cases of quantification operators

Version 1.4 of UML-RSDS introduced *forAll*, *exists*, *exists*1 quantification over *Integer.subrange*(st, en) sequences, e.g.:

$$result = Integer.subrange(1, 10) \rightarrow exists(x \mid x * x > 50)$$

and $Set(E)$ for entities E, for both query and update uses, e.g.:

$$(s \rightarrow subcollections()) \rightarrow forAll(x \mid x \rightarrow display())$$

exists quantification is supported for query uses.

Note that *select*, *collect* and *reject* cannot be used with collections of numbers or strings, or collections of collections, but only with collections of class instances. Ordered *forAll* quantification over entities can be specified when a constraint is created (the last field in the dialog of Fig. 4.1), and indicates that the executable implementation of the quantification should iterate over the collection elements in ascending order of the specified expression on these elements (this facility is for type 1, 2 and 3 postcondition constraints for general use cases only).

4.2 Type checking

For each expression in a specification, its type and element type (for a collection-valued expression) are determined, according to Tables 4.10, 4.11 and 4.12. The most general numeric type of two numeric values x and y is given by Table 4.9. The least common supertype (LCS) of the types of $x1$, $x2$ is the most specific type which includes both types.

Table 4.9: Numeric type generalisation

x type	y type	*General numeric type*
double	double	double
double	int or long	double
int or long	double	double
long	long	long
long	int	long
int	long	long
int	int	int

The OCL standard does not define - or ∩ when the first argument is a sequence, or ∪ for the union of a sequence and a set. For convenience we define these as:

$$
\begin{aligned}
sq - col &= sq{\rightarrow}reject(x \mid col{\rightarrow}includes(x)) \\
sq \cap col &= sq{\rightarrow}select(x \mid col{\rightarrow}includes(x)) \\
sq \cup st &= sq{\rightarrow}asSet() \cup st
\end{aligned}
$$

A subtle aspect of the semantics of *collect* is that it always returns a Sequence, even when applied on sets: the result of $st{\rightarrow}collect(e)$ can contain duplicate values for sets st, and the cardinality of the result always equals that of st. This is in accordance with the OCL behaviour of *collectNested*, which should return a Bag of the evaluation results.

Table 4.10: Numeric operator types

Expression	Type	Element type
x + y	String (if one of x, y is a string), or general numeric type of x, y	–
x - y	General numeric type of x, y	–
x * y	General numeric type of x, y	–
x / y	General numeric type of x, y	–
x mod y	int	–
x.sqr	double	–
x.sqrt	double	–
x.floor	int	–
x.round	int	–
x.ceil	int	–
x.abs	double	–
x.exp	double	–
x.log	double	–
x.pow(y)	double	–
x.sin	double	–
x.cos	double	–
x.tan	double	–
Integer.subrange(st,en)	Sequence	int

4.3 Differences to OCL

UML-RSDS supports most features of the OCL standard library [2]. Omitted are:

■ OclAny, OclVoid, OclInvalid: omitted due to absence of suitable semantics. The implementation of OCL in UML-RSDS (and for B, SMV, Z3 and code translations) has a two-valued logic. Association ends of multiplicity 0..1 are treated as sets (or sequences, if ordered) of maximum size 1. There are no explicit null or invalid elements. Null elements cannot be defined, and are not permitted to be members of association ends or other collections.

■ OclMessage: replaced by invocation instance expressions on sequence diagrams.

■ UnlimitedNatural: not needed for internal use within models.

■ Integer, Real: replaced by int, long, double. The reason for this is to ensure that the specification semantics of these types corresponds to their semantics in the generated executable (in Java and C#) and in B.

Table 4.11: Collection operators types

Expression	Type	Element type
$Set\{\}$	Set	–
$Sequence\{\}$	Sequence	–
$Set\{x1, x2, ..., xn\}$	Set	LCS of types of $x1$ to xn
$Sequence\{x1, x2, ..., xn\}$	Sequence	LCS of types of $x1$ to xn
s->including(x)	Type of s	LCS of type of x and element type of s
s->excluding(x)	Type of s	Element type of s
s - t	Type of s	Element type of s
s->prepend(x)	Sequence	LCS of type of x and element type of s
s->append(x)	Sequence	LCS of type of x and element type of s
s->count(x)	Integer (int)	–
s->indexOf(x)	Integer (int)	–
$x\backslash/y$	Sequence if x, y ordered, otherwise Set	LCS of element types of x, y
$x/\backslash y$	Type of x	Element type of x
$x \frown y$	Sequence	LCS of element types of x and y
x->union(y)	Same as $x\backslash/y$	Same as $x\backslash/y$
x->intersection(y)	Same as $x/\backslash y$	Same as $x/\backslash y$
x->symmetricDifference(y)	Set	LCS of element types of x, y
x->any()	Element type of x	–
x->subcollections()	Set	Type of x
x->reverse()	Sequence	Element type of x
x->front()	Sequence	Element type of x
x->tail()	Sequence	Element type of x
x->first()	Element type of x	–
x->last()	Element type of x	–
x->sort()	Sequence	Element type of x
x->sortedBy(e)	Sequence	Element type of x
x->sum()	String if any element of x is a String, otherwise LCS of x element types	–
x->prd()	General numeric type of elements of x	–
Integer.Sum(a,b,x,e)	Type of e	–
Integer.Prd(a,b,x,e)	Type of e	–
x->max()	Element type of x	–
x->min()	Element type of x	–
x->asSet()	Set	Element type of x
x->asSequence()	Sequence	Element type of x
s->isUnique(e)	Boolean	–
x->isDeleted()	Boolean	–

Table 4.12: Selection/collection operators types

Expression	Type	Element type
s->select(P)	Type of s	Element type of s
s->select(x | P)	Type of s	Element type of s
s->reject(P)	Type of s	Element type of s
s->reject(x | P)	Type of s	Element type of s
s->collect(e)	Sequence	Type of e
s->collect(x | e)	Sequence	Type of e
s->selectMaximals(e)	Type of s	Element type of s
s->selectMinimals(e)	Type of s	Element type of s
s->unionAll(e)	Sequence if s type and e type Sequence, otherwise Set	Element type of e
s->intersectAll(e)	Set	Element type of e

- max, min between two values: expressed instead by generalised max, min operations on collections. These apply also to collections of strings.

- oclIsTypeOf(T), flatten(), and equalsIgnoreCase() (to be included in future tool versions).

- The xor logical operator: this can be expressed using the other logical operators. The operators and, implies are written as &, =>.

- Set, sequence and string subtraction uses the - operator, extending OCL in the case of sequences and strings.

- OrderedSet and Bag are omitted: both can be represented by sequences. In the future, sorted sets will be introduced (the {*sorted*} constraint on association ends).

- Tuples and the cartesian product of two collections: these are very rarely used in modelling. The same effect can be achieved by introducing a new class with many-one associations directed to the tuple component entities, and similarly for ternary or higher-arity associations. Sequences can be used to represent tuple values.

- *collectNested* in OCL is the same as *collect* in UML-RSDS, i.e., no flattening takes place.

- The *one* operator of OCL is expressed by *exists*1.

The OCL *substring* and *subsequence* operators are combined into a single *subrange* operation in UML-RSDS.

Sets can be written with the notation $\{x1, ..., xn\}$ instead of $Set\{x1, ..., xn\}$. Intersection and union can use the mathematical operators $\cap$ and $\cup$ written as $/\backslash$ and $\backslash/$. Likewise, subtraction on collections is written using -.

Additional to standard OCL are the operators $s \rightarrow isDeleted()$, $s \rightarrow unionAll(e)$, $s \rightarrow intersectAll(e)$, $s \rightarrow selectMinimals(e)$, $s \rightarrow selectMaximals(e)$ and $s \rightarrow subcollections()$, $Integer.Sum(a, b, i, e)$, $Integer.Prd(a, b, i, e)$, and the $Integer.subrange(i, j)$ type constructor.

Qualified or composition associations and association classes are not yet fully supported: Java, C#, C++ and B can be defined for these associations, but their values cannot be stored in or retrieved from instance models. Only binary associations are supported.

Summary

This chapter has introduced the OCL notation supported by UML-RSDS, and given examples of specifications using OCL. The rules for expression types and constraint semantics have been defined.

References

[1] K. Lano, *UML-RSDS manual*, http://www.dcs.kcl.ac.uk/staff/kcl/umlrsds.pdf, 2015.

[2] OMG, *Object Constraint Language 2.4 Specification*, www.omg.org/spec/OCL/2.4, 2014.

Chapter 5

Use Cases

Use cases define the services which a system or component provides to its clients or users. In UML-RSDS use cases are precisely specified using OCL, and their effects are defined in terms of the modifications they make to the class diagram data (and possibly calls to external applications). Use cases are shown on the system class diagram together with the classes they relate to.

5.1 Specification of use cases

The use cases of a system represent the externally available services that it provides to clients, either directly to users, or to other parts of a larger system. Two forms of use case can be defined in UML-RSDS:

- EIS use cases – simple operations such as creating an instance of an entity, modifying an instance, etc., intended to be implemented using an EIS platform such as Java Enterprise Edition. These are described in Chapter 20.

- General use cases – units of functionality of arbitrary complexity, specified by constraints (pre and postconditions of the use case). These are particularly used to specify model transformations (Chapter 7). They are visually represented as ovals in the class diagram. They may have their own attributes and operations, since use cases are classifiers in UML. Use case invariants can also be defined for general use cases.

General use cases can be structured and composed using several different mechanisms:

- *extend*: one use case can be declared as an extension of another, to provide additional functionality to the base use case.

- *include*: one use case can be included in one or several other use cases, to define a sub-operation or process of the base use cases. This can be used to factor out common sub-processes.

- *Parameterisation*: a use case can be given typed parameters to make it generic and reusable.

- *Inheritance*: a use case can inherit another, to specialise its effect. Inheritance of use cases is not currently supported by UML-RSDS as we have not found it a useful facility in practice.

The elementary example of a "Hello world" program can be defined as a single postcondition

```
"Hello world!"->display()
```

of a use case on an empty metamodel.

A simple example of a use case for our teaching system (Fig. 3.1) could have the single postcondition (with no entity context):

```
Lecturer->exists( k | k.name = "Mike" )
```

which creates a lecturer object with name "Mike".

The option *Use Case Dependencies* on the *View* menu allows the dependencies between use cases and classes to be seen: a red dashed line is drawn from a use case to each class whose data it may modify, and a green dashed line is drawn from each class read by the use case, to the use case.

5.2   General use cases

A general use case can be introduced into a UML-RSDS system to represent any service provided by that system, or a subpart of such a service. An example is the correlation calculator of Chapter 1.

Figure 5.1 shows the UML-RSDS dialog for creating use cases. For general use cases only the name needs to be entered, along with any parameters.

Figure 5.2 shows the UML-RSDS dialog for modifying use cases.

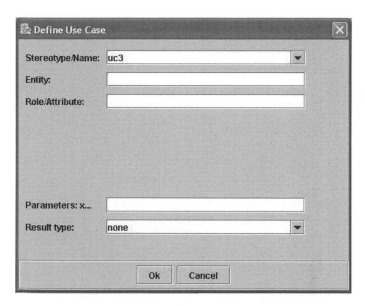

Figure 5.1: Use case dialog

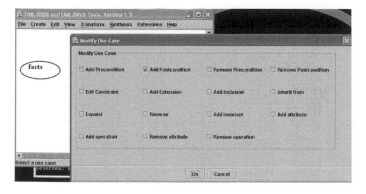

Figure 5.2: Use case edit dialog

A use case has:

- A name: this should be unique among the use cases of the system, and distinct from any class name. It should usually have a lower case initial letter. There is an implicit class associated with any use case: this class has the same name as the use case, but with the first letter capitalised, so this version of the name should also not conflict with any existing class name.

- Parameters, specified by their name and type. These are restricted to numeric, boolean or string types.

- Assumptions (preconditions): constraints *Asm* defining when the use case may be validly invoked. The default is *true*.

- Postconditions: a sequence of constraints *Post* defining the effect of the use case. The sequential order of the constraints is used as the order of the corresponding code segments.

Use cases may also have:

- *Invariants*: constraints expressing which properties are preserved during the use case.

- *Activity*: an activity in pseudocode defining the behaviour of the use case, for example, in terms of included use cases. The default, if no explicit activity is defined, is the sequential composition of the included use cases, following the code *stat(Post)* of the use case itself.

- *Operations and attributes*: these are static features owned by the use case and only available within its postcondition constraints.

5.2.1 Use case post-conditions

Use case post-conditions must be written in particular orders, to ensure that data which is needed by one constraint is available (e.g., because it has been produced by an earlier constraint) at the point where it is used. The correlation calculator example (Section 2.1) illustrates this principle.

For each predicate P we define the *write frame* $wr(P)$ of P, and the *read frame* $rd(P)$ (Table 5.1). These are the sets of entities and features which the procedural interpretation $stat(P)$ of P may update or access, respectively. The *write frame* $wr(P)$ of a predicate is the set of features and entities that it modifies, when interpreted as an activity (an activity $stat(P)$ to establish P). This includes object creation. The *read frame* $rd(P)$ is the set of entities and features read in P. The read and write frames can help to distinguish different implementation strategies for constraints (Chapter 6). $var(P)$ is the set of all features and entity type names used in P.

Table 5.1: Definition of read and write frames

P	$rd(P)$	$wr(P)$
Basic expression e without quantifiers, logical operators or $=, :, E[],$ $\rightarrow includes,$ $\rightarrow includesAll,$ $\rightarrow excludesAll,$ $\rightarrow excludes,$ $\rightarrow isDeleted$	Set of features and entity type names used in P: $var(P)$	$\{\}$
$e1 : e2.r$ $e2.r \rightarrow includes(e1)$ r many-valued $e1, e2$ single-valued	$var(e1) \cup var(e2)$	$\{r\}$
$e2.r \rightarrow excludes(e1)$ $e1 \; / : \; e2.r$ r many-valued $e1, e2$ single-valued	$var(e1) \cup var(e2)$	$\{r\}$
$e1.f = e2$ $e1$ single-valued	$var(e1) \cup var(e2)$	$\{f\}$
$e1.f[i] = e2$ $e1$ single-valued, f sequence-valued	$var(e1) \cup var(e2)$ $\cup \; var(i)$	$\{f\}$
$e1.f \rightarrow last() = e2$ $e1.f \rightarrow first() = e2$ $e1$ single-valued f sequence-valued	$var(e1) \cup var(e2)$	$\{f\}$
$e2.r \rightarrow includesAll(e1)$ $e1 \; <: \; e2.r$ $r, e1$ many-valued $e2$ single-valued	$var(e1) \cup var(e2)$	$\{r\}$
$e2.r \rightarrow excludesAll(e1)$ $r, e1$ many-valued $e2$ single-valued	$var(e1) \cup var(e2)$	$\{r\}$
$E[e1]$	$var(e1) \cup \{E\}$	$\{\}$
$E \rightarrow exists(x \mid Q)$ (E concrete entity type)	$rd(Q)$	$wr(Q) \cup \{E\} \cup$ all superclasses of E
$E \rightarrow exists1(x \mid Q)$ (E concrete entity type)	$rd(Q)$	$wr(Q) \cup \{E\} \cup$ all superclasses of E
$E \rightarrow forAll(x \mid Q)$	$rd(Q) \cup \{E\}$	$wr(Q)$
$x \rightarrow isDeleted()$ x of element type entity type E	$var(x)$	$\{E\} \cup$ all superclasses of $E \cup$ E-valued roles r
$C \; \Rightarrow \; Q$	$var(C) \cup rd(Q)$	$wr(Q)$
$Q \; \& \; R$	$rd(Q) \cup rd(R)$	$wr(Q) \cup wr(R)$

$e2.r \rightarrow excludes(e1)$ for single-valued r is treated as $e2 \rightarrow excludesAll$ $(e2 \rightarrow select(r = e1))$, and $e2.r \rightarrow excludesAll(e1)$ for single-valued r is treated as $e2 \rightarrow excludesAll(e2 \rightarrow select(r : e1))$. $e1.f \rightarrow first() = e2$ has the same read and write frames as $e1.f \rightarrow last() = e2$ (see Section 14.5). In computing $wr(P)$ we also take account of the features and entity types which depend upon the explicitly updated features and entity types of Cn, such as inverse association ends. If there is an invariant constraint φ of the class diagram which implicitly defines a feature g in terms of feature f, i.e.: $f \in rd(\varphi)$ and $g \in wr(\varphi)$, then g depends on f. In particular, if an association end $role2$ has a named opposite end $role1$, then $role1$ depends on $role2$ and vice-versa. Creating an instance x of a concrete entity type E also adds x to each supertype F of E, and so these supertypes are also included in the write frames of $E \rightarrow exists(x \mid Q)$ and $E \rightarrow exists1(x \mid Q)$ in Table 5.1. Deleting an instance x of entity type E by $x \rightarrow isDeleted()$ may affect any supertype of E and any association end owned by E or its supertypes, and any association end incident with E or incident with any supertype of E. Additionally, if entity types E and F are related by an association which is a composition at the E end, or by an association with a mandatory multiplicity at the E end, i.e., a multiplicity with lower bound 1 or more, then deletion of E instances will affect F and its features and supertypes and incident associations, recursively. The read frame of an operation invocation $e.op(pars)$ is the read frame of e and of the $pars$ corresponding to the input parameters of op together with the read frame of the postcondition $Post_{op}$ of op, excluding the formal parameters v of op. Its write frame is that of the actual parameters corresponding to the outputs of op, and $wr(Post_{op}) - v$. $wr(G)$ of a set G of constraints is the union of the constraint write frames, likewise for $rd(G)$.

A dependency ordering $Cn < Cm$ is defined between constraints by

$$wr(Cn) \cap rd(Cm) \neq \{\}$$

"Cm depends on Cn". A use case with postconditions $C_1, \ldots, C_n$ should satisfy the *syntactic non-interference* conditions:

1. If $C_i < C_j$, with $i \neq j$, then $i < j$.

2. If $i \neq j$ then $wr(C_i) \cap wr(C_j) = \{\}$.

Together, these conditions ensure that the activities $stat(C_j)$ of subsequent constraints C_j cannot invalidate earlier constraints C_i, for $i < j$.

A use case satisfies *semantic non-interference* if for $i < j$:

$$C_i \implies [stat(C_j)] C_i$$

where $[act]P$ is the weakest-precondition of P with respect to act. Syntactic non-interference implies semantic non-interference, but not conversely. Under either condition we can deduce that the use case achieves the conjunction of its postconditions [1].

The UML-RSDS tools give warnings if the syntactic non-interference conditions fail for two constraints. If both $C_i < C_j$ and $C_j < C_i$ hold, with $i \neq j$, then these constraints are placed in a constraint group $\{C_i, C_j\}$, and implemented as a unit (Chapter 6).

A typical form of postcondition for a refinement or migration transformation is "for all instances of source entity type ST that satisfy condition $Ante$, create an instance of target entity type TT satisfying P": $(R1)$

$\qquad ST ::$
$$Ante \;\Rightarrow\; TT \rightarrow exists(t \mid P)$$

P typically defines the feature values of the new instance t in terms of the feature values of $self : ST$. The implementation of this constraint is a bounded loop which iterates over all instances $self$ of the context entity ST, checks $Ante$ for $self$, and if this holds, applies the succedent to create a new t corresponding to the source instance. Subsequent constraints in the use case postconditions can then read instances of TT to assist in the construction of other target entity type instances. But later constraints should not write to ST or to its features (in a refinement or migration, the source model is normally read-only in any case).

It would break syntactic non-interference to have a second constraint which also creates and sets TT instances. However this may still be correct with regard to semantic non-interference. For example, if a constraint $(R2)$

$\qquad ST ::$
$$not(Ante) \;\Rightarrow\; TT \rightarrow exists(t \mid P1)$$

is included together with $R1$, then these do not interfere semantically as only one of $R1$ and $R2$ is executed for each instance of ST, and disjoint collections of TT instances are created for $ST \rightarrow select(Ante)$ and for $ST \rightarrow select(not(Ante))$.

More complex postconditions may be used for refactorings or other categories of transformation. In such cases the constraints express requirements of the form "for all instances of source entity type ST that satisfy condition $Ante$, update or restructure the model to achieve the condition $Succ$":

$\qquad ST ::$
$$Ante \;\Rightarrow\; Succ$$

For a refactoring, $Succ$ may contradict $Ante$, because $Ante$ will express some situation or structure in the model that should be removed by applying $Succ$, as in the example of Section 2.3.

Such constraints will typically be implemented by an unbounded loop

```
while some s : ST satisfies s.Ante
do
   (select such an s;
    apply stat(s.Succ)
   )
```

5.3   Composition and features of use cases

Basic use cases (use cases without activities or included use cases) can be composed together using *extend*. This has the effect of conjoining the postconditions of the extension and extended use cases to form the postconditions of the composed use case, and likewise for preconditions and invariants. This operator acts like a conjunction combinator of use cases (assumed to be mutually consistent). A new use case with the conjoined postconditions is added to the system model. More complex use cases/services can be composed from these basic use cases using *include* and use case activities. If use cases uc1, ..., ucn are included in use case uc, in that order, then the composed effect of uc includes executing uc1, ..., ucn after uc's own effect. An explicit activity for *uc* can alternatively be defined to invoke the included use cases according to an algorithm.

There are the following restrictions on extend/include:

- A use case cannot be an extension of two or more other use cases, nor both an extension and an inclusion.

- Cycles in the include/extend relationships (or cycles involving combinations of include/extend) are not permitted.

- The parameters of an included or extension use case must be a subset of those of the including/extended use case.

An elementary example of a use case is a transformation which calculates the square of some data values (Fig. 5.3). For each instance $a : A$, the use case $a2b$ creates a new $b : B$ instance with $b.y$ equal to $(a.x)^2$. The transformation has postcondition:

$$B \rightarrow exists(b \mid b.y = x * x)$$

on context class A.

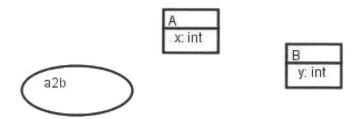

Figure 5.3: A to B Transformation τ_{a2b}

Another use case, $a2c$, could instead compute the cube of the $a.x$:

$$C \rightarrow exists(c \mid c.z = x * x * x)$$

on context class A, where C is an additional class, with an attribute $z : int$.

5.3.1 Extend-composition

These two use cases could be added as extensions ≪ *extend* ≫ of a base use case uc which has no postconditions of its own. Effectively, uc has postconditions

$$A :: \quad B \rightarrow exists(b \mid b.y = x * x)$$
$$A :: \quad C \rightarrow exists(c \mid c.z = x * x * x)$$

or (equivalently)

$$A :: \quad C \rightarrow exists(c \mid c.z = x * x * x)$$
$$A :: \quad B \rightarrow exists(b \mid b.y = x * x)$$

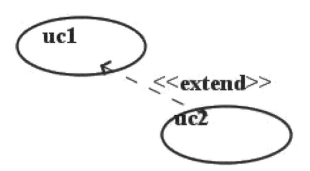

Figure 5.4: Use case extension of $uc1$ by $uc2$

The *extend*-composition of two use cases $uc1$, $uc2$ (Fig. 5.4) is a new use case whose *Post* is a sequence of constraints such that:

- *Post* consists of the constraints of $Post_{uc1}$ and $Post_{uc2}$

- The constraints of $uc1$ appear in the same order in *Post* as in $Post_{uc1}$, likewise for $uc2$.

- If $uc1$ and $uc2$ satisfy syntactic non-interference, and $wr(uc1)$ is disjoint from $wr(uc2)$, and either $wr(uc1)$ and $rd(uc2)$ are disjoint, or $wr(uc2)$ and $rd(uc1)$ are disjoint, then *Post* also satisfies syntactic non-interference.

The assumptions of the composite transformation are the union of the assumptions of its components, likewise for the invariants.

5.3.2 Include-composition

An *extend*-composition is semantically a conjunction or parallel composition of the main use case and its extensions. In contrast, an *include*-composition is a sequential composition of its main use case, followed by the included use cases, in order. For example, a strategy for mapping a class diagram to a relational database schema is to perform the following transformations:

- Replace inheritance by many-one associations

- Add primary key attributes to all classes

- Replace many-many associations by a new class and two many-one associations

- Replace many-one associations by foreign keys.

These could be expressed by separate transformations $uc1$ to $uc4$. The appropriate order for their use is as given above, and they could be defined as ≪ *include* ≫ use cases of a use case uc in this order, to define an overall transformation that applies the included transformations in this order.

5.3.3 Use case inversion

Given a use case uc whose postconditions are all of type 0 or type 1, an inverse use case $uc^\sim$ can be derived. This use case has inverse postcondition constraints $Cn^\sim$ for each postcondition constraint Cn of uc, listed in the same order as in uc (Section 7.4). The aim of this use case is to reverse the effect of uc, and permit the recovery of an input model of *uc* from an output model of its processing. In addition, $Cn^\sim$ is a candidate transformation invariant which should be preserved by the transformation steps of *stat(Cn)*. The inverse of a use case can be generated using the option *reverse* on the use case edit dialog.

The inverse of the simple A-to-B example given above is a constraint with the postcondition

$$A\to exists(a \mid a.x = y\to sqrt())$$

on context class *B*.

Constraints with multiple quantifiers, and with additional quantified variables and let variables can be inverted, however all *exists* quantifiers in the succedent should be grouped together. For example:

A ::
$$a1 : A \ \& \ a1.x = 2 * x \ \Rightarrow$$
$$C\to exists(c \mid D\to exists(d \mid$$
$$c.cId = aId \ \& \ d.dId = a1.aId \ \&$$
$$c.z = x \ \& \ d.w = a1.x \ \& \ d : c.dr))$$

can be inverted to:

C ::
$$d : D \ \& \ d : dr \ \Rightarrow$$
$$A\to exists(ax \mid A\to exists(a1 \mid$$
$$ax.aId = cId \ \& \ a1.aId = d.dId \ \& \ ax.x =$$
$$z \ \& \ a1.x = d.w \ \& \ a1.x = 2 * ax.x))$$

Transformation and use case inversion is discussed in more detail in Chapter 14.

5.3.4 *Use case parameters*

Use cases may have parameters of numeric, boolean or string type. The values of the parameters are supplied to the use case when it is executed. The parameters may be used in the assumption and postcondition constraints of the use case. For example, a use case *calculateSqRoot* could have an integer parameter $x : int$, assumption

$$x \geq 0$$

and a postcondition

$$x\to sqrt()\to display()$$

5.3.5 *Generic use cases*

Parameterisation may also be used to substitute part of the specification text of a use case with variant texts. A generic use case can be created from the *Create* menu, and should have a boolean parameter. The name of this parameter can then be used within the constraints of the use case as a subformula. For example, the *a2b* use case could be made into a generic use case with parameter p. The use case could have postcondition:

$$B \rightarrow exists(b \mid b.y = x * x \ \& \ p)$$

on context class A.

When the use case is instantiated, an actual predicate must be provided as the value for p: this could be some tracing or logging of the use case actions, such as

$$(``Mapped" + x + ``to" + b.y) \rightarrow display()$$

5.3.6 *Use case attributes*

According to the UML standard, use cases may own attributes, and UML-RSDS also permits this. Such attributes can be used to store the result of a computation performed in one constraint, for use in subsequent constraints. An attribute can be added to a use case using the modify use case dialog. It will be a static attribute. A use case attribute *att* can be referred to via the notation $Uc.att$ in the post conditions of its use case *uc* (*att* actually belongs to the class Uc associated with *uc*).

5.3.7 *Use case operations*

Use cases can own operations, to perform some calculation which is used internally in the use case. Such operations can help to avoid duplicated complex expressions in different constraints: an operation can be introduced which evaluates the expression, and this operation is then called in place of the expression within the constraints. The operation will be a static operation, and can be referred to in the postconditions of its use case *uc* by the notation $Uc.op(params)$.

The following use case is an example of parameterisation and use case operations: display factorial(i) for all i from 1 up to a parameter p. This could be specified as a parameterised UML-RSDS use case $fact(p : int)$ with one postcondition

$$Integer.subrange(1, p) \rightarrow forAll(i \mid Fact.factorial(i) \rightarrow display())$$

where *factorial* is a use case operation

```
static query factorial(i : int) : int
pre: i ≥ 1
post:
```
$$(i \leq 2 \Rightarrow result = i) \&$$
$$(i > 2 \Rightarrow result = i * factorial(i-1))$$

and this is defined as a $\ll$ *cached* $\gg$ operation, to avoid repeated evaluation of the factorial for the same argument value.

Summary

In this chapter we have described how system functionality can be specified in UML-RSDS using use cases. The elements of use cases, and the composition operators for use cases, have been explained.

References

[1] K. Lano, S. Kolahdouz-Rahimi and T. Clark, *A framework for model transformation verification*, BCS FACS Journal, 2014.

Chapter 6

Design Synthesis

This chapter examines in detail the design and code synthesis process in UML-RSDS. This process is automated, using a built-in synthesis strategy, but there is scope for user configuration and selection of alternative options in different cases. The process takes as input a logical system specification defined by a class diagram and use cases, and produces a language-independent design in a pseudocode activity language. In turn, this design can be directly mapped into implementations in Java, C#, C++, and potentially many other languages.

6.1 Synthesis of class diagram designs

The structure of the specification class diagram of a UML-RSDS system is directly followed in the design and implementation of the system: for each specification class E there is an implementation class E, with corresponding features: for each specification-level owned attribute $att : T$, the implementation class has an owned attribute att of type T', the implementation type corresponding to T. For each 1-valued role r owned by E, at the F end of a E to F association, there is a F-valued owned attribute of E's implementation. Table 6.1 summarises the specification to implementation mapping for class diagrams. The close structural correspondence between the UML-RSDS specification and the implementation code facilitates debugging of the specification: errors that arise in the code can usually be traced back to an error in the corresponding part of the specification. Of course, such code errors should not be corrected at the code level, but at the specification level.

Table 6.1: Mappings from UML/OCL to programming languages

UML/OCL	Java 4	Java 6	C#	C++
Class E	Class E	Class E	Class E	Class E
Interface I	Interface I + inner class *IOps*	Interface I + inner class *IOps*	Interface I + class *IOps*	Class I
Attribute *att* : T	instance variable T' att	instance variable T' att	instance variable T' att	instance variable T' att
1-valued role r to class F	instance variable F r	instance variable F r	instance variable F r	instance variable F* r
many-valued role r to class F (unordered)	instance variable List r	instance variable HashSet r	instance variable ArrayList r	instance variable set<F*>* r
many-valued role r to class F (ordered)	instance variable List r	instance variable ArrayList r	instance variable ArrayList r	instance variable vector<F*>* r
instance scope operation op(p : T) : RT of class E	operation public RT' op(T' p) of class E	operation public RT' op(T' p) of class E	operation public RT' op(T' p) of class E	operation public: RT' op(T' p) of class E
Inheritance of class F by class E	class E extends F	class E extends F	class E : F	class E : public F

6.2 Synthesis of constraint code

Constraints (boolean-valued expressions/logical predicates) are used in UML-RSDS both to express a required property which an operation or use case should establish, and to guide the generation of the executable code which *ensures* that the property is established. Thus an equation

$$v = e$$

where v is a variable or other assignable expression, is interpreted as an assignment $v := e$ at the design level, and as the corresponding programming language assignment statement at the implementation level. An expression $x : v.r$ is interpreted as a design $v.r := v.r{\rightarrow}including(x)$ which adds x to $v.r$, thereby establishing the expression as true. The same principle applies to a wide range of specification constraints. In particular, an existential quantifier $E{\rightarrow}exists(x \mid P)$ for concrete class E corresponds to the creation of an instance x of E.

The basis for the synthesis of operational behaviour from a UML-RSDS specification is the operational interpretation $stat(P)$ of OCL expressions, shown in Table 6.2. This interpretation is an activity which is intended to establish P, i.e., $[stat(P)]P$ holds true, where $[\;]$ is the weakest-precondition operator.

Updates to association ends may require additional further updates to inverses of the association ends (Table 3.2), updates to entity type extents or to features may require further updates to derived and other data-dependent features, and so forth. These updates are all included in the *stat* activity. In particular, for $x{\rightarrow}isDeleted()$, x is removed from every association end in which it resides, and further cascaded deletions may occur if these ends are mandatory/composition ends.

The clauses for $X{\rightarrow}exists(x \mid x.id = v \ \& \ P1)$ test for existence of an x with $x.id = v$ before creating such an object: this has implications for efficiency but is necessary for correctness: two distinct X elements with the same primary key value should not exist. This design strategy

Table 6.2: Definition of $stat(P)$

P	$stat(P)$	$Condition$
$x = e$	$x := e$	x is assignable, $x \notin var(e)$
$e : x$ $x \rightarrow includes(e)$	$x := x \rightarrow including(e)$	x is assignable, collection-valued, $x \notin var(e)$
$e \ / : x$ $x \rightarrow excludes(e)$	$x := x \rightarrow excluding(e)$	x is assignable, collection-valued, $x \notin var(e)$
$e <: x$ $x \rightarrow includesAll(e)$	$x := x \rightarrow union(e)$	x is assignable, collection-valued, $x \notin var(e)$
$e \ / <: x$ $x \rightarrow excludesAll(e)$	$x := x - e$	x is assignable, collection-valued, $x \notin var(e)$
$x \rightarrow isDeleted()$ (single object x)	; -composition of $E := E \rightarrow excluding(x)$ $y.r := y.r \rightarrow excluding(x)$	Each entity type E containing x each association end $y.r$ containing x
$obj.op(e)$	$obj.op(e)$	Single object obj
$objs.op(e)$	for $x : objs$ do $x.op(e)$	Collection $objs$
$P1$ & $P2$	$stat(P1);\ stat(P2)$	$wr(P2) \cap wr(P1) = \{\}$ $wr(P2) \cap rd(P1) = \{\}$
$E \rightarrow exists(x \mid x.id = v$ $\&\ P1)$ $E \rightarrow exists(x \mid P1)$	if $E.id \rightarrow includes(v)$ then $x := E[v];\ stat(P1)$ else $(x : E;$ $\quad stat(x.id = v\ \&\ P1))$ $(x : E;\ stat(P1))$	E is a concrete entity type with $E \rightarrow isUnique(id)$ E is a concrete entity type, $P1$ not of form $x.id = v\ \&\ P2$ for unique id attribute of E

$e \rightarrow exists(x \mid x.id = v$
 $\&\ P1)$
 	
 $e \rightarrow exists(x \mid P1)$
	if $e \rightarrow includes(E[v])$ then
	 $(x := E[v];\ stat(P1))$
	 else skip
	 if $e \rightarrow notEmpty()$ then
	 $(x := e \rightarrow any(true);$
	 $\quad stat(P1))$ else skip
		Non-writable expression e with element entity type E, $E \rightarrow isUnique(id)$
		 Non-writable expression e, $P1$ not of above form

$E \rightarrow exists1(x \mid P1)$	if $E \rightarrow exists(x \mid P1)$ then skip else $stat(E \rightarrow exists(x \mid P1))$	E is an entity type or non-writable expression
$E \rightarrow forAll(x \mid P1)$	for $x : E$ do $stat(P1)$	
$P1 \Rightarrow P2$	if $P1$ then $stat(P2)$ else skip	$P1$ side-effect free $wr(P2) \cap var(P1) = \{\}$

is a case of the well-known principle of 'check before enforce' used in QVT, ETL, ATL and other transformation languages. The write frame of $stat(P)$ is equal to $wr(P)$, the read frame includes $rd(P)$. As an example of these definitions, $stat(R)$ for the postcondition R of the transformation of Fig. 5.3 is:

```
for a : A
do
  (b : B;
  b.y := a.x*a.x;
  )
```

It is invalid to write the same data in both arguments of a conjunction: $x = 5$ & $x = 7$ has no defined procedural form, nor should later conjuncts write data read in earlier conjuncts: $y = x$ & $x = 7$ is also invalid. It is acceptable to read data written in earlier conjuncts: $x = 5$ & $y = x + 7$ has procedural interpretation $x := 5;\ y := x + 7$. It is also possible to use pre-forms of data to read their values prior to the effect of the statement being specified: $y = x@pre$ & $x = 7$ is valid and has procedural interpretation $y := x$; $x := 7$.

6.3   Synthesis of use case designs

Each use case is mapped to a global operation of the system, implemented as a public operation of the *Controller* class of the system. The code of the operation for use case *uc* is derived from the use case postconditions. Specific design and implementation strategies are used for use case postcondition constraints, as defined in Table 6.3. The postcondition constraints *Cn* are generally of the form

$$Ante \Rightarrow Succ$$

on some context entity type (classifier) S_i. *Ante* denotes the antecedent (condition) of the constraint, *Succ* the succedent (effect). We include S_i in $rd(Cn)$. The choice of design strategy depends upon the internal data dependencies of the constraint *Cn*: if the constraint modifies a disjoint collection $wr(Cn)$ of model features (entities and their features) to the collection $rd(Cn)$ of model features that it reads, then it can be implemented by a bounded loop (a for-loop in Java, C# or C++). Otherwise a fixed-point iteration is required, which applies the constraint until it is established, using a while-loop.

Table 6.3: Implementation choices for constraints *Cn*

	Data dependencies	Implementation choice
Type 0	No contextual classifier	$stat(Cn)$
Type 1	$wr(Cn) \cap rd(Cn) = \{\}$	for loop over S_i
Type 2	Succedent *Succ* has $wr(Succ) \cap rd(Succ) \neq \{\}$ but $wr(Succ) \cap rd(Ante) = \{\}$	while-iteration of for loop over S_i
Type 3	$wr(Succ) \cap rd(Ante) \neq \{\}$	while iteration of search-and-return loop

The higher the constraint type number, the more thorough is the implementation in attempting to establish the constraint – and the more time-consuming and complex is the implementation. Type 2 and 3 constraints are not guaranteed to terminate.

Unless fixed-point iteration is essential for a problem, constraints should be written as type 1 where possible. One technique for enforcing the use of a bounded loop is to use $f@pre$ throughout the constraint, whenever a feature is read. For example, a constraint that increments the $x : Integer$ attribute of every A object could be written (incorrectly) as

$$x = x + 1$$

on context class A. But this reads and writes $A :: x$ and so will have a fixed-point implementation that attempts to make the equality $a.x = a.x + 1$ true for every $a : A$. This would not terminate. The constraint should instead be written as:

$$x = x@pre + 1$$

on context class A. The term $x@pre$ denotes the read-only value of x at the start of execution of the constraint. The write and read frames are now disjoint and a bounded loop implementation is synthesised, which iterates once through the existing instances of A.

If $wr(C_j) \cap rd(C_i)$ and $wr(C_i) \cap wr(C_j)$ are empty, the sequence C_i, C_j of constraints can be implemented by $stat(C_i); \ stat(C_j)$. The structure of the generated design is therefore closely aligned with the specification structure, which helps in relating code generation issues back to the UML specification level.

6.3.1 Type 1 constraints

In the simple case where a constraint Cn of the form $Ante \Rightarrow Succ$ on context class S_i satisfies the type 1 condition:

$$wr(Cn) \cap rd(Cn) \ = \ \{\}$$

the constraint can be implemented by a bounded loop

for $s \ : \ S_i$ **do** $s.op_i()$

over S_i. In S_i we introduce a new instance-scope operation of the form:

$op_i()$
post:
$\quad Ante \quad \Rightarrow \quad Succ$

We refer to this strategy as constraint implementation approach 1. Confluence of this implementation can be shown, if the updates of written data in different executions of the loop body are independent of the order of the executions. The time complexity of the implementation is linear in the size $\#\overline{S_i}$ of the source domain. More precisely the worst case complexity is linear in

$$\#\overline{S_i} * (cost_{eval}(Ante) + cost_{act}(Succ))$$

where $cost_{eval}(e)$ is the time required to evaluate e, and $cost_{act}(e)$ the time required to execute $stat(e)$. If additional source domains D (from quantified variables $v : D$) also need to be iterated over, the cost is also multiplied by their size. This shows that multiple element matching or complex expressions in the constraint should be avoided for efficiency reasons. If ordered iteration over S_i is needed, i.e., an iteration which selects S_i elements in ascending order of the value of an expression e with context S_i, then a sorted version of S_i can be precomputed before the above iteration:

$sisorted$:= $S_i {\rightarrow} sortedBy(e)$;
for s : $sisorted$ do $s.op_i()$

The data features occurring in e count as data read in the antecedent of Cn.

6.3.2   Type 2 constraints

A more complex implementation strategy is required for type 2 and type 3 constraints. In the case where

$$wr(Cn) \cap rd(Succ)$$

is non-empty but the other conditions of non-interference still hold (i.e., a type 2 constraint), a fixed-point iteration of the form:

$running$:= $true$;
while $(running)$ do
  $(running$:= $false$;
    for s : S_i do
      if $s.Ante$ then
        [if $s.Succ$ then skip
        else] $(s.op()$; $running$:= $true)$
      else skip)

can be used, where $op()$ is a new operation of S_i defined as:

$op()$
pre: $Ante$
post: $Succ$

In the conditional test within the *for* loop, $Succ$ is evaluated in a non side-effecting manner.

We refer to this fixed-point strategy as constraint implementation approach number 2. The conditional test of $Succ$ and the code between [and] can be omitted if it is known that $Ante \Rightarrow not(Succ)$. The UML-RSDS tools perform algebraic simplification to check if $Ante$ contradicts

Succ. This is the Omit Negative Application Conditions design pattern (Chapter 9). The design synthesiser prompts the user to confirm if this optimisation should be used.

In order to establish termination and confluence, it is necessary to define a measure $Q : \mathbb{N}$ over the source and target models, which is a *variant* for the while loop (2):

$$\forall \nu : \mathbb{N} \cdot Q = \nu \wedge running = true \wedge \nu > 0 \;\Rightarrow\; [body](Q < \nu)$$

where *body* is the body of the while loop.

Q is also necessary to prove correctness: while there remain $s : S_i$ with *Ante* true but *Succ* false, then $Q > 0$ and the iteration will apply *op* to such an s. At termination, $running = false$, which can only occur if there are no $s : S_i$ with *Ante* true but *Succ* false, so the constraint therefore holds true, and $Q = 0$. Confluence also follows if $Q = 0$ is only possible in one unique state of the source and target models which can be reached from the initial state by applying the constraint: this will be the state at termination regardless of the order in which elements were transformed.

The time complexity of the implementation depends on the value of Q on the starting models *smodel*, *tmodel*, and on the size $\#\overline{S_i}$ of the domain. The worst case complexity is of the order

$$Q(smodel, tmodel) * \#\overline{S_i} * (cost_{eval}(Ante) + cost_{eval}(Succ) + cost_{act}(Succ))$$

since the inner loop may be performed Q times. Optimisation by omitting the successor test reduces the complexity by removing the term $cost_{eval}(Succ)$. Again in the case of an ordered iteration, precomputation of a sorted version of the source domain can be used:

```
running   :=   true;
sisorted  :=   Si→sortedBy(e);
while (running) do
  (running  :=  false;
   for s : sisorted do
     if s.Ante then
        [if s.Succ then skip
        else] (s.op();  running  :=  true)
     else skip)
```

The cost of the sorting is then added to the overall execution time.

6.3.3 Type 3 constraints

If the other conditions of non-interference fail (a type 3 constraint), then the application of a constraint to one element may change the elements to which the constraint may subsequently be applied to, so that a fixed *for*-loop iteration over these elements cannot be used. Instead, a schematic iteration of the form:

while *some source element s satisfies a constraint lhs* do
select such an s and apply the constraint

can be used. This can be explicitly coded as:

running := *true*;
while *running* do
  running := *search*()

where *search* is a new static operation of S_i defined as:

```
static search() : Boolean
   (for s : Sᵢ do
      if s.Ante then
        [if s.Succ then skip
        else] (s.op(); return true));
   return false
```

and the new operation *op* of S_i has postcondition *Succ*. We call this approach 3, iteration of a search-and-return loop. As with approach 2, the conditional test of *Succ* and code between [and] can be omitted if it is known that $Ante \Rightarrow not(Succ)$, or if the user confirms this optimisation.

As in approach 2, a Q measure is needed to prove termination and correctness. Termination follows if Q is a variant of the while loop: applying $op()$ to some $s : S_i$ with *Ante* and $not(Succ)$ decreases Q, even if new elements of S_i are generated. Correctness holds since *search* returns false exactly when $Q = 0$, i.e., when no $s : S_i$ falsifying the constraint remain. As for type 2 constraints, confluence can be deduced from uniqueness of the termination state. The worst case execution time complexity is of the order

$$Q(smodel, tmodel) * maxS * (cost_{eval}(Ante) + cost_{eval}(Succ) + cost_{act}(Succ))$$

where *maxS* is the maximum size of $\#\overline{S_i}$ reached during the computation. Again, optimisation can remove the $cost_{eval}(Succ)$ term.

For a sorted iteration, the sorted version of S_i must be recomputed each time S_i or e are modified:

```
static search() : Boolean
   (sisorted := Sᵢ→sortedBy(e);
      for s : sisorted do
      if s.Ante then
        [if s.Succ then skip
        else] (s.op(); return true));
   return false
```

This can result in high time complexities, because the cost of sorting is now included in the cost of each individual iteration. Thus sorted iteration with type 3 constraints should be avoided if at all possible: if neither S_i nor the data of e is written by Cn, then the ordering of the S_i elements will not change, and *sisorted* can be precomputed.

In the case that two or more constraints are mutually data-dependent, i.e.,

$$wr(Ci) \cap rd(Cj) \neq \{\}$$

and

$$wr(Cj) \cap rd(Ci) \neq \{\}$$

then the constraints are combined into a constraint group $\{Ci, Cj\}$, and such groups are amalgamated. Such groups will be implemented by a generalised form of the type 2 or type 3 fixed-point iterations described above. The execution will attempt C_i as many times as possible before attempting C_j, and then repeat this behaviour while either remains applicable to the source model.

6.3.4 *Type 0 constraints*

Type 0 constraints are those constraints without an entity context. They represent a single action, such as an initialisation step at the beginning of a use case. Even if they do contain expressions of the form

$$E \rightarrow forAll(e \mid P)$$

in their conclusion, for an entity type E, this is interpreted as a bounded (for) loop over E, not a fixed-point loop. The interpretation of a type 0 constraint Cn is $stat(Cn)$ as defined in Table 6.2.

A common form of type 0 constraint is an iteration over a finite range of integers, for example:

$$Integer.subrange(1, 10) \rightarrow forAll(i \mid (i * i) \rightarrow display())$$

which displays the squares of integers from 1 to 10.

6.3.5 *Quantified and let variables*

Use case post-condition constraints may have additional quantified variables $v : e$ or let variables $v = e$ in their antecedents, where v is a new identifier not occurring as a feature name of the use case or context class, and distinct from other parameter, let or quantifier variable names of the use case, and e is an expression not involving v.

For example, the constraint (C1) iterating over the *Sudoku* class:

```
Sudoku::
  sq : square & sq.value = 0 & v = sq.possibleValues() & v.size = 1  =>
                               sq.value = v->min() & self.showBoard()
```

from the Sudoku solver of Chapter 2 has quantified variable sq and let variable v. These variables are computed as an additional part of the design and implementation of the constraint. A quantified variable $v : e$ introduces a bounded loop

```
for v : e
do
   (stat)
```

where $stat$ is the design for the remainder of the constraint following the quantified variable.

A let variable $v = e$ introduces an additional creation and assignment statement:

$$v : T := e;$$
$$stat$$

where T is the type of v deduced from e, and $stat$ is the design for the remainder of the constraint following the let variable.

As discussed previously in this chapter, the use of quantified variables has implications for the efficiency of the constraint implementation, and the use of a pattern such as Restrict Input Ranges (Chapter 9) is recommended to ensure that the smallest possible quantification range e is chosen for an additional quantified variable $v : e$. Let variables $v = e$ will also be recomputed on each application of the constraint, and so the complexity of the expression e defining the variable should also be reduced where possible. Let definitions should be moved before quantified variables unless they depend upon those variables (in $C1$ above, v's definition depends on sq, so this optimisation cannot be made in this case).

6.3.6   Specification and design guidelines

The following are useful guidelines to follow when constructing a UML-RSDS specification or design:

Avoid type 2 or 3 constraints if possible: use a pattern such as Replace Fixed-point Iteration by Bounded Iteration (Chapter 9) to avoid writing and reading the same data in a constraint, unless this is necessary for the problem. Type 2 and type 3 constraints are more difficult to analyse than type 0 or type 1 constraints, and cannot generally be inverted.

Avoid collection matching: quantified variables of the form v : $Set(e)$ should be avoided by using a simple quantified variable $x : e$ and defining the required set as some collection based on x: $v = f(x)$. See Sections 2.3 and 13.2 for examples.

Avoid operation calls in succedents of type 2 or 3 constraints: these can lead to incorrect implementations.

Avoid ordered iteration of type 3 constraints: as discussed above, this can lead to highly inefficient implementations.

Summary

This chapter has described how platform-independent designs are synthesised from specifications. The synthesis rules for different cases of constraints have been explained. We have also provided guidelines for improving the efficiency of designs.

Chapter 7

Model Transformations

Model transformations are a central element of model-based development approaches. Transformations can be used to improve the quality of models, to refactor models, to migrate or translate models from one representation to another, and to generate code or other text from models. In UML-RSDS, transformations are defined by use cases and are treated as a special case of software system, to which all the normal development facilities of UML-RSDS can be applied.

7.1 Model transformation concepts

Model transformations operate on one or more models, each model m conforms to a language or metamodel M which defines the structure of the model: what kinds of element it can contain and how these are linked (Fig. 7.1). We write $m : M$ to express that model m conforms to/is an instance of metamodel/language M. Typically a transformation τ maps a single model m which is an instance model of a source language S, to an instance model n of the target language T (a *mapping* or *separate-models* transformation), or updates a model $m : S$ in-place to form a new model $m' : S$ (an *update-in-place* transformation). Transformations operating on more than one language are termed *exogenous*, transformations that only involve a single language are termed *endogenous*. Figure 7.1 shows a *model-to-model* transformation, where source models are mapped to target models. Code generation transformations may instead generate text from models, this is referred to as a *model-to-text* transformation.

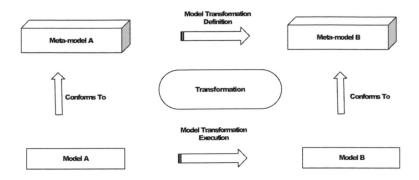

Figure 7.1: Model transformation context

Table 7.1 gives some examples of different kinds of transformations in these categories.

Table 7.1: Examples of transformation applications

	Endogenous	*Exogenous*
Update-in-place	Refactoring Reactive Simulation	–
Separate-models	Enhancement Model copying	Migration, Refinement, Code generation, Reverse-engineering/Abstraction

The categories of transformations include:

- *Code generation/refinement*: these produce a more implementation-specific model or code from an implementation-independent representation. E.g., mapping of UML to Java, or UML to C++, etc.

- *Migration*: these transform one version of a language to another/or to a similar language. E.g., mapping Java to C#, or UML 1.4 to UML 2.3, or from one EHR (Electronic Health Record) format to another, etc.

- *Refactoring/restructuring*: these rewrite a model to improve its structure or quality. E.g., removing redundant inheritance, introducing a design pattern, etc.

- *Enhancement*: these map a model of a system into a model of an enhanced system, e.g., to add access control facilities to a system.

- *Reactive*: transformations which compute a response to input events, e.g., to calculate an optimal move in a game in response to an opponent's move.

- *Reverse-engineering/Abstraction*: producing a more abstract/design or specification-oriented model from an implementation. For example, to produce a class diagram or architecture diagram from source code.

The category of update-in-place exogenous transformations is unusual, one example is the State machine/Petri Net transformation of [4] which uses simultaneous rewrites of the source and target models. Transformations can be *incremental*: applied to incremental changes in a source model to make corresponding changes in a (pre-existing) target model, or *bidirectional*: applicable in either source to target or target to source directions.

A key principle of UML-RSDS is that transformations can be considered to be use cases, and specified and developed using the same techniques as other UML-RSDS applications:

> *Model transformations can be specified as use cases, with use case postconditions expressing the transformation rules.*

The postcondition constraints are both a specification of the postconditions of the transformation, and a definition of the implementation of the transformation rules.

Transformations are naturally expressed as UML use cases: since a Use Case is a Classifier it is also a Namespace for its elements, and may have its own attributes and operations – such as local functions in QVT-R, helper functions and attributes in ATL, etc. Use cases may have invariants, and can be related by inheritance and by relations such as *extend* and *include*, permitting composition of transformations from subtransformations. Most importantly, a Use Case has an associated Behavior, which can represent the synthesised design of a transformation.

7.2 Model transformation languages

A large number of MT languages have been devised – it sometimes seems that each different MT research group or individual researcher has their own particular language – but only a few MT languages have wide usage. MT languages span a wide range of styles, from *declarative languages* expressing transformation rules in a logical high-level manner, most often using a version of OCL, or a graph formalism, to *procedural languages*, defining detailed low-level processing steps. *Hybrid*

MT languages can use both styles. Declarative languages include TGG and QVT-R, while Kermeta and QVT-O are examples of procedural MT languages. Hybrid languages include ATL [1], ETL [3] and GrGen [2]. Our view is that it is not necessary to invent a new specialised language for transformations: UML (with a formalised semantics for class diagrams and use cases) is already sufficient to define all practical cases of transformations. In terms of the classification of MT languages, UML-RSDS is a hybrid language since it contains both declarative logical and procedural imperative facilities: transformations can be defined by the logical postconditions of use cases, together with operations, which may be defined by explicit UML activities. Table 7.2 compares the scope of UML-RSDS with other model transformation languages.

Table 7.2: Comparison of transformation languages

Language	*Mapping*	*Update-in-place*	*Bidirectionality*	*Change-propagation*
UML-RSDS	√√	√√	√	√
ATL	√√	√	×	×
QVT-R	√√	√	√	√
ETL, GrGen	√√	√√	×	×

ATL has a restricted form of update-in-place processing, called *refining mode*. This makes a copy of the source model and then updates this copy based on the (read-only) source model. Thus the effects of updates cannot affect subsequent rule applications. QVT-R also adopts this approach, but repeatedly applies the copy and update process until no further changes occur. In contrast, UML-RSDS and ETL directly apply updates to the source model. Bidirectionality in UML-RSDS is partly supported by the synthesis of inverse transformations (use cases) from mapping transformations. Only transformations consisting of type 0 or type 1 postconditions can be reversed in this way. QVT-R provides the capability to apply a transformation in different directions between the domains (parameters) of the transformation rules. However, as with UML-RSDS, this capability is essentially limited to bijective mapping transformations [6]. QVT-R additionally supports change-propagation, by deleting, creating and modifying target model objects when an incremental change to the source model takes place. UML-RSDS supports change-propagation via the incremental execution mode for use cases (Chapter 14).

Table 7.3 compares ATL and UML-RSDS as transformation languages. Generally, ATL is better suited to separate-models transformations such as migrations, whereas UML-RSDS has full support for update-in-place transformations such as refactorings.

Table 7.3: Comparison of ATL and UML-RSDS

	ATL	*UML-RSDS*
System modularisation	Modules, rules, libraries, helpers	Use cases, operations, constraints, classes
Rule modularisation	Inheritance, called rules	Called operations
Rule scheduling/ priorities	Implicit	Explicit ordering
Multiple input elements in rules	No	Yes
Direct update of input models	No	Yes
Transformation implementation	In ATL interpreter	In Java, C#, C++
Analysis	Runtime rule conflicts detected	Data dependency, confluence, determinacy, rule conflicts

7.3   Model transformation specification in UML-RSDS

Model transformations in UML-RSDS are defined by use cases, the postconditions of these use cases define the transformation effect. Both the source and target metamodels are represented as parts (possibly disjoint and unconnected parts) of the same class diagram. In terms of Fig. 7.1, the source metamodel A and target metamodel B are defined as class diagrams. The transformation definition is given by a use case, consisting of postconditions which define transformation rules. Each use case postcondition constraint Cn usually has context some source metamodel entity E, and defines how elements of E are mapped to target model elements.

Figure 7.2 shows an example where the source metamodel consists of a single entity A with attribute $x : int$, and the target metamodel consists of entity B with attribute $y : int$, and there is a use case $a2b$ with a single postcondition constraint:

```
x > 0  =>  B->exists( b | b.y = x*x )
```

on context A. The constraint specifies that a new B object b is created for each $ax : A$ with $ax.x > 0$, and $b.y$ is set to the square of $ax.x$.

Assumptions of a transformation can also be defined, as precondition constraints of its use case. In this example we assume that the target model is initially empty, i.e.:

```
B->size() = 0
```

A valid transformation invariant constraint could be:

```
A->exists( a | a.x > 0 & y = a.x*a.x )
```

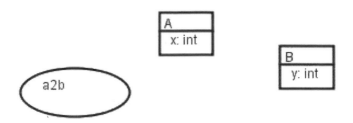

Figure 7.2: A to B transformation

on *B*. This expresses that every *B* must have been derived from a corresponding *A*.

The following steps are taken to define a transformation in UML-RSDS:

- Define the metamodels, as a single class diagram or separate class diagrams.

- Create a general use case, for the transformation.

- Edit the use case, adding pre and postcondition and invariant constraints as required. The order of the postcondition constraints determines the order of execution of the corresponding code segments.

- On the synthesis menu, select Generate Design to analyse the use case and generate a design-level description as operations and activities.

- Select Generate Java (Java 4) to produce an executable version of the transformation, which will be contained in the *output* directory files *Controller.java*, *GUI.java*, *ControllerInterface.java* and *SystemTypes.java*.

- The transformation implementation can be compiled using *javac GUI.java*, and then executed by the command *java GUI*. This opens up a simple dialog to load the input model and execute individual transformations (Fig. 3.13).

  Input models are specified in a file `in.txt`, output models are created in `out.txt`, together with XMI versions in `xsi.txt`.

The instance models Model A and Model B in Fig. 7.1 are represented in the files in.txt and out.txt. The transformation execution is an execution of the GUI class (for Java implementations). As described in Chapter 3, the text format for instance models in `in.txt` and `out.txt` is very simple, consisting of lines of text of three possible forms:

```
e : T
```

declaring that *e* is an instance of concrete entity *T*,

```
e.f = v
```

declaring that the attribute or 1-multiplicity role *f* of *e* has value *v*, and

```
obj : e.role
```

declaring that *obj* is a member of the many-valued role *role* of *e*. For sequence-valued roles, the order in which these membership assertions occur in the file is the order of elements in *role*.

For example, we could have the input model

```
a1 : A
a1.x = 5
a2 : A
a2.x = 3
b1 : B
b1.y = 2
```

for our elementary transformation example (this model does not satisfy the transformation assumption because there is already a B object in the model). Running the transformation on this input model produces the following output model:

```
a1 : A
a1.x = 5
a2 : A
a2.x = 3
b1 : B
b1.y = 2
b2 : B
b2.y = 25
b3 : B
b3.y = 9
```

Qualified associations and association classes cannot be represented in models, however these could be used for internal processing of a transformation, as auxiliary metamodel elements.

7.3.1 *Transformation constraints*

Four categories of postconditions *Cn* for transformations are distinguished, corresponding to the constraint categories defined in Chapter 6:

1. Type 0: Cn has no context classifier, for example

```
"Hello world!"->display()
```

The constraint dialog field for the context entity is left empty when defining such constraints (the first field in the dialog of Fig. 4.1).

2. Type 1: a context classifier E exists, and $wr(Cn)$, the set of entity types and features written by Cn, is disjoint from $rd(Cn)$, the set that it reads (write and read frames are defined in Table 5.1). Such Cn are implemented by a for-loop over E. For example, the constraint

```
x > 0  =>  B->exists( b | b.y = x*x )
```

given above is of type 1. E (in this case A) is specified in the context entity field of the constraint dialog (Fig. 4.1).

3. Type 2: $wr(Cn)$ has common elements with $rd(Cn)$, but the context classifier E itself is not in $wr(Cn)$, nor are other entity types/features in the condition/antecedent (LHS) of Cn. These are implemented by a simplified fixed-point iteration over E.

4. Type 3: as type 2, but $wr(Cn)$ includes the context classifier or other condition entity types/features. For example, to delete all A objects with negative x values, we could write:

```
x < 0  =>  self->isDeleted()
```

on context A. For such constraints a general fixed-point implementation is used, however it is often the case that this can be optimised by omitting checks that the conclusion of Cn already holds (in the above example, the conclusion obviously never holds for some $self : A$ before the application of the constraint). A dialog box is presented asking for confirmation of this optimization, during the Generate Design step. Answer y to confirm the optimisation.

The most common form of constraints for migrations and refinements are type 0 or type 1, because such transformations normally only write the target model, and do not update the source model. In constructing the target model normally the data that is read is disjoint from the data that is written, or this separation can be achieved by using a pattern such as Map Objects Before Links (Chapter 9). For refactorings, type 2 or 3 constraints may be necessary because of the update-in-place nature of the transformation processing.

As for other general use cases, distinct postcondition constraints should be ordered so that Cm preceeds Cn if $wr(Cm)$ has common elements with $rd(Cn)$. For the above example this means that the correct order is:

```
x < 0  =>  self->isDeleted()
```

```
x > 0  =>  B->exists( b | b.y = x*x )
```

since the first constraint writes A and the second reads A: this order ensures that the invariant identified above actually is maintained by the transformation. Constraint analysis during the Generate Design step identifies any potential problems with the ordering of constraints.

7.3.2 Transformation specification techniques

For migration and refinement transformations, the postcondition constraints are typically of type 0 or type 1, and have informal specifications such as:

> For each instance of source entity Si, that satisfies Cond, instantiate a corresponding instance t of target entity Tj, and set t's features based on the source instance.

Such a mapping requirement would be formalised as a postcondition constraint

```
Si::
  Cond  =>  Tj->exists( t | Post )
```

The a2b example given above fits exactly into this pattern:

```
A::
  x > 0  =>  B->exists( b | b.y = x*x )
```

More realistically, some means of tracing the target elements back to their corresponding source elements is often necessary. To support tracing, we use the principal primary keys of source and target entities (introducing such keys if they do not already exist). If such keys were added to the classes A and B, we could write:

```
A::
  x > 0  =>  B->exists( b | b.bId = aId & b.y = x*x )
```

The A instance corresponding to a B instance b is then $A[b.bId]$.

For comparison, the a2b transformation example could be specified as follows in ATL:

```
rule a2b1 {
  from a : A (a.x > 0)
  to b : B
    ( bId <- a.aId,
      y <- a.x*a.x )
}
```

ATL is appropriate for the definition of migrations and refinements, although migration between similar languages may involve substantial amounts of copying. In such cases a specialised migration language such as Epsilon Flock may be more appropriate.

Refinements and migrations may involve *entity splitting*, where multiple elements in the target model may be produced from each single source element. An example would be the production of HTML forms, JSP files, beans, and database interfaces from UML classes, as in the UML to web system mappings of Chapter 20. *Entity merging* may also occur, where multiple source elements contribute to the definition of single target elements. The basic form of type 1 constraint given above can also be used for entity splitting and merging, with identity attributes being used to correlate the appropriate sources and targets.

Migrations and refinements are often structured based on the compositional structure of the source language: a source entity $E1$ can be considered to be at a higher compositional level relative to a source entity $E2$ if there is a one-to-many association directed from $E1$ to $E2$. A transformation may then map $E2$ instances to target instances in one constraint, then map $E1$ instances to target instances in a second constraint, which also links the $E1$-targets to their corresponding $E2$-targets. This style of specification is called the Phased Construction pattern (Chapter 9).

For example, the a2b transformation can be elaborated by the addition of another composition level to the languages, and the addition of primary keys to all entities (Fig. 7.3). The specification of ac2bde can be organised as a Phased Construction by relating the entities C and D at one composition level, and then A and B at the next higher level:

C ::
$$D{\rightarrow}exists(d \mid d.dId = cId \ \& \ d.w = z + 5)$$
A ::
$$B{\rightarrow}exists(b \mid b.bId = aId \ \& \ b.y = x * x \ \& \ b.dr = D[cr.cId])$$

In the second constraint, the D instances corresponding to cr are looked-up by their primary key values: $D[cr.cId]$. The second constraint assumes that all C objects have a corresponding D object – this is ensured by the first constraint.

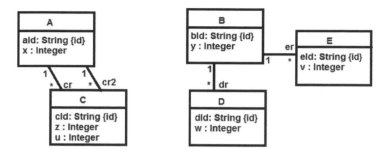

Figure 7.3: Extended a2b example: ac2bde

In ATL, this style of specification is also directly supported, with the linking process being carried out implicitly:

```
rule ac2bde1 {
  from c : C (true)
  to d : D
    ( dId <- c.cId,
      w <- c.z + 5 )
}

rule ac2bde2 {
  from a : A (true)
  to b : B
    ( bId <- a.aId,
      y <- a.x*a.x,
      dr <- a.cr )
}
```

In the to clause of ac2bde2, the assignment of *a.cr* to *dr* actually assigns the *D* instances corresponding to *a.cr*. This involves an implicit lookup of these instances. We consider migrations in more detail in Chapter 11, and refinements in Chapter 12.

Refactorings and other update-in-place transformations are typically more complex than refinements and migrations. Their postcondition constraints are typically of type 2 or type 3, and have informal specifications such as:

> For each source model situation that satisfies condition Cond, rewrite or replace the situation to achieve condition Post.

Such a refactoring requirement would be formalised as a postcondition constraint

```
Si::
  Cond  =>  Post
```

where *Si* is a source model entity type which is appropriate to use as a *pivot* or main element to refer to the source model structure which is to be rewritten. Usually, *Post* implies *not(Cond)*, and may involve object deletion using the →*isDeleted*() operator. Such constraints cannot usually be represented in ATL, nor in QVT-R, which does not have explicit object deletion. Unlike refinements and migrations, refactoring transformations may be structured on the basis of the different cases of source model situations/structures which need to be rewritten. In particular, a constraint *C*1 which deals with a specialised case of a situation, should normally precede a constraint *C*2 which deals with a more general case, and constraints which express a higher-priority rewrite for a given situation should precede constraints expressing a lower-priority rewrite. We consider refactoring transformations in detail in Chapter 13.

7.3.3 Pre-state expressions in constraints

Pre-state expressions *e@pre* in use case postcondition constraints refer to the values of entity types or to the values of features of individual objects at the start of execution of individual applications of the constraint. A prestate feature *obj.f@pre* should only be applied to instances *obj* of a prestate entity *E@pre*, unless *E* itself is not written by the constraint. It is bad practice to both read *x.f@*pre and write *x.f* for the same object *x* in the same constraint, this can lead to a failure of confluence, and to constraint implementations that do not establish the constraint (or at least, not those parts of the constraint that use *f@*pre). *f@pre* can be used for features *f* of the context classifier of the constraint, but cannot be used for features of variables *x* of *exists(x | P)*, etc., *self* of *select(P)*, etc., or other internal variables within a constraint. They should not be used in the condition of type 3 constraints (*e* by itself denotes *e@pre* in such conditions).

An example of the use of prestate entities and features is the computation of the one-step composition of pairs of edges in a graph: if a pair of edges *e*1 and *e*2 are joined head-to-tail at the same node, then create a new edge that directly links *e*1's source to *e*2's target (but do not iterate this process any further):

```
e1 : Edge@pre  &  e2 : Edge@pre  &  e2.src@pre = e1.trg@pre  =>
    Edge->exists1( e3 | e3.src = e1.src@pre & e3.trg = e2.trg@pre )
```

The iterations of *e*1 and *e*2 over *Edge@pre* restricts the composition step to operate only upon pre-existing edges, not upon any *e*3 created by the step itself. The use of *src@pre* and *trg@pre* emphasises that the features of pre-existing edges are not changed by the constraint. Taken together, these annotations allow a simple double for-loop implementation of the constraint (because its set of written entities and features are disjoint from its set of read entities and features) rather than a fixed-point implementation. This is an example of the Replace Fixed-point by Bounded Iteration pattern (Chapter 9).

Care is needed in the use of pre-state expressions in constraints, as their use can make constraints harder to understand. Their main use is to serve as annotations to indicate that a type 1 bounded loop implementation should be used, for a constraint which otherwise would be of type 2 or 3 and use fixed-point iteration.

Variables may also be used to express *let* definitions, by placing an equation $v = exp$ in the assumption of a constraint. v can then be used in place of exp in the conclusion. Such v should only be used in read-only contexts after their definition.

7.4 Specifying bidirectional transformations

Support for *bidirectional* transformations is provided by the option to *reverse* a use case (on the edit use case menu). This option generates a new use case whose postconditions are derived as inverses of the postconditions of the original use case: these inverse constraints are often also invariants of the original use case. A type 1 postcondition constraint

$$S_i ::$$
$$SCond(self) \;\Rightarrow\; T_j \rightarrow exists(t \mid TCond(t) \;\&\; P_{i,j}(self,t))$$

is inverted to a constraint of the form

$$T_j ::$$
$$TCond(self) \;\Rightarrow\; S_i \rightarrow exists(s \mid SCond(s) \;\&\; P^{\sim}_{i,j}(s,self))$$

where the predicates $P_{i,j}(s,t)$ define the features of t from those of s, and are invertible: an equivalent form $P^{\sim}_{i,j}(s,t)$ should exist, which expresses the features of s in terms of those of t.

A type 0 postcondition constraint

$$S_i \rightarrow forAll(s \mid SCond(s) \;\Rightarrow\; T_j \rightarrow exists(t \mid TCond(t) \;\&\; P_{i,j}(s,t)))$$

is inverted to

$$T_j \rightarrow forAll(t \mid TCond(t) \;\Rightarrow\; S_i \rightarrow exists(s \mid SCond(s) \;\&\; P^{\sim}_{i,j}(s,t)))$$

Tables 7.4, 7.5 and 7.6 show examples of inverses $P^\sim$ of predicates P.

Table 7.4: Inverse of predicates

$P(s,t)$	$P^\sim(s,t)$	Condition
$t.g = s.f$	$s.f = t.g$	Data features f, g
$t.g = s.f.sqrt$	$s.f = t.g.sqr$	f, g non-negative
$t.g = s.f.sqr$	$s.f = t.g.sqrt$	f, g non-negative
$t.g = s.f.exp$	$s.f = t.g.log$	g positive
$t.g = s.f.log$	$s.f = t.g.exp$	f positive
$t.g = s.f.pow(x)$	$s.f = t.g.pow(1.0/x)$	x non-zero, independent of $s.f$
$t.g = s.f.sin$	$s.f = t.g.asin$	$-1 \leq t.g \leq 1$
$t.g = s.f.cos$	$s.f = t.g.acos$	$-1 \leq t.g \leq 1$
$t.g = s.f.tan$	$s.f = t.g.atan$	
$t.b2 = not(s.b1)$	$s.b1 = not(t.b2)$	Boolean attributes $b1$, $b2$
$t.g = K * s.f + L$ Numeric constants K, L $K \neq 0$	$s.f = (t.g - L)/K$	f, g numeric
$t.g = s.f + SK$	$s.f = t.g.subrange(1, t.g.size - SK.size)$	String constant SK
$t.g = SK + s.f$	$s.f = t.g.subrange(SK.size + 1, t.g.size)$	String constant SK
$t.r = s.f \rightarrow characters()$	$s.f = t.r \rightarrow sum()$	String feature f, sequence r
$R(s,t)$ & $Q(s,t)$	$R^\sim(s,t)$ & $Q^\sim(s,t)$	

Table 7.5: Inverse of predicates on associations

$P(s,t)$	$P^\sim(s,t)$	Condition
$t.rr = s.r \rightarrow reverse()$	$s.r = t.rr \rightarrow reverse()$	r, rr ordered association ends
$t.rr = s.r \rightarrow last()$	$s.r \rightarrow last() = t.rr$	rr single-valued, r ordered
$t.rr = s.r \rightarrow first()$	$s.r \rightarrow first() = t.rr$	rr single-valued, r ordered
$t.rr = s.r \rightarrow including(s.p)$	$s.r = t.rr \rightarrow front()$ &	rr, r ordered association ends
$t.rr = s.r \rightarrow append(s.p)$	$s.p = t.rr \rightarrow last()$	p 1-multiplicity end
$t.rr = s.r \rightarrow prepend(s.p)$	$s.r = t.rr \rightarrow tail()$ &	rr, r ordered association ends
	$s.p = t.rr \rightarrow first()$	p 1-multiplicity end
$t.rr = Sequence\{s.p1, s.p2\}$	$s.p1 = t.rr[1]$ & $s.p2 = t.rr[2]$	rr ordered association end $p1$, $p2$ 1-multiplicity ends
$t.rr = s.r \rightarrow select(P)$	$s.r \rightarrow excludesAll(x \mid P(x)$ & $t.rr \rightarrow excludes(x))$ $\rightarrow includesAll(t.rr \rightarrow select(P))$	r, rr set-valued
$t.rr = s.r \rightarrow reject(P)$	$s.r \rightarrow excludesAll(x \mid not(P(x))$ & $t.rr \rightarrow excludes(x))$ $\rightarrow includesAll(t.rr \rightarrow reject(P))$	r, rr set-valued
$t.rr = s.r \rightarrow sort()$	$s.r = t.rr \rightarrow asSet()$	r set-valued, rr ordered
$t.rr = s.r \rightarrow asSequence()$		

Table 7.6: Inverse of predicates (extended)

$P(s,t)$	$P^\sim(s,t)$	*Condition*
$t = T_j[s.idS]$	$s = S_i[t.idT]$	idS primary key of S_i idT primary key of T_j
$t = T_j[s.r.idS]$	$s.r = S_i[t.idT]$	idS primary key of S_i idT primary key of T_j
$t.rr = TRef[s.r.idS]$ idS primary key of $SRef$, idT primary key of $TRef$	$s.r = SRef[t.rr.idT]$	rr association end with element type $TRef$, r association end with element type $SRef$
$t.rr = TRef[s.r{\rightarrow}collect(idS)]$	$s.r =$ $SRef[t.rr{\rightarrow}collect(idT)]$	As above
$t.g = s.r.idS$ Attribute g	$s.r = SRef[t.g]$	idS primary key of $SRef$, r association end with element type $SRef$
$t.rr = TRef[s.f]$ f is an attribute	$s.f = t.rr.idT$	idT primary key of $TRef$, rr association end with element type $TRef$
$T_j[s.idS].rr = TRef[s.r.idSRef]$ r has element type $SRef$, rr has element type $TRef$	$S_i[t.idT].r =$ $SRef[t.rr.idTRef]$	$idS, idSRef$ primary keys of S_i, $SRef$ $idT, idTRef$ primary keys of T_j, $TRef$

The meaning of assignments of the form $f{\rightarrow}last() = g$ is dealt with in Chapter 14.

More details of bidirectional transformation specification in UML-RSDS are given in Chapter 14.

7.5   Transformation examples

In this section we describe some simple examples of transformation specification using UML-RSDS.

7.5.1   *Refinement example: UML to relational database*

The UML to relational database refinement transformation has been used as an archetypical transformation example in many different languages, for example in QVT-R [5]. Figure 7.4 shows the source and target language metamodels of a basic version of this transformation. UML packages are mapped to RDB schemas, classes are mapped to tables, and attributes to columns. In this version the transformation can also be regarded as a structure-preserving migration.

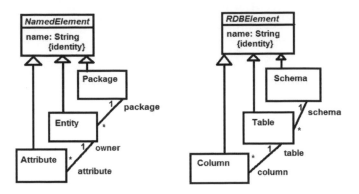

Figure 7.4: UML to relational database metamodels

A specification of the transformation can be written as a use case *uml2rdb* in UML-RSDS as follows. An assumption is that *name* is a primary key for *NamedElement*. This could be explicitly written as:

$$NamedElement \rightarrow isUnique(name)$$

However this is not necessary as *name* is already declared as an *identity* attribute in the source language class diagram.

The property

$$RDBElement \rightarrow isUnique(name)$$

could be asserted as a transformation invariant, that no two target objects with duplicate names should exist/be created. This property is part of the target language theory, and hence is required for the transformation to be syntactically correct (Chapter 18).

The following constraints define the mapping rules performed by *uml2rdb*, and are written in this order in its postconditions:

$$Schema \rightarrow exists(s \mid s.name = name)$$

This constraint has context entity *Package*, and maps packages 1-1 to schemas. For each package p a new schema s is created and its name is set equal to p's name.

$$Table \rightarrow exists(t \mid t.name = name \ \& \ t.schema = Schema[package.name])$$

This constraint has context *Entity*. Each entity instance e is copied to a table t with the same name, and t's schema is set equal to the schema corresponding to e's package: such a schema exists because of the effect of the previous constraint (it guarantees that for every package there is a corresponding schema with the same name).

Finally, the following constraint is iterated over *Attribute* to create columns:

$$Column{\rightarrow}exists(cl \mid cl.name = name \ \& \ cl.table = Table[owner.name])$$

Again, this relies on the preceding constraint to establish that for every class there is a corresponding table, so that *Table[owner.name]* is well-defined.

This specification structure is an example of the Phased Construction transformation design pattern (Chapter 9), where the source entities at each level of composition are related by a single constraint to target entities, and subsequent constraints can then lookup instances of the constructed target entities to create target instances at a higher (or lower) level of composition. This can be described by a *language mapping*:

$$Package \ \longmapsto \ Schema \ \ (via \ constraint \ 1)$$
$$Entity \ \longmapsto \ Table \ \ (via \ constraint \ 2, reads \ Schema)$$
$$Attribute \ \longmapsto \ Column \ \ (via \ constraint \ 3, reads \ Table)$$

In general, if the sequence $C_1 \ \& \ ... \ \& \ C_n$ of use case postcondition constraints satisfies the syntactic or semantic non-interference conditions, then each constraint may assume that all of its precedessors hold true at its initiation.

7.5.2 *Migration example: trees to graphs*

This transformation [3] maps tree structures into corresponding node and edge structures, and has the source and target metamodels shown in Fig. 7.5.

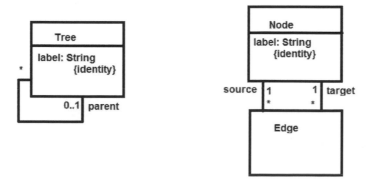

Figure 7.5: Tree to graph metamodels

The transformation is defined as a UML-RSDS use case *tree2graph* with two postconditions. The first constraint has context *Tree*, and creates nodes for each tree:

$$(C1): \quad Node \rightarrow exists(n \mid n.label = label)$$

A second constraint then creates edges for each link between parent and child trees. It is a double iteration over *Tree*:

$$(C2): \quad p : parent \Rightarrow$$
$$Edge \rightarrow exists(e \mid e.source = Node[label]$$
$$\& \quad e.target = Node[p.label])$$

For each pair of a tree (*self*) and its parent *p*, an Edge instance is created corresponding to the link from *self* to *p* in the source model. This transformation is also an example of a bidirectional transformation, because a reverse mapping *graph2tree* can be directly derived from *tree2graph*. The reverse mapping has postconditions:

$$(I1): \quad Tree \rightarrow exists(t \mid t.label = label)$$

on *Node* and

$$(I2): \quad Tree \rightarrow exists(t \mid Tree \rightarrow exists(p \mid p : t.parent \&$$
$$t.label = source.label \& p.label =$$
$$target.label))$$

on *Edge*. These postconditions are derived mechanically from *tree2graph* using Tables 7.4, 7.5 and 7.6.

The specification structure is an example of the Map Objects Before Links transformation design pattern (Chapter 9): trees are mapped to nodes, and then the parent links between trees are mapped by a separate constraint to links (edges) between nodes. Similarly for the inverse transformation.

Summary

We have described how transformations can be defined in UML-RSDS, and we have also compared UML-RSDS with other model transformation languages. Guidelines for defining refinements, migrations and refactorings were given, and simple examples of transformation definitions in UML-RSDS were presented.

References

[1] Eclipsepedia, *ATL User Guide*, http://wiki.eclipse.org/ATL/ User_Guide_-_The_ATL_Language, 2014.

[2] S. Kolahdouz-Rahimi, K. Lano, S. Pillay, J. Troya and P. Van Gorp, *Evaluation of model transformation approaches for model refactoring*, Science of Computer Programming, 2013, http://dx.doi.org/10.1016/j.scico.2013.07.013.

[3] D. Kolovos, R. Paige and F. Polack, *The Epsilon Transformation Language*, in ICMT 2008, LNCS Vol. 5063, pp. 46–60, Springer-Verlag, 2008.

[4] K. Lano, S. Kolahdouz-Rahimi and K. Maroukian, *Solving the Petri-Nets to Statecharts Transformation Case with UML-RSDS*, TTC 2013, EPTCS, 2013.

[5] OMG, *MOF 2.0 Query/View/Transformation Specification v1.1*, 2011.

[6] P. Stevens, *Bidirectional model transformations in QVT*, SoSyM, Vol. 9, No. 1, 2010.

Chapter 8

Case Study: Resource Scheduler

This chapter illustrates the UML-RSDS development process and tools by showing the complete development of a non-trivial example.

8.1   Case study description

This problem was the assessed coursework for the second year undergraduate course Object-oriented Specification and Design at King's College London in 2015/16. The system class diagram and system operations need to be specified in UML-RSDS, and an executable implementation synthesised in Java.

The system is intended to carry out release planning for an agile development process. The development or modification project to be implemented is divided into a number of *Story* objects, which have a *storyId : String* unique key. Each story has an ordered list *subtasks* of *Task* objects, which define particular work tasks. Tasks have a unique *taskId : String* key, and an Integer *duration*. A task may depend on other tasks (which must be completed before it is started, but could be completed in parallel with each other). A task has a set, *needs*, of *Skill* objects which represent skills needed to carry out the task. In turn, a *Skill* has a unique *skillId : String*. An entity type *Staff* represents staff, and has a unique *staffId : String*, and an Integer *costDay*. A set, *has*, of skills is associated to each staff object. Finally, the task schedule for an iteration is represented by a class *Schedule*, with an attribute *totalCost :*

Integer, and an ordered list *assignment* of *Assignment* objects, where each *Assignment* has associated staff and task objects.

The required system operations are:

- *allocateStaff*: for each unallocated task t, all of whose *dependsOn* tasks have already been allocated, find an available (unallocated) staff member who has all the skills required by t, and assign the task to the cheapest such staff member, s. Create a new assignment for t and s, and add this to the schedule.

- *calculateCost*: add up the products *s.costDay* ∗ *t.duration* for the assignments of the schedule and add this to the *totalCost* of the schedule.

- *displaySchedule*: print the list of assignments in order, with information of the *staffId*, *costDay*, *taskId*, *duration* for each assignment.

The solution is to be evaluated and tested on several test cases of planning problems. The solution is expected to always find a schedule with minimal total cost. Further additional requirements are introduced during the system development: (i) To add a *duration* : *Integer* attribute to *Schedule*, and to compute this as part of the *calculateCost* operation. (ii) To extend the system to calculate schedules for a series of iterations: an iteration schedule is complete when all possible allocations to available staff have been made: that is, when no further allocation of a staff member to a task can be made. Define a use case *nextIteration* to continue a schedule with a further iteration.

8.2 Solution

An initial class diagram, expressing the core data and functionality of the problem, could be defined as in Fig. 8.1.

To display assignments of staff to tasks, a *toString* operation is defined for *Assignment*, overriding the default version of this operation:

```
Assignment::
query toString() : String
pre: true
post:
  result = task.taskId + ", " + task.duration + ", " + staff.staffId
  + ", " + staff.costDay
```

The key use case of the system is *allocateStaff*. We decide therefore to make this the highest-priority development task. The use case can be viewed as a refactoring transformation, which operates to assign as many tasks to staff as possible – this will need a fixed-point iteration,

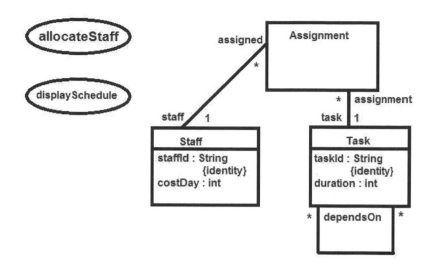

Figure 8.1: Initial schedular class diagram

since allocating one task may then make further tasks (that depend upon the allocated task) allocatable, and will remove the task itself from consideration for allocation. Informally, the scenario handled by this use case could be expressed as:

> If a task *self* is not yet assigned to a staff member, but all of the tasks it depends on have been, and there are some staff who have the skills to work on *self*, then: choose such a staff member of minimal cost and assign *self* to that person, and add the assignment to the schedule.

We specify this scenario using evolutionary prototyping, increasing the functionality of the prototype use case until it achieves all the scenario requirements. In this case the functional requirement is quite clear – if there had been ambiguity or incompleteness in the requirement, then it would be necessary to use requirements elicitation techniques, such as exploratory prototyping and interviews, to identify the true requirements.

Initially, we could write a simple version of the postcondition of *allocateStaff*, on context class *Task*:

```
Task::
  st : Staff & assignment.size = 0 & st.assigned.size = 0   =>
        Assignment->exists( a | a.task = self & a.staff = st )
```

This is a transformation rule that maps *Task* and *Staff* to *Assignment*: for each pair of an unassigned task *self* : *Task*, and an unassigned staff member *st*, the rule creates a new assignment which assigns *st* to work on *self*. It is of type 3 because *assignment* and *assigned* are read in the constraint condition, and implicitly written in the succedent (they are inverse association ends of *task* and *staff*).

This version could map the task and staff data (in *in.txt*):

```
t1 : Task
t1.taskId = "t1"
t1.duration = 10
t2 : Task
t2.taskId = "t2"
t2.duration = 5
t1 : t2.dependsOn
s1 : Staff
s1.staffId = "Mike"
s2 : Staff
s2.staffId = "Amy"
```

to the data (in *out.txt*):

```
a1 : Assignment
a1.task = t1
a1.staff = s1
a2 : Assignment
a2.task = t2
a2.staff = s2
```

If there were 3 tasks and 2 staff, one task would remain unallocated. This initial version fails to meet all the scenario requirements:

- No account is taken of *dependsOn* or *duration*: a task should only be allocated if all its preceding tasks have already been allocated:

$$dependsOn{\rightarrow}forAll(d \mid d.assignment.size > 0)$$

  or, equivalently:

$$dependsOn.assignment.size = dependsOn.size$$

- We want to assign long-duration tasks first.

- No account is taken of staff skills or cost.

The second prototype addresses the first two points:

```
Task::  (ordered by -duration)
  assignment.size = 0 &
  dependsOn.assignment.size = dependsOn.size &
  st : Staff & st.assigned.size = 0   =>
      Assignment->exists( a | a.task = self & a.staff = st )
```

This considers longer-duration tasks first (because it iterates over *Task* in increasing order of $-duration$, i.e., tasks are considered in *decreasing* order of duration), and gives a task a higher priority than tasks that depend on it. Given the input data

```
t1 : Task
t1.taskId = "t1"
t1.duration = 10
t2 : Task
t2.taskId = "t2"
t2.duration = 15
t1 : t2.dependsOn
t3 : Task
t3.taskId = "t3"
t3.duration = 16
t1 : t3.dependsOn
s1 : Staff
s1.staffId = "Mike"
s2 : Staff
s2.staffId = "Amy"
```

task $t1$ is allocated first, then $t3$, because $t3$ has a longer duration than $t2$.

To base assignments on skills, we need to enrich the simple data model of Fig. 8.1 with representation of skills. Figure 8.2 shows the completed system class diagram after formalisation of the initial and additional requirements.

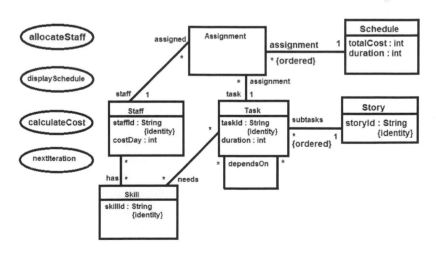

Figure 8.2: Schedular class diagram

Staff skills can now be considered: we should only allocate $st : Staff$ to $t : Task$ if $t.needs \subseteq st.has$, i.e., if st has all the skills that t needs. Instead of $st : Staff$ & $st.assigned.size = 0$ in the antecedent, we should therefore use the restricted quantification range

$$st : Staff \rightarrow select(assigned.size = 0 \;\&\; needs \subseteq has)$$

Finally, we want a staff member of minimal cost in this set. One way to do this is to sort the possible staff in increasing order of cost and take the first element of this sorted sequence:

$$availStaff \rightarrow sortedBy(costDay) \rightarrow first()$$

where $availStaff$ is a let variable holding the set $Staff \rightarrow select(assigned.size = 0 \;\&\; needs \subseteq has)$.

The complete scenario specification is as follows. In this version the postcondition refers to the schedule instance (which must exist prior to the execution of $allocateStaff$):

```
Task:: (ordered by -duration)
  s : Schedule & assignment.size = 0 &
  dependsOn.assignment->size() = dependsOn.size &
  availStaff = Staff->select(assigned.size = 0 & needs <: has) &
  availStaff.size > 0  =>
      Assignment->exists( a | a : s.assignment & a.task = self &
                 a.staff = availStaff->sortedBy(costDay)->first() )
```

The constraint only applies to tasks which do not already have allocated staff ($assignment.size = 0$) and whose preceding tasks have all been allocated ($dependsOn.assignment \rightarrow size() = dependsOn.size$). The variable $availStaff$ is then calculated as the set of possible staff who could be allocated to the task: staff who have all the needed skills, and who have not yet been allocated. If this set is non-empty, a new assignment a is created (the succedent of the constraint), assigned to the task, added to the schedule, and the staff member chosen for this assignment is someone from $availStaff$ with minimum cost. As an optimization, this constraint is iterated in order of $-duration$. This means that the longest tasks are considered first and assigned to cheap developers and scheduled before shorter tasks where possible.

Note that the succedent of this constraint contradicts the antecedent, because the task is assigned (to a) in the succedent, whilst it is required to have no assignment in the antecedent. This means that the constraint will iterate until no task satisfies the antecedent, i.e., until there is no remaining task that can be allocated. At its termination, all possible tasks that can be allocated in this iteration have been allocated, and the constraint is therefore established for all tasks.

The *calculateCost* use case computes the schedule cost (for a single iteration) as the sum of costs for each assignment (the first postcondition), and the schedule duration as the maximum of the assignment durations (the second postcondition):

```
Schedule::
  totalCost = assignment->collect(staff.costDay * task.duration)->sum()

Schedule::
  assignment.size > 0  =>
      duration = assignment.task.totalDuration()->max()
```

The calculation of schedule durations requires task durations to be calculated, which can be done using the following operation of *Task* :

```
query totalDuration() : int
pre: true
post:
  ( dependsOn.size = 0 => result = duration ) &
  ( dependsOn.size > 0 => result = duration + dependsOn.totalDuration
  ()->max() )
```

The total duration of a task is its own duration, plus the maximum of the durations of the tasks that it directly depends upon. The concept of task and schedule duration was not made clear in the requirements – so some elicitation or research work would be needed to identify the precise functionality required here.

The *displaySchedule* use case displays the assignments of each schedule:

```
Schedule::
  assignment->forAll( a | a->display() )
```

The *nextIteration* use case simply deletes all the tasks of existing assignments (i.e., the tasks which have already been assigned to staff in previous iterations). This also has the effect of deleting all the assignments themselves (because each assignment has a mandatory task and cannot exist without its task), and of making the staff allocated to these assignments available once more:

```
Assignment::
  task->isDeleted()
```

Previously allocated tasks are also removed from the *dependsOn* sets of unallocated tasks. Thus the situation is ready for a further application of *allocateStaff* to compute the next iteration.

8.3 Scheduling examples

The system can be tested with a number of examples. A simple test case involves three tasks, *t1*, *t2* and *t3*, with *t3* depending on *t1*, *t2*, and three staff members, with varying skills and costs:

```
s : Schedule
st1 : Story
st1.storyId = "st1"
t1 : Task
t1.taskId = "t1"
t1.duration = 5
t1 : st1.subtasks
t2 : Task
t2.taskId = "t2"
t2.duration = 10
t2 : st1.subtasks
t3 : Task
t3.taskId = "t3"
t3.duration = 7
t3 : st1.subtasks
t1 : t3.dependsOn
t2 : t3.dependsOn
s1 : Staff
s1.staffId = "s1"
s1.costDay = 3
s2 : Staff
s2.staffId = "s2"
s2.costDay = 7
s3 : Staff
s3.staffId = "s3"
s3.costDay = 2
sk1 : Skill
sk1.skillId = "Java"
sk2 : Skill
sk2.skillId = "JSP"
sk3 : Skill
sk3.skillId = "C++"
sk1 : t1.needs
sk2 : t1.needs
sk3 : t2.needs
sk1 : t3.needs
sk1 : s1.has
sk1 : s2.has
sk2 : s2.has
sk3 : s2.has
sk1 : s3.has
sk2 : s3.has
sk3 : s3.has
```

The first allocation assigns *s*3 to *t*2, and then *s*2 to *t*1. Notice that *s*2 could have carried out *t*2, but this would have been a more expensive choice: by allocating the most time-consuming tasks before lower duration tasks, there are a wider choice of developers available to assign to the high duration tasks, and a lower-cost schedule will result.

The output from *displaySchedule* in this case is:

```
t2, 10, s3, 2
t1, 5, s2, 7
```

with a total cost of 55 and a duration of 10 (since the two tasks can proceed in parallel).

After applying nextIteration and performing allocation again, the new iteration

```
t3, 7, s3, 2
```

is displayed, with a total cost of 14 and duration of 7.

A more complex example has four tasks, with a linear dependency of t4 on t3, t3 on t2, and t2 on t1:

```
s : Schedule
st1 : Story
st1.storyId = "st1"
t1 : Task
t1.taskId = "t1"
t1.duration = 5
t1 : st1.subtasks
t2 : Task
t2.taskId = "t2"
t2.duration = 10
t2 : st1.subtasks
t3 : Task
t3.taskId = "t3"
t3.duration = 7
t3 : st1.subtasks
t1 : t2.dependsOn
t2 : t3.dependsOn
t4 : Task
t4.taskId = "t4"
t4 : st1.subtasks
t4.duration = 11
t3 : t4.dependsOn
sk3 : t4.needs
```

The iterations for this example are:

```
t1, 5, s3, 2
--------------------
```

```
t2, 10, s3, 2
t3, 7, s1, 3
--------------------
t4, 11, s3, 2
```

8.4   Optimisation

The solution is functionally correct, however it involves the use of sorted iteration with a type 3 constraint, which is intrinsically quite inefficient: the list of tasks is re-sorted each time the constraint is applied. In this case such re-sorting is unnecessary because the duration of tasks does not change during the *allocateStaff* use case, nor does the extent of *Task*, and so the *allocateStaff* constraint can be optimised by pre-sorting the tasks and using a standard type 3 constraint over this pre-sorted list (this is an application of the Auxiliary Metamodel pattern of Chapter 9). An auxiliary *—* association *sortedtasks : Schedule → Task* is introduced, which is ordered at the *Task* end. This is initialised to *Task→sortedBy(−duration)*, and then iterated over by the main allocation constraint:

```
Schedule::
  sortedtasks = Task->sortedBy(-duration)

Schedule::
  t : sortedtasks & t.assignment.size = 0 &
  t.dependsOn.assignment->size() = t.dependsOn.size &
  availStaff = Staff->select(assigned.size = 0 & t.needs <: has) &
  availStaff.size > 0   =>
      Assignment->exists( a | a : assignment & a.task = t &
                      a.staff = availStaff->sortedBy(costDay)->first() )
```

In the same way, the list of staff could be pre-sorted by *costDay*, to avoid sorting the available staff in each constraint application:

```
Schedule::
  sortedtasks = Task->sortedBy(-duration)

Schedule::
  sortedstaff = Staff->sortedBy(costDay)

Schedule::
  t : sortedtasks & t.assignment.size = 0 &
  t.dependsOn.assignment->size() = t.dependsOn.size &
  availStaff = sortedstaff->select(assigned.size = 0 & t.needs <: has)
  & availStaff.size > 0   =>
      Assignment->exists( a | a : assignment & a.task = t &
                      a.staff = availStaff.first )
```

Table 8.1 shows the effect of these two optimisations, on large scheduling examples.

Table 8.1: Test cases of scheduling

Test case	Unoptimised	Optimised
100 tasks, 100 staff	608ms	515ms
200 tasks, 200 staff	3.8s	2.8s
500 tasks, 500 staff	28.5s	21.4s

Summary

This chapter has illustrated development using UML-RSDS, with development steps shown for a case study of a resource scheduler. Initial exploratory and evolutionary prototyping was used to produce a working solution, then optimisation was carried out to produce an improved production-quality solution.

Chapter 9

Design Patterns and Refactorings

Design patterns are a well-known technique for organising the structure of a software system in order to achieve quality or efficiency goals [3]. Several design patterns are built-in to UML-RSDS and are automatically incorporated into systems synthesised using the tools. Other patterns can be optionally selected by the developer, and there are further patterns which are recommended for UML-RSDS developments, but which need to be manually encoded. Refactorings are system restructurings which aim to improve the quality of the system specification or design, whilst preserving its semantics [2].

9.1 Design patterns

Software design patterns were identified in [3] and in subsequent research work to provide solutions to characteristic problems encountered during software development, and specifically during object-oriented software development. Many of these classical patterns, such as Facade, Singleton, Observer, Model-View-Controller are relevant to UML and to UML-RSDS in order to organise the structure of system class diagrams:

- Facade: defines a 'function-oriented' class which provides a simplified interface to the functionalities of a subsystem by means of its public operations. Client systems can use the Facade class to avoid linking directly to the internal classes of the subsystem.

This pattern is used by the UML-RSDS code generators to define the Controller class of a system as a Facade.

■ Singleton: defines a class which has one unique instance, thus providing a globally available resource. Again, the Controller class in UML-RSDS is implemented as a Singleton.

■ Observer: provides a structure linking observable objects to view objects which present some view of the observable object data. Updates to observables are automatically propagated to view updates.

■ Model-View-Controller (MVC): a generalisation of Observer in which a Controller class co-ordinates the Model-View interaction. This pattern is used in the 'generate web applications' options of UML-RSDS (Chapter 20).

More recently, patterns specific to model transformations have been identified [4, 5]:

1. **Rule modularisation patterns:** Phased Construction; Structure Preservation; Entity Splitting/Structure Elaboration; Entity Merging/Structure Abstraction; Map Objects Before Links; Parallel Composition/Sequential Composition; Auxiliary Metamodel; Construction and Cleanup; Recursive Descent; Replace Explicit Calls by Implicit Calls; Introduce Rule Inheritance.

2. **Optimization patterns:** Unique Instantiation; Object Indexing; Omit Negative Application Conditions; Replace Fixed-point by Bounded Iteration; Decompose Complex Navigations; Restrict Input Ranges; Remove Duplicated Expression Evaluations; Implicit Copy.

3. **Model-to-text patterns:** Model Visitor; Text Templates; Replace Abstract by Concrete Syntax.

4. **Expressiveness patterns:** Simulate Multiple Matching; Simulate Collection Matching; Simulate Universal Quantification; Simulate Explicit Rule Scheduling.

5. **Architectural patterns:** Phased Model Construction; Target Model Splitting; Model Merging; Auxiliary Models; Filter Before Processing.

6. **Bidirectional transformation patterns:** Auxiliary Correspondence Model; Cleanup before Construct; Unique Instantiation; Phased Construction for bx; Entity Merging/Splitting for bx; Map Objects Before Links for bx (Chapter 14).

It is a principle of UML-RSDS development to use such patterns to help to organise and optimize specifications:

> *Use specification patterns where possible to improve the clarity, compositionality and efficiency of UML-RSDS systems.*

The MT design patterns described in [4] and on the MT design pattern repository (http://www.dcs.kcl.ac.uk/staff/kcl/mtdp) form a *pattern language*: the patterns can be combined and composed together to solve problems. For example, Simulate Explicit Rule Ordering and Auxiliary Metamodel are combined in [6]. Figure 9.1 shows the relationships between some of the transformation patterns.

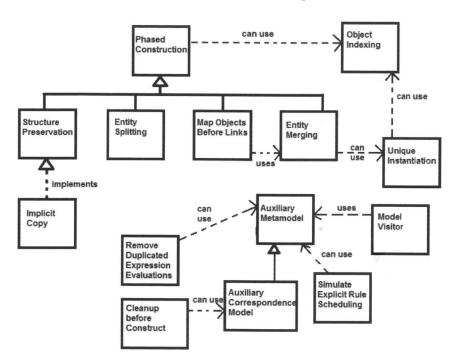

Figure 9.1: Transformation pattern relationships

Phased Construction

This pattern defines a standard organisation of transformation postconditions, based on the composition structure of the source or target languages of the transformation. If there is a composition structure $T1 \longrightarrow_r T2$ of entity types in the target language (that is, an association from $T1$ to $T2$ with a role name r at the $T2$ end), then a transformation creating models of this language could have a rule creating instances of $T2$:

> $S2 ::$
>> $SCond2 \Rightarrow T2\rightarrow exists(t \mid TCond2 \;\&\; Post2)$

preceding a rule creating instances of $T1$:

> $S1 :$
>> $SCond1 \Rightarrow T1\rightarrow exists(t \mid TCond1 \;\&\; Post1 \;\&\; t.r = T2[e.id])$

The $T2$ instances are created first and then linked to the $T1$ instances by means of a lookup based on the source language features (the object or object collection expression e) and a string-valued primary key id of the element type/type of e. An example of this pattern is the UML to RDB transformation (Section 7.5.1).

Map Objects Before Links

This is a related pattern which applies if there are self-associations $E \longrightarrow_r E$ in the source language which need to be mapped to the target language. In this case the pattern defines an organisation of the transformation into two phases: (1) map E to its target entity T, without considering r; (2) map r to the target model, using lookup of T instances. An example of this pattern is the Tree to Graph example of Section 7.5.2. It is also used in the GMF migration example of Chapter 11.

Entity Merging/Splitting

These patterns are variations of Phased Construction which apply if multiple elements in the source model are to be combined into a single element in the target (for Entity Merging), or if a single element in the source produces multiple elements in the target (for Entity Splitting). An example of Entity Splitting is the generation of multiple web application components from a single logical entity type, as in the synthesis of EIS applications in UML-RSDS (Chapter 20).

Auxiliary Metamodel

This pattern defines entity types and attributes, additional to those in the source or target metamodels, in order to support the transformation processing. The auxiliary elements can be used to record traces or source-target correspondence models, or intermediate transformation results.

An example of this would be an alternative form of the UML to relational database transformation which takes account of inheritance in the source model, and only creates relational tables for root classes in the source model inheritance hierarchy, the data of subclasses is then merged into these tables (Fig. 9.2). This is also an example of Entity Merging.

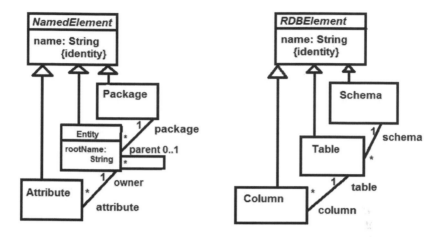

Figure 9.2: UML to relational database metamodels (enhanced)

The attribute *rootName* is a new auxiliary attribute which records the name of the root class of each class. It can be computed using a transformation *setRoots* as follows:

Entity ::
$$parent = Set\{\} \;\Rightarrow\; rootName = name$$
Entity ::
$$parent \neq Set\{\} \;\&\; rootName = \text{``''} \;\&\; parent.any.rootName \neq \text{``''} \;\Rightarrow$$
$$rootName = parent.any.rootName$$

Both postcondition constraints iterate over *Entity*, the second constraint is of type 3, and is iterated until all non-root classes have an assigned non-empty root name.

Sequential Composition

This pattern is used to organise a transformation into a sequential application of modular sub-transformations.

For example, the extended version of the UML to RDB transformation can be split into a sequence of two transformations: (i) *setRoots* to compute the root class name of each class; (ii) *mapUML2RDB* to perform the main mapping, using the auxiliary *rootName* to map subclasses of a root class to the table of the root class.

mapUML2RDB has the postconditions:

$$parent = Set\{\} \;\Rightarrow\; Table{\rightarrow}exists(t \mid t.name = name)$$

on *Entity* creates tables for each root class.

$$a : attribute \Rightarrow$$
$$Column \rightarrow exists(cl \mid$$
$$cl.name = a.name \ \& \ cl : Table[rootName].column)$$

on *Entity* copies the attributes of each entity to columns of the table corresponding to the entity's root class. Thus the attributes of all subclasses (direct and indirect) of a given root class are all merged together into the single table for the root class.

9.2 Design pattern implementation in UML-RSDS

Several design patterns are provided on the UML-RSDS tools *Transform* menu to assist developers. Some (Singleton and Facade) are applicable to systems in general, whilst others are specialised for transformations:

- *Singleton*: constructs a singleton class, following the classic GoF pattern structure.

- *Facade*: identifies if a Facade class would improve the modularity of a given class diagram.

- *Phased Construction*: converts a transformation postcondition which has a nested *forAll* clause within an *exists* or *exists1* succedent into a pair of postconditions without the nested clause, and using instead an internal trace association.

- *Implicit Copy*: looks for a total injective mapping from the source language entities and features to the target language and defines a transformation which copies source data to target data according to this mapping.

- *Auxiliary Metamodel*: constructs an auxiliary trace class and associations linking source entity types to the trace class and linking the trace class to target entity types.

Other patterns from [4] are incorporated into the design generation process:

Unique Instantiation: as described following Table 4.2, the update interpretation of $E \rightarrow exists(e \mid e.id = val \ \& \ P)$ where *id* is a unique/identity attribute or primary key of E checks if there is already an existing $e : E$ with $e.id = val$ before creating a new object. The design for $E \rightarrow exists1(e \mid P)$ checks if there is an existing $e : E$ satisfying P before creating a new object.

Object Indexing: indexing by unique/primary key is built-in: if entity type E has attribute $att : String$ as its first primary key (either inherited or directly declared in E), then lookup by string values is supported: $E[s]$ denotes the unique $e : E$ with $e.att = s$, if such an object exists. Lookup by sets st of string is also supported: $E[st]$ is the set of E objects with att value in st. If there is no identity attribute/primary key defined for E, but some string-valued attribute satisfies $E{\rightarrow}isUnique(att)$, then lookup by string value can also be used for the first such att.

Omit Negative Application Conditions (NACs): if type 2 or 3 (Chapter 6) constraints $Ante \Rightarrow Succ$ have that $Ante$ and $Succ$ are mutually inconsistent, then the design generator will simplify the generated design by omitting a check for $Succ$ if $Ante$ is true. It will also prompt the user to ask if this simplification should be applied. For example, any constraint with the form

$$Ante \Rightarrow P \ \& \ self{\rightarrow}isDeleted()$$

can be optimized in this way, likewise for

$$x : E \ \& \ Ante \Rightarrow P \ \& \ x{\rightarrow}isDeleted()$$

Constraints with a *true* antecedent cannot be optimized using this pattern, for example the computation of the transitive closure *ancestor* of a many-many reflexive association $parent : E \rightarrow_* E$ on an entity E:

```
E::
  parent <: ancestor
```

```
E::
  parent.ancestor <: ancestor
```

The first constraint is of type 1, the second is of type 2. The NAC of the second constraint is $not(parent.ancestor \subseteq ancestor)$, and this needs to be checked before attempting to perform $stat(parent.ancestor \subseteq ancestor)$, otherwise the implementation will not terminate.

Note that the use of operation calls within constraints to define update functionality may prevent correct implementation of type 2 or 3 constraints, if NACs are needed. The implementation of a constraint

$$G \Rightarrow Post \ \& \ op(pars)$$

in such cases tests the NAC G & $not(Post)$ before applying the constraint, meaning that cases where G and $Post$ both hold will not result in application of the constraint, even if the effect of $op(pars)$ has not been established. A partial solution to this problem is to use Auxiliary Metamodel to introduce a new attribute to keep an explicit record of those source elements par for which $op(pars)$ has been completed, and use this to avoid re-application of the constraint to such elements.

Replace Fixed-point Iteration by Bounded Iteration: Again, for type 2 or 3 constraints $Ante \Rightarrow Succ$, which would normally be implemented by a fixed-point iteration, a simpler and more efficient implementation by a bounded loop is possible if the effect of $Succ$ never produces new cases of objects satisfying $Ante$ which did not exist at the start of the constraint implementation. In some cases this can be automatically detected, e.g.:

$$Ante \Rightarrow self \rightarrow isDeleted()$$

on entity E where there is no data-dependency of $Ante$ upon E. The user is prompted to confirm such optimizations.

Developers can enforce the use of bounded iteration by using expressions of the form $E@pre$, $e@pre$ instead of E, e in read expressions within the constraint. In particular, if there are two mutually data-dependent postcondition constraints $C1$, $C2$ where $C1$ reads entity type E, and $C2$ creates instances of E, we can assert that the instances created by $C2$ are irrelevant to $C1$ by using $E@pre$ in $C1$, denoting the set of E objects created before $C1$ begins execution, thus potentially removing the need for fixed-point iteration of the constraint group $\{C1, C2\}$.

Whenever possible, the use of fixed-point solutions should be avoided. Although it is possible to write a (type 3) constraint such as

$$x < 7 \Rightarrow x = x + 1 \ \& \ P$$

to mean "increment x until it becomes 7, executing $stat(P)$ for each x value", such a loop is better expressed as a type 1 constraint

$$Integer.subrange(x@pre + 1, 7) \rightarrow forAll(i \mid P(i)) \ \& \ x = 7$$

which is clearer and easier to understand as well as requiring only a bounded loop implementation.

Factor out Duplicated Expressions: complex duplicated read-only expressions *e* in constraints can be factored out by defining a let variable *v* as $v = e$ in the constraint antecedent, and using *v* in place of the repeated occurrences of *e*.

9.3 Refactorings

Refactorings are an important technique in agile development [1]. On the *Transform* menu a set of class diagram refactorings are provided to help in improving the structure of a class diagram:

- Remove redundant inheritance: removes generalisations which link classes which already have a generalisation relationship via an intermediate class.

- Introduce superclass: implements the 'Extract superclass' refactoring to identify common parts of two or more classes.

- Pushdown abstract features: used to copy 'virtual' data features of interfaces down to subclasses, in order to implement a form of multiple inheritance.

There are also inbuilt refinement transformations, mainly used for web application construction (transforming a UML class diagram into a relational database schema):

- Express statemachine on class diagram: creates an enumerated type and conditional expressions within the owning entity of a statemachine, in order to express the statemachine semantics.

- Introduce primary key: adds a String-valued identity attribute to the specified classes (Fig. 9.3).

- Remove many-many associations: replaces a many-many association with a new class and two many-one associations.

- Remove inheritance: replaces an inheritance by an association (Fig. 9.4).

Figure 9.3: Introducing a primary key

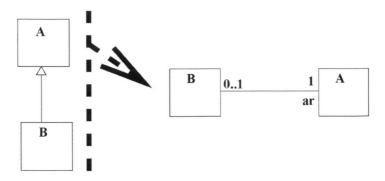

Figure 9.4: Replace inheritance by an association

■ Aggregate subclasses: merges all subclasses of a given class into the class, in order to remove inheritance.

■ Remove association classes: replaces an association class by two many-one associations.

■ Introduce foreign key: define a foreign key to represent a many-one association (Fig. 9.5).

■ Matching by backtracking: introduces a search algorithm for constructing a mapping.

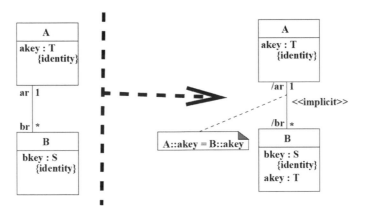

Figure 9.5: Introducing a foreign key

Summary

This chapter has described the design patterns and refactorings that can be used in the UML-RSDS development process. Guidelines for using patterns have been given, and the tool support for applying patterns has been described.

References

[1] K. Beck et al., *Principles behind the Agile Manifesto*, Agile Alliance, 2001. http://agilemanifesto.org/principles.

[2] M. Fowler, K. Beck, J. Brant, W. Opdyke and D. Roberts, *Refactoring: Improving the Design of Existing Code*, Addison-Wesley, 1999.

[3] E. Gamma, R. Helm, R. Johnson and J. Vlissides, *Design Patterns: Elements of Reusable Object-Oriented Software*, Addison-Wesley, 1994.

[4] K. Lano and S. Kolahdouz-Rahimi, *Model-transformation Design Patterns*, IEEE Transactions in Software Engineering, Vol. 40, 2014.

[5] Model-transformation Design Patterns repository, http://www.dcs.kcl.ac.uk/staff/kcl/mtdp, 2015.

[6] W. Smid and A. Rensink, *Class diagram restructuring with GROOVE*, TTC 2013.

Chapter 10

System Composition and Reuse

Medium or large scale systems should ideally be constructed as modular compositions of components, with well-defined interfaces and client-supplier relationships between components. Such components must be at a useful level of granularity, offering a collection of related services to client systems via a convenient interface of operations. To facilitate reuse, the specifications of these operations must be precise and clear, as must the specifications of any data they operate upon. In this chapter we describe ways in which system composition using components can be achieved with UML-RSDS.

10.1 Component-based and service-oriented composition

In component-based design (CBD), a system is formed out of subsystems in a hierarchical manner, with its subcomponents themselves potentially constructed from smaller components. Ideally, as much as possible of the new system should be constructed from reusable components obtained from component libraries. This form of composition and reuse is supported by UML-RSDS, since each UML-RSDS system can be viewed as a component operating on data structured according to the system class diagram, and providing a set of top-level operations characterised by its use cases. These services may be invoked by external client systems in addition to direct users. The external system may be another Java/C#/C++ application which uses the UML-RSDS synthesised system as a subcomponent, or may be an application running on a remote machine and which invokes the use case operations via remote method invocation (RMI) or as web services.

An external system/application M used by another UML-RSDS system is defined in the client system as a class with the stereotype *externalApp*. This signifies that M has been developed as a UML-RSDS application with system name M. The class M acts as a facade or proxy for the supplier system. For Java implementations, the code of system M will be contained in a package with package name M, and should be located in a subdirectory with this name. Calls $M.op(p)$ within the client system are interpreted as $M.Controller.inst().op(p)$ in the complete generated code, and therefore correspond to use cases of the supplier system. The operations of M which are used in the client system should be declared in the M class in the client system class diagram (M may have additional operations – corresponding to use cases of the supplier system M – that are not used in the client, and these do not need to be listed).

Libraries of useful use cases can be developed for reuse as external applications in this manner, for example statistical operations such as the correlation calculator of Chapter 2 could be packaged into a library component for use in other applications. An example of the use of such a library component is the *StatLib* class of the CDO application (Fig. 21.8).

Regarding reuse of components, there is the following principle for UML-RSDS:

> *When a functionality or set of related functionalities have been developed, and which seem to be of potential utility in other systems, construct a reusable component consisting of these functionalities as use cases, supported by the local data. This component can be declared as an externalApp in other UML-RSDS systems.*

Service-based composition, or service-oriented architectures (SOA), achieve reuse and composition by the combination of existing services in workflows (activities) or by other forms of service coordination. UML-RSDS supports this form of composition by enabling use cases to be published as web services (Section 10.4), which can then be externally invoked and combined, including composition with services not developed using UML-RSDS.

10.2 Language extensions and importing libraries

The UML-RSDS language can be extended with new binary and unary $\rightarrow$ operators, and external Java libraries and classes may be declared in the class diagram for use by a UML-RSDS specification. For example, to use Java regular expressions, the `java.util.regex.*` library package would be declared as a new import, and the classes `Pattern` and `Matcher` of this package declared as *external* classes in the class diagram, along with any methods that we wish to use from them, e.g., the static `matches(p : String, s : String) : boolean` operation of `Pattern`. The *external* stereotype on an entity type indicates that the entity type is defined in executable code which is in an external library, or which has been provided by some other source, and that it is not a complete UML-RSDS application. Classes from a UML-RSDS development may be exported as library components via the option "Export system as library" on the Extensions menu. This saves the code of the classes E of the system in separate files *output/E.java*, and these classes can then be used as *external* classes in a different UML-RSDS development.

These extension/import mechanisms are usually language-specific, and there is no support for formal analysis of system elements that depend upon extension/imported components. They are a convenience to support rapid code generation of systems.

10.2.1   *External classes and operations*

Each external class used by the system should be added to the class diagram, with the stereotype *external*. Any operations of these classes used by the system should also be added to their class. Note that currently, array input and output parameters are not permitted, and only the non-collection types supported by UML-RSDS (boolean, int, long, double, String, enumerations and class types) can be used for parameters of such operations. In expressions, declared operations of external entities may be invoked as with any other operation, e.g., `result = Pattern.matches(".a.", "bar")`. Their form in the generated Java code is the same as in the UML-RSDS expression. Instances of external entity types may be created locally, for example, an activity language statement

```
p : Pattern := Pattern.compile(".a.")
```

defines a local variable p holding a *Pattern* object.

Provided that the external entity type E has a zero-argument constructor, objects of the entity may be created in constraints by using an $E{\rightarrow}exists(e \mid ...)$ construct. For example:

```
Date->exists( d | d.getTime()->display() )
```

The generated code initialises d with the *Date*() constructor.

Existing methods of the String class may be called without declaration, e.g., *str.replaceAll*(*p, s*) can be used as an expression within a specification to be implemented in Java. Operations of the Java *Math* class (additional to those already provided in UML-RSDS) may be used by defining *Math* as an *external* class, and the necessary operator *op* as a static query operation of *Math*. For example, the *random*() : *double* operation for generating random numbers in the interval 0 to 1 could be introduced in this way. The expression *Math.random*() could then be used within the system and would compile to a call on the Java operator. Figure 10.1 shows a simple example of a system using *Math.random*() to generate random series, e.g., for a Monte Carlo simulation of share prices.

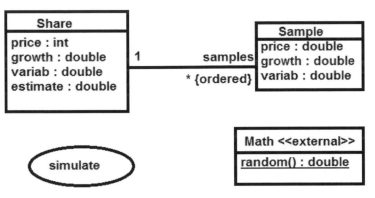

Figure 10.1: System using random numbers

The use case *simulate* has a postcondition

```
Share::
  Integer.subrange(1,10)->forAll( j |
     Sample->exists( s | s.price = price & s.growth = growth &
                        s.variab = variab & s : samples ) )
```

to create 10 samples of the share price trend, and to initialise the share price simulation samples for each share. A second constraint computes the simulations for each sample, using 100 time points, and with random variation in prices simulated by *Math.random*():

```
Sample::
    Integer.subrange(1,100)->forAll( t |
               price = price@pre + price@pre * growth +
                  price@pre * variab * ((Math.random() * 2) - 1) )
```

This models share price changes as a *stochastic process*, with the price at time *t* derived from the price at time *t*−1 as the sum of the current price, a growth component, and a variable component subject to random variation (both positive and negative) of degree $varib * price$ about mean 0.

Finally, an overall estimate for the price at time 100 is calculated as the average of the sample prices:

```
Share::
  estimate = (samples.price->sum())/10
```

For example, with a starting price of 100 for a share, growth as 0.1 (10% growth) and variability as 0.05 (5% variability), one run produces a range of price estimates from 105 to 114, and an average of 111. A full Monte Carlo simulation might use 10,000 samples instead of 10.

Another example of an *external* class is *XMLParser* in the XML to code transformation of Fig. 21.2. This class is an external component whose code has been hand-written. No code is generated by UML-RSDS for *external* or *externalApp* classes, because they are assumed to already possess executable implementations.

10.2.2   *Adding an import*

The Add import option allows the user to add access to a library package to their system, either a standard Java library or a package containing an *external* class or *externalApp* application. The exact text required should be entered, e.g.:

```
import java.util.regex.*;
```

or

```
import mylibrary.*;
```

for a Java import.

10.2.3   *Adding a new operator*

New unary and binary $\to$ operators can be added. The dialog asks for the name of the operator, including the arrow, and the result type. For an operator application $\_1 \to op(\_2)$ the default text in Java and C# is $\_1.op(\_2)$. If an alternative is needed, this should be specified in the following text areas. For example, an operator $str \to time()$ to compose the current time with a string message could be given the Java template text

```
(_1 + (new Date()).getTime())
```

The operator can then be used as a string expression within constraints.

Operators can be used for query expressions, or as new forms of update expression, in which case the Java/C# form of *stat*() for the operator should be entered. For example:

```
JOptionPane.getInputDialog(_1);
```

for a new unary operator →*ask*().

10.3 Example of library creation and use: mathematical functions

A developer could define an *external* library of useful mathematical functions using UML-RSDS, as follows. They may have found the functions *factorial*(*n* : *int*) : *int*, *combinatorial*(*n* : *int*, *m* : *int*) : *int* "n choose m", *gcd*(*n* : *int*, *m* : *int*) : *int* and *lcm*(*n* : *int*, *m* : *int*) : *int* useful and want to define them in a language-independent manner to use in several different applications. A class should be created with these functions as static operations (Fig. 10.2). Since these functions are to be widely used, particular care should be taken over their efficiency and correctness.

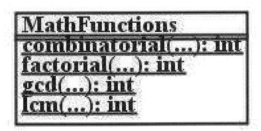

Figure 10.2: Mathematical functions library

For *factorial* and *combinatorial*, the *Integer.Prd*(*a*, *b*, *i*, *e*) operator can be used to compute the product $\Pi_{i=a}^{b}\ e$, and to optimize the computation of these operations:

```
static query combinatorial(n: int, m: int): int
pre: n >= m & m >= 0 & n <= 25
post:
  ( n - m < m =>
      result = Integer.Prd(m + 1,n,i,i) / Integer.Prd(1,n - m,j,j) ) &
  ( n - m >= m =>
      result = Integer.Prd(n - m + 1,n,i,i) / Integer.Prd(1,m,j,j) )
```

```
static query factorial(x: int): int
pre: x <= 12
post:
  ( x < 2 => result = 1 ) &
  ( x >= 2 => result = Integer.Prd(2,x,i,i) )
```

The definition of the combinatorial is optimized to avoid duplicate evaluation of products. For example, if $n \geq 2m$, then the second case applies and

$$combinatorial(n, m) = \frac{n*(n-1)*...*(n-m+1)}{m*(m-1)*...*1}$$

An alternative would be to use a recursive computation for *factorial*, and then use this to compute the *combinatorial*, using the equation

$$combinatorial(n, m) = \frac{n!}{m!(n-m)!}$$

But this approach would be less efficient – as recursion is usually more computationally expensive than iteration – and would lead to numeric overflow in the *combinatorial* computation for cases of $n \geq 13$ or $m \geq 13$. The limit on the input value for *factorial* and for the input values of *combinatorial* are expressed in the preconditions: callers of the operations should ensure these preconditions are satisfied. In a more complete library, probably operation versions using *long* integers would also be provided. In addition, *cached* versions of the operations could be provided, to provide additional optimization.

For the gcd, there is a well-known recursive computation:

```
static query gcd(x: int, y: int): int
pre: x >= 0 & y >= 0
post:
  (x = 0  =>  result = y) &
  (y = 0  =>  result = x) &
  (x = y  =>  result = x) &
  (x < y  =>  result = gcd(x, y mod x))  &
  (y < x  =>  result = gcd(x mod y, y))
```

This is considered too inefficient in general for use in the library, and is replaced by an explicit iterative algorithm, defined using the *Create* menu option *Operation Activity*:

```
static query gcd(x: int, y: int): int
pre: x >= 0 & y >= 0
post: true
activity:
```

```
l : int ; k : int ; l := x  ; k := y  ;
while l /= 0 & k /= 0 & l /= k
do
    if l < k then k := k mod l
    else l := l mod k ;
if l = 0 then result := k
else result := l ;
return result
```

This version is derived from the recursive version by the well-known program transformation 'replace recursion by iteration', and the clear relation between the activity and its declarative version increases confidence in its correctness. Formal proof using B refinement could be used if a high degree of assurance was needed. Note that activities should be written without using brackets, and with spaces used around all operators, including the sequence operator ';'.

From the gcd, the lcm can be directly calculated:

```
static query lcm(x: int, y: int): int
pre: x >= 1 & y >= 1
post: result = ( x * y ) / gcd(x,y)
```

To make this system into a library, set the system name to "mathfunctions" and select "Save system as library" after generating the design. This will produce separate Java files MathFunctions.java, SystemTypes.java and Controller.java in the output directory. Move these to a subdirectory called "mathfunctions" and compile them there. The specification file *mm.txt* of a library should also be placed in its directory, for reference by library users.

The library can be imported into another UML-RSDS application by defining an *external* class MathFunctions with the required operations declared (but without activities or detailed postconditions), and then using the *Add import* option to add the library as an imported package:

```
import mathfunctions.*;
```

The library operations can then be used in use cases of the importing system, for example in a postcondition:

```
MathFunctions.combinatorial(10,5)->display() &
MathFunctions.factorial(7)->display() &
MathFunctions.gcd(6,10)->display() &
MathFunctions.lcm(12,20)->display()
```

which tests the operations for different input values.

The output from these tests is:

252
5040
2
60

which is correct.

10.4 Publishing UML-RSDS applications as web services

Web services are applications which can be accessed by client systems via the internet. They provide operations which, in principle, any client system on any computer connected to the internet can call, independently of the platform and technology used at the client end. Web services are very powerful for connecting applications together and enabling reuse, however they have some limitations:

- Because they are invoked across the internet, there may be delays in web service request and response communications, and hence web services should not be used for time-critical functionalities, nor should frequent fine-grain requests be made. It would be a mistake to try to access a mathematical library such as *MathFunctions* as a web service.

- The data transmitted should be serialisable and not involve platform-specific objects.

UML-RSDS provides two alternative ways to publish an application as a (Java) web service:

REST or *Representational State Transfer* – services are accessed by URLs, and data transfer is by means of the HTTP protocol.

SOAP or *Simple Object Access Protocol* – services are described using a Web Service Description Language (WSDL) specification in an XML file. The services communicate with clients via XML messages in the SOAP format.

In either case, the communication between the client and web service supplier/host involves the client locating the service, constructing a request message to send to the supplier, and then receiving any response message from the supplier.

The share price estimator use case from Section 10.2.1 could be appropriate as a web service. To make it useful to remote callers, all its data needs to be supplied as parameters, so that it is independent of server-side data:

- *currentPrice* : *double*

- *timeDays* : *int* – the length of period considered for the prediction

- *growthRate* : *double*

- *variation* : *double*

- *runs* : *int* – the number of samples to be generated

The result parameter gives the estimated future price as a double. The name of the use case is changed to the more meaningful *estimateFuturePrice*, and the constraints are modified to be:

```
Share->exists( s | s.price = currentPrice & s.growth = growthRate &
                         s.variab = variation )
```

```
Share::
  Integer.subrange(1,runs)->forAll( j |
      Sample->exists( s | s.price = price & s.growth = growth &
                          s.variab = variab & s : samples ) )
```

```
Sample::
  Integer.subrange(1,timeDays)->forAll( t |
      price = price@pre + price@pre * growth +
              price@pre * variab * ( ( Math.random() * 2 ) - 1 ) )
```

```
Share::
  estimate = ( samples.price->sum() ) / runs
```

```
result = Share.estimate->any()
```

The final constraint copies the estimated price of the single *Share* instance to the *result* parameter of the use case. As an alternative to *Math.random*(), the Apache math library class *NormalDistribution* and operation *sample* could preferably be used to obtain samples from the normal distribution N(0,1) [1].

Table 10.1 shows the time complexity of this version, using *initialPrice* = 100, *timeDays* = 50, *growth* = 0.1, *variability* = 0.09, and varying the number of samples. It can be concluded that the service is of adequate efficiency to use in practice.

Table 10.1: Execution time for share price estimator service

Number of samples	Execution time (Java 4)
100	40ms
1000	160ms
10,000	5,140ms

10.4.1 REST web service

This is generated by the option *Web Service, REST* on the Synthesis menu. This option produces a web interface for the system, consisting of a web page and JSP file for each use case, and a bean class which invokes the system controller. The architecture of Fig. 20.3 is used, with a facade for *Controller* instead of entity beans in the business tier. A web page and JSP for each use case are generated. These should be placed in a server directory *webapps/app/servlets*, where *app* is the system name of the UML-RSDS system.

Figure 10.3 shows the web page for the *estimateFuturePrice* web service. This submits a GET HTTP request to the following JSP:

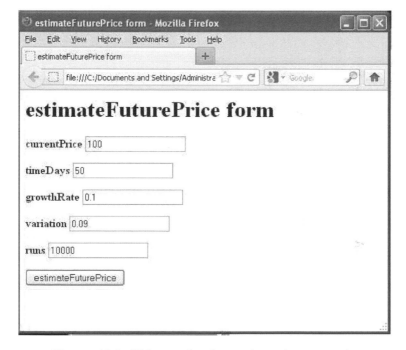

Figure 10.3: Web page for share price estimator service

```
<jsp:useBean id="bean" scope="request"
 class="beans.ControllerBean"/>
<jsp:setProperty name="bean"
property="currentPrice"  param="currentPrice"/>
<jsp:setProperty name="bean"
property="timeDays"  param="timeDays"/>
<jsp:setProperty name="bean"
property="growthRate"  param="growthRate"/>
<jsp:setProperty name="bean"
property="variation"  param="variation"/>
```

```
<jsp:setProperty name="bean"
property="runs"  param="runs"/>

<html>
<head><title>estimateFuturePrice</title></head>

<body>

<h1>estimateFuturePrice</h1>
<% bean.estimateFuturePrice(); %>
<h2>estimateFuturePrice performed</h2>
<strong> Result = </strong> <%= bean.getResult() %>

<hr>

</body>
</html>
```

The request is:

http://127.0.0.1:8080/app/servlets/estimateFuturePrice.jsp?
    currentPrice=100&timeDays=50&growthRate=0.1&variation=
    0.09&runs=10000

and this request could also be issued programmatically, e.g., using the Java URL class, instead of via a browser.

The JSP calls operations of *ControllerBean* to transfer the service parameters and to invoke the service:

```
package beans;

import java.util.*;

public class ControllerBean
{ Controller cont;

  public ControllerBean() { cont = Controller.inst(); }

  double currentPrice;
  int timeDays;
  double growthRate;
  double variation;
  int runs;
  String result;

  public void setcurrentPrice(String _s)
  {
    try { currentPrice = Double.parseDouble(_s);
    } catch (Exception _e) { return; }
  }
```

```
public void settimeDays(String _s)
{
  try { timeDays = Integer.parseInt(_s);
    } catch (Exception _e) { return; }
}

public void setgrowthRate(String _s)
{
  try { growthRate = Double.parseDouble(_s);
    } catch (Exception _e) { return; }
}

public void setvariation(String _s)
{
  try { variation = Double.parseDouble(_s);
    } catch (Exception _e) { return; }
}

public void setruns(String _s)
{
  try { runs = Integer.parseInt(_s);
    } catch (Exception _e) { return; }
}

public void estimateFuturePrice()
{ result = "" + cont.estimateFuturePrice(currentPrice,
        timeDays,growthRate,variation,runs); }

public String getResult() { return result; }
}
```

This class should be located in the *webapps/app/WEB-INF/classes/beans*
directory, together with the *Controller* class and other Java files of the
system. The *bean* object has *request* scope in the JSP, which means
that it only exists for the specific service request, and its data is not
retained for subsequent requests.

Figure 10.4 shows the result page returned by the *estimateFuturePrice*
web service.

10.4.2   SOAP web service

This is generated by the option *Web Service, SOAP* on the Synthesis
menu. This produces a SOAP web service specification in Java for the
current system, with each use case defined as a web service method.
For example, the share price estimator has the following SOAP specification:

```
import java.util.*;
```

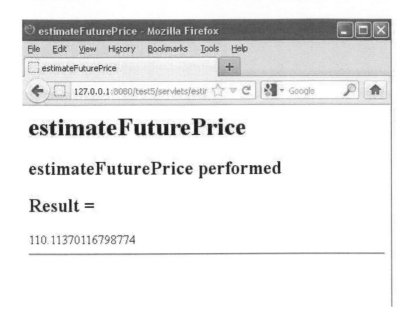

Figure 10.4: Share price estimator result page

```
import javax.jws.WebService;
import javax.jws.WebMethod;
import javax.jws.WebParam;

@WebService( name = "ControllerWebBean",
serviceName = "ControllerWebBeanService" )
public class ControllerWebBean
{ Controller cont;

  public ControllerWebBean() { cont = Controller.inst(); }

  @WebMethod( operationName = "estimateFuturePrice" )
  public String estimateFuturePrice
   (double currentPrice, int timeDays, double growthRate,
                 double variation, int runs)
  { return "" + cont.estimateFuturePrice
   (currentPrice,timeDays,growthRate,variation,runs); }

}
```

This instantiates the system controller and invokes it, in order to carry out requests to the web service. The class annotation @WebService declares ControllerWebBean as a Java web service, and the method annotation @WebMethod declares estimateFuturePrice as a operation which can be called as a web service.

Summary

This chapter has described how UML-RSDS systems can be composed together and how they can use external applications. We have given examples to show how libraries can be created and used, and how UML-RSDS applications can be used as components in other systems, or published as globally-available web services.

References

[1] Apache Commons Math library, http://commons.apache.org/proper/commons-math/apidocs/ org/apache/commons/maths3/distribution/NormalDistribution. html.

Chapter 11

Migration Transformations

Migration transformations occur in many situations in MBD: data migration where existing business data stored in legacy repositories needs to be migrated into a new form of storage with an updated data schema; model migration where models structured according to one language/metamodel need to be translated into models structured according to an evolved/updated metamodel. Related operations are data cleansing and model merging, where errors in data need to be detected and removed, or where related data in different models need to be merged and mapped to a new model.

11.1 Characteristics of migration transformations

Migration transformations are typically separate-models transformations, with read-only source models. They should therefore normally consist of type 0 or type 1 constraints only, that is, constraints which write and read separate data items, and have bounded loop implementations. The functional requirements for migration transformations concern how elements of the source language (the entity types and entity type features) should be mapped to elements of the target language, for example "for each instance of source entity type $S1$ there should exist a corresponding instance of target entity type $T1$ such that ...". Such requirements can be expressed at a high level by *language mappings* which define the corresponding target language elements of each source language element in the scope of the transformation. For example, a mapping χ

$$S1 \longmapsto T1$$
$$S2 \longmapsto T1$$
$$S1 :: f \longmapsto T1 :: g$$
$$S2 :: h \longmapsto T1 :: p$$

indicates that source entity types $S1$ and $S2$ map to target entity type $T1$ (any instance of the source types should be migrated to an instance of $T1$), and that feature f of $S1$ is represented by feature g of $T1$, and feature h of $S2$ is represented by feature p of $T1$. From such abstract requirements, outline UML-RSDS rules can be derived:

```
S1::
  T1->exists( t1 | t1.g = f )
```

```
S2::
  T1->exists( t1 | t1.p = h )
```

Transformation patterns such as Phased Construction, Structure Preservation, Entity Merging, Entity Splitting and Map Objects before Links are particularly relevant for migration transformations. The above example is a case of Entity Merging. Object Indexing and Unique Instantiation are also important, to support tracing of target model elements back to source model elements, and to avoid creating duplicated target elements.

In this chapter we consider two migration examples: (i) migration of Eclipse GMF graphical data models from GMF version 1.0 to GMF version 2.1, and (ii) mapping of ATL transformation specifications to UML-RSDS.

11.2   Case study: GMF model migration

This case study is a re-expression transformation which involves a complex restructuring of the data of a model: indirection between objects is introduced in the target language, so that actual figures in the source model are replaced by references to figures in the target model, and references from a figure to its subfigures are recorded by explicit objects.

Eclipse GMF (Graphical Modeling Framework) is a model-based approach for generating customised graphical editors for modelling languages (www.eclipse.org/modeling/gmp). Between versions 1.0 and 2.1 of GMF there were significant changes in how graphical languages were represented, leading to the need to perform migration from the old to the updated versions of GMF. Figure 11.1 shows the unified metamodels of the source (GMF version 1.0) and target (GMF version 2.1) languages. Since most of the data of a model may remain unchanged by the transformation, we specify the transformation as an update-in-place mapping on this combined metamodel. An alternative would be to copy the unchanged data to the target model, using a pattern such as Structure Preservation. *Figure*1 is the target metamodel version of the *Figure* class, *figures*1 is the target version of the gallery figure list association end.

The migration can be abstractly expressed by the language mapping:

$$Figure \longmapsto RealFigure$$
$$Figure :: name \longmapsto RealFigure :: name$$
$$Figure :: children \longmapsto RealFigure :: children$$
$$FigureGallery \longmapsto FigureGallery$$
$$FigureGallery :: figures \longmapsto FigureGallery :: figures1$$

The entity types *DiagramElement*, *Node*, *Compartment*, *Connection*, *DiagramLabel*, *Canvas* and their source language features are mapped identically to the target language. In this transformation there are also refinement aspects, with new entity types (*FigureDescriptor* and *ChildAccess*) being introduced in the target language to hold more detailed information than is present in the source language.

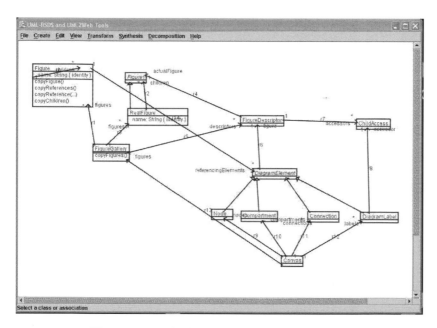

Figure 11.1: GMF metamodels in UML-RSDS

We assume in *Asm* that the input model is a syntactically correct GMF version 1.0 model and that the new entities have no instances:

$Figure1 = Set\{\}$
$FigureDescriptor = Set\{\}$
$ChildAccess = Set\{\}$

We also assume that *name* is an identity attribute (unique identifier) for *Figure* and for *RealFigure*:

$Figure \rightarrow isUnique(name)$
$RealFigure \rightarrow isUnique(name)$

For simplicity of specification, we decompose the transformation into a first transformation which creates the new data from the old, without deleting any data, and a second transformation which removes the version 1.0 data which is not in version 2.1. This is an example of the Construction and Cleanup design pattern (Chapter 9).

The first transformation is specified by a use case *createTarget* with the following postcondition constraints (C1), (C2), (C3), (C4). (C1) is:

```
Figure::
  RealFigure->exists( rf | rf.name = name &
    FigureDescriptor->exists( fd | fd.actualFigure = rf ) )
```

For each source model figure, there is a unique target model real figure, with an associated figure descriptor.

(C2) is:

```
Figure::
  RealFigure[name].children = RealFigure[children.name]
```

For each source model figure *f*, the corresponding target model real figure *RealFigure[f.name]* has as its children the children (real figures) corresponding to the children of *f*. This is an example of the Map Objects Before Links pattern: Figures are mapped to RealFigures by (C1), then parent-child links between RealFigures are created from those of Figures by (C2). The pattern is needed because *children* is a reflexive association in the source language. Both (C1) and (C2) are of type 1.

(C3) is:

```
FigureGallery::
  figures1 = RealFigure[figures.name]  &
  descriptors = FigureDescriptor->select(actualFigure : figures1)
```

For each figure gallery, its figures (*figures1*) in the target model are the real figures corresponding to the source model figures of the gallery, its descriptors are the descriptors of these figures. Although in this constraint *figures1* is both written and read, the update only affects the local data of one *FigureGallery* object *fg*, and no other object is modified, so no other application of the rule is affected. Thus the rule is effectively of type 1: it could be written equivalently (but less efficiently) as:

```
FigureGallery::
  figures1 = RealFigure[figures.name]  &
  descriptors = FigureDescriptor->select(actualFigure :
  RealFigure[figures.name])
```

Another alternative way of expressing this constraint is to use a let variable:

```
FigureGallery::
  fs = RealFigure[figures.name]  =>
                        figures1 = fs &
                        descriptors = FigureDescriptor->
                         select(actualFigure : fs)
```

(C4) is:

```
Figure::
fd : FigureDescriptor & d : referencingElements & fd.actualFigure =
RealFigure[name]   =>
    d.figure = fd &
    (d : DiagramLabel  =>
        ChildAccess->exists( ca | d.accessor = ca & ca :
        fd.accessors) )
```

The figure descriptor *fd* of a diagram element *d* in the target model is that corresponding to the figure which contained the element in the source model. If the diagram element is a label of a nested figure (the condition *d* : *DiagramLabel*), then an explicit child access object is created to record the access.

The second transformation, *cleanSource*, removes all instances of *Figure* and other source model data which is not needed in the target model:

```
Figure@pre->forAll( f | f.referencingElements = {} )
FigureGallery->forAll( fg | fg.figures = {} )
Figure->isDeleted()
```

11.3 Case study: migration of ATL specifications to UML-RSDS

The UML-RSDS tools provide an option to import ATL modules. This facility enables ATL developers to use UML-RSDS to analyse the ATL transformations, and to generate code for these in Java, C# or C++. It also provides a way to write UML-RSDS specifications (of a restricted kind) using ATL syntax. The translation from ATL to UML-RSDS maps from the abstract syntax of ATL (Fig. 11.2) into the UML-RSDS metamodel (Figs. 11.3, 11.4, and A.2), and can be viewed as a language migration transformation *atl2uml* similar to a programming language migration (e.g., from Visual Basic to Java).

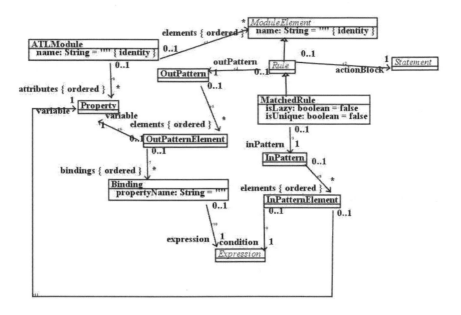

Figure 11.2: ATL metamodel

The informal initial idea of the mapping can be described as follows. Given an ATL module M consisting of a set of rules r1, ..., rn:

```
module M;
create OUT : T from IN : S;
rule r1
{ from s1 : S1, ..., sm : Sm (SCond)
  to t1 : T1 (TCond1), ..., tk : Tk (TCondk)
  do (Stat)
}
...
rule rn { ... }
```

the equivalent UML-RSDS specification is a use case M' with post-conditions for each of the ri, and with owned attributes for the local attributes of *M*. A normal MatchedRule r1:

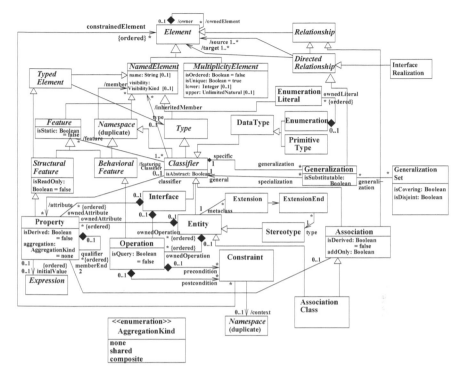

Figure 11.3: UML-RSDS class diagram metamodel

```
rule r1
{ from s1 : S1, ..., sm : Sm (SCond)
  to t1 : T1 (TCond1), ..., tk : Tk (TCondk)
  do (Stat)
}
```

is represented by a postcondition constraint $r1'$ of M':

$$S1 ::$$
$$s2 : S2 \& ... \& sm : Sm \& SCond' \Rightarrow$$
$$T1 \rightarrow exists(t1 \mid t1.\$id = \$id \& ... \&$$
$$Tk \rightarrow exists(tk \mid tk.\$id = \$id \& TCond1' \& ... \&$$
$$TCondk' \& s1.opr1(s2, ..., tk))...)$$

where each expression E in ATL is mapped to a corresponding expression E' in UML-RSDS, and $opr1$ is an operation that represents the action block (*do* clause) if this is present. New identity attributes $\$id : String$ are introduced as new principal primary keys for each of the Si and Tj. Lazy and unique lazy rules are translated to operations – such rules are subordinate to matched rules and only execute if invoked from the matched rules.

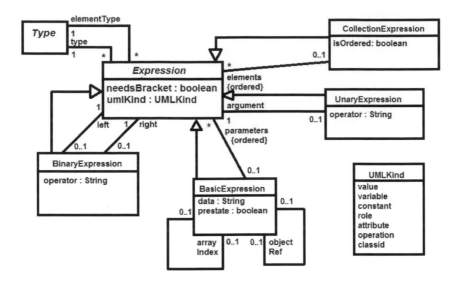

Figure 11.4: UML-RSDS expression metamodel

In order to correctly express the semantics of ATL, each ATL matched rule needs to be translated to two separate constraints in UML-RSDS: the first simply creates the *tj* objects and sets their $id values, the second performs the remaining actions of the rule, using object lookup on the *tj*.$id. This corresponds to the ATL semantics in which a matching (target object creation) phase precedes initialisation (target object linking). This strategy is an example of the Map Objects Before Links pattern, and means that all ATL rules should translate to type 1 constraints in UML-RSDS.

As an example of the migration, the *a2b* transformation of Section 7.3 expressed in ATL would be written as:

```
module M;
create OUT : T from IN : S;
rule r {
  from a : A (a.x > 0)
  to b : B
    ( y <- a.x*a.x )
}
```

This would translate into a UML-RSDS use case with two constraints:

$$A ::$$
$$x > 0 \implies$$
$$B \rightarrow exists(b \mid b.\$id = \$id)$$

and

$$A ::$$
$$x > 0 \Rightarrow$$
$$B \rightarrow exists(b \mid b.\$id = \$id \ \& \ b.y = x * x)$$

In the second constraint b is looked-up, and not re-created, since the object $B[\$id]$ has been created by the first constraint.

More formally, the migration from ATL to UML-RSDS can be described by a language mapping:

$$
\begin{array}{rcl}
ATLModule & \longmapsto & UseCase \\
MatchedRule & \longmapsto & Constraint + Constraint \\
(isLazy = false) & & \\
MatchedRule & \longmapsto & Operation \\
(isLazy = true) & & \\
InPattern & \longmapsto & Expression \ (conjunction \ of \ InPatternElement') \\
InPatternElement & \longmapsto & Expression \\
OutPattern & \longmapsto & Expression \ (conjunction \ of \ OutPatternElement') \\
OutPatternElement & \longmapsto & Expression \ (conjunction \ of \ Binding') \\
Binding & \longmapsto & Expression
\end{array}
$$

The output conditions $TCondj$ of an ATL rule are expressed as UML-RSDS expressions $TCondj'$ as follows. A Binding of *propertyName* f of tj to expression e:

$$f \leftarrow e$$

is interpreted as

$$tj.f = e'$$

where e' is the UML-RSDS interpretation of e. Any implicit type conversion from an expression p in e of a source entity type $SEnt$ to a target entity type $TEnt$ is expressed as

$$TEnt[p.\$id]$$

in e'. This is the target object corresponding to p. Likewise for implicit type conversions from $Set(SEnt)$ to $Set(TEnt)$ and from $Sequence(SEnt)$ to $Sequence(TEnt)$.

If an action block with code *Stat* is specified, then a new update operation $opri(s2 : S2, ..., sm : Sm, t1 : T1, ..., tk : Tk)$ is introduced to $S1$, and this operation has activity given by the interpretation *Stat'* of *Stat* as a UML-RSDS activity. The translation of lazy and called rules r is similar to matched rules, except that the translated constraint r' is used as the postcondition of an operation r of the first input entity type of the rule. Calls *thisModule.r(v1, ..., vm)* to the rule are interpreted as calls $v1.r(v2, ..., vm)$ of this operation.

This migration transformation *atl2uml* can itself be written in UML-RSDS (this is an example of a *higher-order transformation*: a transformation that produces transformations). The language mapping provides a good guide for the structure of the transformation, which could either be written in a top-down or bottom-up Phased Construction form. We have found that language translations of this kind are more naturally specified in a top-down manner, because there is usually some context information from an enclosing construct which needs to be passed down to the mapping rules for enclosed (subordinate) constructs. E.g., to process a Binding, we need to know the variable of its enclosing OutPatternElement.

At the topmost level, for each ATLModule, a corresponding UseCase must be created:

> *ATLModule* ::
> > *UseCase→exists(uc | uc.name = name &*
> > *uc.ownedAttribute = attributes)*

For all non-lazy rules of the ATLModule, a postcondition constraint of the corresponding use case needs to be created:

> *ATLModule* ::
> *uc = UseCase[name] & r : MatchedRule & r : elements &*
> > *r.isLazy = false   ⇒ Constraint→exists(c | c.id =*
> > *r.name & c : uc.orderedPostconditions)*

In turn, the InPattern of the matched rule forms the antecedent of the corresponding constraint:

> *MatchedRule* ::
> *isLazy = false & c = Constraint[name] & ipe : inPattern.elements ⇒*
> > *BasicExpression→exists(varexp | varexp.data = ipe.variable.name &*
> > *varexp.type = ipe.variable.type &*
> > *varexp.umlKind = variable &*
> > *BasicExpression→exists(typeexp | typeexp.data = ipe.variable.*
> > *type.name &*
> > > *typeexp.type = SetType & typeexp.umlKind = entity &*
> > > *typeexp.elementType = ipe.variable.type &*
> > > *BinaryExpression→exists(inexp | inexp.operator = ":" &*
> > > *inexp.left = varexp & inexp.right = typeexp &*
> > > *BinaryExpression→exists(condexp | condexp.operator*
> > > *= "&" &*
> > > > *condexp.left = inexp &*
> > > > *condexp.right = ipe.condition &*
> > > > *c.conjoinCondition(condexp)))))*

This constraint conjoins the formula $si : Si$ & $SCondi$ to the constraint antecedent for the rule. This shows how prolix working in abstract syntax can be: each target language element has to be created and its features set in complete detail (in fact some details are omitted here for readability). Similar (but more complex) mapping rules handle OutPatterns and lazy rules. The completed transformation has been incorporated into UML-RSDS, along with similar transformations for mapping ETL, Flock and QVT-R into UML-RSDS.

Summary

In this chapter we have considered the special aspects of migration transformations, and we have given two examples of how these can be specified in UML-RSDS.

Chapter 12

Refinement and Enhancement Transformations

Refinement transformations are an example of a *vertical* transformation: they map a model at one level of abstraction to a model at a lower level of abstraction. Such transformations are used in MDA and MDD to produce Platform-specific Models (PSMs) from Platform-independent Models (PIMs), and to generate executable code from PSMs. A code generation transformation is a refinement transformation that generates source code text in a programming language. It is an example of a *model-to-text* transformation. A refinement transformation can also be used to enrich a model with more specific and detailed information. For example, a transformation could map syntax-oriented descriptions into semantics-oriented descriptions. In this case it can be considered to be an enhancement transformation and to not change the abstraction level (a *horizontal transformation*).

UML-RSDS makes use of several refinement transformations in its processing: central to the UML-RSDS process is a specification to design transformation which derives a procedurally-oriented version of each use case and operation from their logical specifications (the transformation maps postcondition expressions E to activities $stat(E)$, and determines what algorithm should be used to implement use case postconditions – fixed-point or bounded iterations). There are also code generation transformations which start from the design model and produce Java 4, Java 6, C# or C++ code. Specialised transformations map EIS descriptions to EIS code (Chapter 20).

Refinement transformations are usually separate-models transformations, operating on a read-only source model and producing a target model which is initially empty. Thus their constraints in UML-RSDS should normally be of type 0 or type 1. Each constraint would not normally be re-applied to the same element more than once in a transformation execution (all constraints are implemented by bounded loops). Refinement transformations may be expected to satisfy the property of *conservativeness* (also termed *model coverage*): all information in the target model is derived from the source model, and no new information has been added. To prove such a property, we use transformation invariants to express that all elements of the target model are derived from source model elements. Traceability of target elements back to the source elements they originate from is typically implemented by means of primary key attributes: target element $t : T_j$ corresponds to source element $s : S_i$ if $s.sId = t.tId$ for their respective principal primary keys, where the transformation maps S_i to T_j. In UML-RSDS, the S_i element corresponding to $t : T_j$ is $S_i[t.tId]$, and the T_j element corresponding to $s : S_i$ is $T_j[s.sId]$, when these elements exist.

Enhancement transformations may write new information to the source model – for example to derive all acyclic paths through a graph given by nodes and edges – but leave the initial data unchanged, and so their constraints can also satisfy the type 1 condition. The analysis of refinement and enhancement transformations is therefore technically simpler than for refactoring or bx transformations, however the size and complexity of code-generation transformations in particular requires that these transformations are carefully organised and structured. Transformation patterns such as Phased Construction, Entity Splitting, and Map Objects before Links are relevant for refinements, as are Object Indexing and Unique Instantiation. Sequential Composition, Auxiliary Metamodel and other modularisation patterns are often useful for decomposing a transformation into smaller sub-transformations, and to compose these sub-transformations into a complete transformation. Model-to-text patterns are relevant for code generators.

12.1 Enhancement transformation: computing inheritance depth

This transformation computes the inheritance depth of each class in a UML class diagram, and adds this information as an auxiliary attribute value *depth* to each generalisation. The class diagram metamodel of Fig.

2.5 is used, with *depth* : *int* added to *Generalization*. It is assumed that the generalisation relationship is acyclic.

The first postcondition constraint of this transformation sets the generalisation depth to 1 if the generalisation points to a root class (*C*1):

```
Generalization::
  general.generalisation.size = 0  =>  depth = 1
```

This constraint is of type 1.

If the superclass is not a root class, set the depth to be one more than the maximum depth of the generalisations starting from the superclass of the generalisation (*C*2):

```
Generalization::
  general.generalisation.size > 0  =>
      depth = 1 + general.generalisation.depth->max()
```

This constraint is of type 2 (*Generalization* :: *depth* is both read and written in the succedent), and hence needs to be implemented by a fixed-point iteration. The constraint is applied repeatedly to all generalisations in the model until the implication holds true for all elements. Because termination and confluence are not immediately satisfied by this transformation, a semi-formal proof of these properties is necessary.

It can be argued (i) by induction on the transformation steps that the value of *depth* is always lower than the actual depth:

$$Generalization ::$$
$$depth \leq actualDepth$$

and that the value of *depth* for a generalisation is always no more than the maximum of the immediately higher generalisations *depth* values, plus 1:

$$Generalization ::$$
$$depth \leq 1 + general.generalisation.depth \rightarrow max()$$

These properties could be proved by invariance proof in B (Chapter 18).

(ii) Each transformation step reduces the difference *actualDepth* − *depth* for at least one generalisation, and does not increase any difference, because some depth is always increased in each step, and none is decreased, and by (i) the depth cannot exceed the actual depth. This means that

$$\Sigma_{g:Generalization}(g.actualDepth - g.depth)$$

is a variant. Since this is an integer quantity bounded below by 0, the transformation terminates.

(iii) Termination coincides with (C2) being true for all non-topmost generalisations, and with the variant being equal to 0. Since there is a unique situation in which this occurs (all depths equal the actual depth), the transformation is confluent.

12.2 Refinement transformation: UML-RSDS to C code generation

UML-RSDS already contains code generators for two versions of Java, and for C# and C++. If a code generator for a new language or language version is required, this can be written as a UML-RSDS transformation from the design (PSM) model of a UML-RSDS application to the abstract and concrete syntax of the new target language. To illustrate this process, we consider the task of generating ANSI C code from UML. Firstly, for each UML-RSDS design language element, the intended C language elements and constructs that should implement this element must be determined (these mapping intents are identified at the informal requirements analysis stage). Various possibilities can be considered, for example the UML-RSDS *boolean* type could be represented by a C `enum`, by a `#define` or by `unsigned char`. Many-multiplicity association ends could be represented by resizable arrays, or by linked list structures. List structures are more flexible, but are less efficient than an array representation. Table 12.1 shows the informal mapping for classes, types and attributes. This shows the schematic concrete grammar for the C elements representing the UML concepts.

Table 12.1: Informal mapping of UML class diagrams to C

UML element e	*C representation* e'
Class *E*	`struct E { ... };`
Property *p* : *T*	member `T' p;` of the struct for *p*'s owner, where `T'` represents *T*
String type	`char*`
int, long, double types	same-named C types
boolean type	`unsigned char`
true	`#define TRUE 1`
false	`#define FALSE 0`
Enumeration type	C `enum`
Entity type *E*	`struct E*` type, and `struct E* newE()` operation
Set(*E*) type	`struct E**` (array of E', without duplicates)
Sequence(*E*) type	`struct E**` (array of E', possibly with duplicates)
Operation *op*(*p* : *P*) : *T* of *E*	C operation `T' op(E' self, P' p)`

These mappings can then be formalised as UML-RSDS rules, defining the postconditions of a transformation *design2C*. This has input language the UML-RSDS metamodels (Figs. 11.3, A.2, A.1) and output language a simple syntax-directed representation of C programs and data declarations (Fig. 12.1 shows a fragment of this).

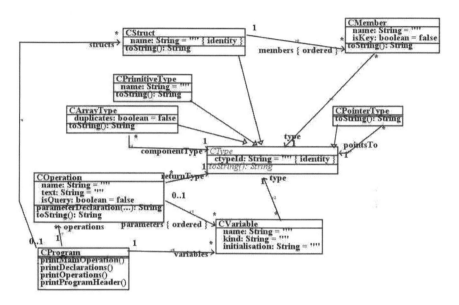

Figure 12.1: C language metamodel

To map classes to struct types, we have the rule:

```
Entity::
  CStruct->exists( c | c.name = name )
```

This rule assumes that class names are unique in the source model.

Then the attributes (and association ends) owned by a class are mapped to members of its corresponding struct:

```
Entity::
  c = CStruct[name] & p : ownedAttribute  =>
       CMember->exists( m | m.name = p.name &
                  m.type = Design2C.type2C(p.type) & m :
                  c.members )
```

where *type2C* is an operation of *design2C* which maps UML types to the text of C types. Note that use case operations and attributes are always static and their names should be preceded by the use case name with an initial capital.

Other rules are also needed to map the C language metamodel elements to text. A model-to-text transformation *genCtext* performs this process:

```
CStruct::
  ("struct " + name)->display() &
  "{"->display() &
  members->forAll( m | ("   " + m.type + "  "
    + m.name + ";")->display() ) &    "};\n"->display()
```

Decomposing the code generator into two sub-transformations improves its modularity, and simplifies the constraints, which would otherwise need to combine language translation and text production. Figure 12.2 shows the resulting transformation architecture.

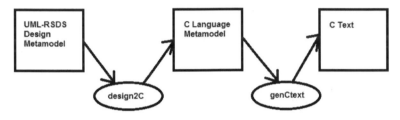

Figure 12.2: C code generator architecture

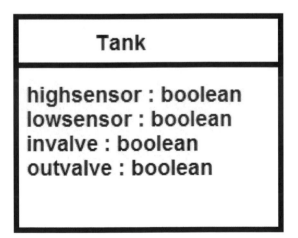

Figure 12.3: Tank class diagram

For the *Tank* class of Fig. 12.3, the code generator produces the declaration in the following program, which also shows the intended mapping of instance operations and of object creation:

```c
#include <stdio.h>
#include <ctype.h>
#include <string.h>
#include <stdlib.h>

#define TRUE 1
#define FALSE 0

struct Tank
{
  unsigned char highsensor;
  unsigned char lowsensor;
  unsigned char invalve;
  unsigned char outvalve;
};

void op(struct Tank* self)
{ if (self->highsensor == TRUE)
  { self->invalve = FALSE;
    self->outvalve = TRUE;
  }
}

int main()
{ struct Tank* t1 = (struct Tank*) malloc(sizeof(struct Tank));
  t1->highsensor = TRUE;
  t1->lowsensor = FALSE;
  op(t1);
  return 0;
}
```

The model data corresponding to Fig. 12.3, and used as input to *design2C*, is the following instance model of the metamodel of Fig. 11.3:

```
Integer : PrimitiveType
Integer.name = "Integer"
Boolean : PrimitiveType
Boolean.name = "Boolean"
Real : PrimitiveType
Real.name = "Real"
String : PrimitiveType
String.name = "String"
SetType : CollectionType
SetType.name = "Set"
SequenceType : CollectionType
```

```
SequenceType.name = "Sequence"
Tank : Entity
Tank.name = "Tank"

highsensor_Tank : Property
highsensor_Tank.name = "highsensor"
highsensor_Tank : Tank.ownedAttribute
highsensor_Tank.type = Boolean
highsensor_Tank.lower = 1
highsensor_Tank.upper = 1
lowsensor_Tank : Property
lowsensor_Tank.name = "lowsensor"
lowsensor_Tank : Tank.ownedAttribute
lowsensor_Tank.type = Boolean
lowsensor_Tank.lower = 1
lowsensor_Tank.upper = 1
invalve_Tank : Property
invalve_Tank.name = "invalve"
invalve_Tank : Tank.ownedAttribute
invalve_Tank.type = Boolean
invalve_Tank.lower = 1
invalve_Tank.upper = 1
outvalve_Tank : Property
outvalve_Tank.name = "outvalve"
outvalve_Tank : Tank.ownedAttribute
outvalve_Tank.type = Boolean
outvalve_Tank.lower = 1
outvalve_Tank.upper = 1
```

The following output (an instance model of Fig. 12.1) is produced from *design2C*:

```
cstructx_0 : CStruct
cstructx_0.name = "Tank"
cmemberx_0 : CMember
cmemberx_0.name = "highsensor"
cmemberx_0.type = "unsigned char"
cmemberx_1 : CMember
cmemberx_1.name = "lowsensor"
cmemberx_1.type = "unsigned char"
cmemberx_2 : CMember
cmemberx_2.name = "invalve"
cmemberx_2.type = "unsigned char"
cmemberx_3 : CMember
cmemberx_3.name = "outvalve"
cmemberx_3.type = "unsigned char"
cmemberx_0 : cstructx_0.members
cmemberx_1 : cstructx_0.members
cmemberx_2 : cstructx_0.members
cmemberx_3 : cstructx_0.members
```

Any code-generator from UML-RSDS designs can be structured into four main parts based on the main UML-RSDS design language divisions:

- Class diagrams (classes, types, attributes, associations, inheritances);

- Expressions;

- Statements (activities);

- Use cases.

Following the usual UML-RSDS code generation approach, UML/OCL expressions should be mapped to C-language strings via two query operations *queryFormC*() : *String* and *updateFormC*() : *String* of *Expression*, which provide the C equivalent of the expression as a query and as an update. Statements may also be mapped to strings, or to a metamodel of C statements, via an operation *updateFormC*() of *Statement*. Use case postconditions will have already been translated to activities via the synthesis process described in Chapter 6.

The UML-RSDS class diagram and use case metamodels are defined in the file `umlrsdscdmm.txt` distributed with the UML-RSDS tools, the expression metamodel is in `umlrsdsexpmm.txt`, and the activity metamodel is in `umlrsdsstatmm.txt`. These metamodels should be loaded into UML-RSDS in this order if the complete language metamodel is needed. Files of specification or design UML-RSDS models (saved using the *Save as* → *Save as model* option on the File menu) conform to this metamodel and can be processed as instance models by transformations such as *design2C*.

In addition to the data features of individual classes, a code generator such as the mapping to C should also handle operations of classes, and generate the *Controller*/Facade code for each application, including:

- Lists of the existing objects of each class;

- Operations to load and save models;

- Indexing maps for classes with identity attributes, to look up their instances by id value;

- Operations for the use cases of the system;

- Global operations on associations (synchronisation of the two ends of bidirectional associations), and on entities (operations to create and delete objects).

As this example shows, developing a code generator is a substantial project, which needs to be organised in a systematic and modular manner based on the source language structure. The three primary considerations for such a transformation are: (i) model-level semantic correctness: does the generated program correctly express the source model semantics? (ii) conformance (syntactic correctness) of the generated text to the target language definition; (iii) efficiency of the resulting program. For critical applications, conservativeness is also required. For new UML-RSDS code generators we recommend following the same translator architecture which has been used for Java/C#/C++ where possible (Fig. 12.4), and to structure the generated code based closely on the source model, so that it is easy for readers of the code to relate code parts to model elements.

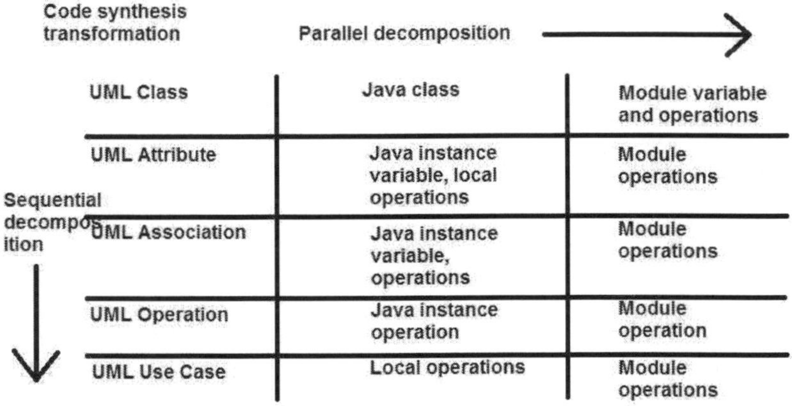

Code synthesis transformation	Parallel decomposition ⟶	
UML Class	Java class	Module variable and operations
UML Attribute	Java instance variable, local operations	Module operations
UML Association	Java instance variable, operations	Module operations
UML Operation	Java instance operation	Module operation
UML Use Case	Local operations	Module operations

Sequential decomposition ↓

Figure 12.4: UML-RSDS code generator structure

To establish conservativeness for the UML to C code generator, we define transformation invariants for *design2C*, these invariants express that the C representation is derived entirely from the source UML-RSDS design. They also provide a form of inverse transformation, and can be derived semi-automatically from the forward transformation rules (Chapter 14):

```
CStruct::
  Entity->exists( e | e.name = name )
```

which expresses that every *CStruct* is derived from a corresponding class, and:

```
CStruct::
  e = Entity[name] & m : members  =>
      Property->exists( p | p.name = m.name &
              p.type = C2Design.type2UML(m.type) & p :
              e.ownedAttribute )
```

which expresses that every member is derived from a corresponding UML Property. *type2UML* is an inverse function for *type2C*.

Summary

We have given examples of enhancement and refinement transformations, and illustrated how UML-RSDS can be extended with new code generators. Guidelines for the organisation of code generation transformations have been provided.

Chapter 13

Refactoring and Update-in-place Transformations

Transformations which update a single model in-place are of wide application, most typically for model refactoring, but also for other uses such as system simulation. Such transformations are usually *horizontal*, because they do not change the level of abstraction of the model they operate upon.

Update-in-place transformations are potentially more complex than separate models transformations, because the source model is both read and written. Conflicts between rules, and failure of confluence are a significant issue for such transformations, and verification is potentially more difficult than for separate-models transformations. Update-in-place transformations may have type 2 and type 3 constraints, with rules that are potentially re-applied multiple times to a single source model element, however in some cases a pattern such as Replace Fixed-point by Bounded Iteration (Chapter 9) can be used to reduce the implementation complexity to a type 1 case. Other optimisation patterns, such as Omit Negative Application Conditions and Restrict Input Ranges, are frequently useful for refactoring transformations. Characteristic of refactoring transformations are constraints whose effect contradicts their condition:

$E ::$

$$A \;\Rightarrow\; B$$

where B logically implies $not(A)$. Such a constraint can only be established by making A false for all applicable instances of E. A good candidate for a variant of the constraint is the number of E instances that satisfy A:

$$E \rightarrow select(A) \rightarrow size()$$

Each application of the constraint should reduce this number.

In this chapter we describe some examples of refactoring transformations, and we give guidelines for reducing the complexity of this form of transformation.

13.1   Case study: repotting geraniums

A simple example of a refactoring is the 'repotting geraniums' example of [4] (Fig. 13.1). This example is however beyond the capabilities of some transformation languages because of its use of nested quantification.

The idea of the transformation is to replace every broken pot p that contains some flowering plant by a new (unbroken) pot p', and to transfer all the flowering plants of p to p'.

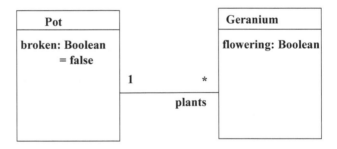

Figure 13.1: Repotting geraniums metamodel

This problem can be specified by a single UML-RSDS rule with context *Pot*:

```
Pot::
  broken = true &
  v = plants->select( flowering = true ) &
  v->size() > 0    =>
        Pot->exists( p1 | p1.plants = v )
```

v is a let-variable which holds the set of flowering plants in the broken pot. It has a constant value throughout the constraint. The introduction of such a variable avoids the need to repeat the complex expression it is defined by, and so helps to make the constraint more readable and more efficient.

Implicit in the effect of the constraint is the removal of the elements of v from *self.plants*: this occurs because of the multiplicity of the *Pot—Geranium* association (a plant cannot belong to two pots). Notice that even though new pots are created by applications of the rule, the collection of pots satisfying the application condition (the antecedent of the constraint) is reduced by each application: after the application there is one less broken pot – *self* – containing flowering plants. This means that a bounded loop can be used for the implementation, instead of a fixed-point iteration. Bounded-loop implementation can be enforced by writing the constraint as an iteration over *Pot*@pre, and using pre-forms for the features that are also written in the constraint:

```
Pot@pre::
  broken@pre = true &
  v = plants@pre->select( flowering = true ) &
  v->size() > 0     =>
      Pot->exists( p1 | p1.plants = v )
```

This is an application of the Replace Fixed-point by Bounded Iteration pattern (Chapter 9) and reduces the constraint to type 1.[1] Termination follows, and confluence holds because there is a unique state where the transformation terminates: the state where all originally broken pots containing flowering plants (call this set *brokenflowering*) now have no flowering plants (their other plants are unchanged), no other original pots are modified, and there are new pots for each of the *brokenflowering* pots.

13.2 Case study: state machine refactoring

UML state machines can be restructured to improve their clarity and to reduce their complexity. For example, if several states each have the same outgoing transition behaviour (they each have a transition with the same event label and the same target state), then these states can be placed in one composite state (if they are not already in such a state) and the multiple transitions replaced by a single transition from the composite state (Fig. 13.2).

---

[1] It is not possible to use @*pre* within a select expression, however.

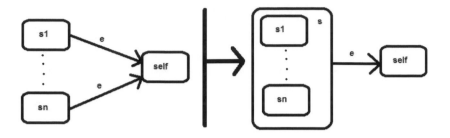

Figure 13.2: Introduce composite state refactoring

The general goal of our state machine refactoring transformation is therefore to introduce composite states to group together states which all have some common outgoing transition. The simplified state machine metamodel of Fig. 13.3 will be used as the source/target language for the transformation.

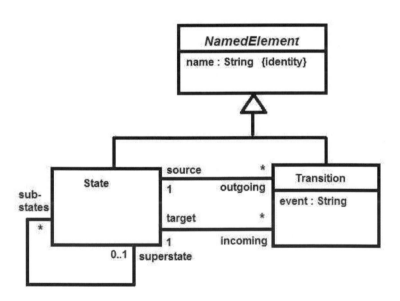

Figure 13.3: Simplified state machine metamodel

Informally, the transformation local functional requirements can be expressed as the following scenario, visually expressed by the concrete grammar sketch of Fig. 13.2:

If there is a set *tt* of two or more transitions, all of which have the same target state *self*, and the same event label *e*, and none of the source states of *tt* are contained in a composite state, then: (i) create a new composite state *s* and make the sources of *tt* the substates of *s*; (ii) create a new transition *t* from *s* to *self*, with event the common event of the *tt*; (iii) delete all the *tt*.

The complexity of the behaviour is evident even in this outline description. One approach to simplify such refactoring rules is to break their action into several steps, implemented as a sequence of separate subrules (e.g., see the class diagram refactoring solution in [5]). However, such an approach requires the introduction of new flag variables or other auxiliary data to enforce a particular flow-of-control, and complicates the implementation and its analysis, so we prefer to implement the informal scenarios by single rules where possible.

There is a non-functional requirement that models of up to 1000 states should be processed within 1 second. Syntactic correctness and termination are essential, but confluence is not required. The informal functional requirements are incomplete (no setting is given for the names of the new state and transition) and vague (should the largest possible set *tt* be taken, or just any set of two or more transitions? Is *self* permitted to be in the set of sources of the *tt*?). After resolving these issues, an initial formalisation can be written as the following prototype rule:

```
State::
   tt : Set(Transition) & tt.size > 1 &
   tt.target = Set{ self } & tt.event->size() = 1 &
   tt.source.superstate->size() = 0  &
   self /: tt.source    =>
       State->exists( s |
           s.name = tt.source.name->sum() &
           tt.source <: s.substates &
           Transition->exists( t |
               t.name = tt.name->sum() &
               t.source = s & t.target = self &
               t.event = tt.event->any() ) ) &
       tt->isDeleted()
```

The intent of the set quantification *tt* : *Set*(*Transition*) is that *tt* should be a maximal set of transitions satisfying the remainder of the antecedent conditions.

Comparing this formalisation to the informal scenario, we can see that all aspects of the intended rule effects are expressed in the formalised version:

■ The application condition "a set *tt* of two or more transitions with a common target state *self* and the same event label, and none of the source states of *tt* are contained in a composite state" is expressed by the constraint antecedent conjuncts: $tt.size > 1$ expresses that *tt* has at least two elements; $tt.target = Set\{self\}$ expresses that all the *tt* have *self* as their target; $tt.event \rightarrow size() = 1$ expresses that the *tt* all have the same event; $tt.source.superstate \rightarrow size() = 0$ expresses that $s1.superstate$ is empty for each $s1 : tt.source$, i.e., that none of these states has a superstate. Note that we have avoided writing quantified formulae for these assumptions, by using navigation expressions and equality instead – in general it is recommended to reduce the number of quantifiers in constraints, in order to improve their comprehensibility.

In addition to these conditions, we require that *self* is not in the set of source states: $self \; / : tt.source$.

■ The succedent (effect) of the constraint expresses the three required scenario updates to the model: update (i) is performed by the succedent part:

```
State->exists( s |
        s.name = tt.source.name->sum() &
        tt.source <: s.substates &
```

The $\rightarrow sum()$ operator applied to a collection of strings concatenates all the strings. It is a convenient means to form new names, but does not guarantee the uniqueness of the composed name, so the syntactic correctness of this constraint (invariance of the state machine language constraints) could not be formally proved.

Update (ii) is performed by the part:

```
Transition->exists( t |
        t.name = tt.name->sum() &
        t.source = s & t.target = self &
        t.event = tt.event->any() ) )    &
```

and update (iii) by the part:

```
tt->isDeleted()
```

We could use this constraint to prototype the transformation and execute it on some simple test cases. While it is correct with respect to the refactoring requirement, this version of the constraint has a number of efficiency problems, and needs to be revised to meet the efficiency requirement.

A quantified variable ranging over an entity type in a constraint antecedent, $q : E$, should be viewed with suspicion, and even more so a variable ranging over collections of E: $qs : Set(E)$. Such quantifications amount to a global search over all the instances of E in the input model, for each instance of the context entity of the constraint, and so can lead to a quadratic or worse time complexity for the constraint implementation. A set quantified antecedent variable (also referred to as *collection matching*) cannot be directly implemented in UML-RSDS for this reason. It can be simulated by using an auxiliary data structure and the Simulate Collection Matching pattern, however this also has severe efficiency limitations. One way to improve the rule is to apply the Restrict Input Ranges pattern (Chapter 9): the quantifier range $tt : Set(Transition)$ can be restricted to the potentially much smaller range $tt : Set(incoming)$, since only transitions incoming to *self* could possibly meet the remaining antecedent conditions. The condition $tt.target = Set\{self\}$ is then redundant and can be omitted. A further improvement is to apply the design principle of *Avoid Collection Matching* (Chapter 6), and replace the search for tt by an explicit construction of tt based on some incoming transition (the same approach was used in the specification of the class diagram refactoring in Chapter 2). This enables the set quantified variable tt to be replaced by an ordinary quantified variable t:

```
State::
  t : incoming &
  tt = incoming->select( event = t.event ) & tt.size > 1 &
  tt.source.superstate->size() = 0  &
  self /: tt.source   =>
      State->exists( s |
          s.name = tt.source.name->sum() &
          tt.source <: s.substates &
          Transition->exists( tr |
              tr.name = tt.name->sum() &
              tr.source = s & tr.target = self &
              tr.event = t.event ) ) &
      tt->isDeleted()
```

tt is the set of incoming transitions which have the same event as the specific transition *t*. Testing of this version shows that it meets the efficiency requirements. For example, a model with 1500 states and 1000 transitions can be processed (with 500 executions of the refactoring rule) in 250 ms. The succedent of the rule contradicts the antecedent (because in the succedent the states of *tt.source* have a superstate, contradicting the antecedent requirement that they do not) so the in-built optimisation pattern Omit Negative Application Conditions can be used in the design generation step (the user is prompted if this optimisation should be applied).

Termination of the transformation is clear because each application of the constraint reduces the number of transitions in the model by at least one. Thus $Transition \rightarrow size()$ is the basis for a variant. Syntactic correctness would follow if some means of generating unique names for the new states and transitions was used. Confluence fails, as some simple counter-examples show. Model-level semantic correctness could be formulated in terms of a *flattening* semantics: the semantics $Sem(m)$ of a state machine m is taken to be the flattened version $flatten(m)$ where all superstates have been removed and transitions from the superstates are replaced by transitions from each of the immediate substates (this is the reverse process of our refactoring rule). It is clear that the introduce composite state refactoring does not change $Sem(m)$.

Other refactorings such as promote substate transitions (if all substates of a state have transitions with the same event and target, replace these transitions by one from the superstate) could be specified as rules of the transformation in the same manner.

13.3   Case study: simulation of BPMN execution semantics

BPMN (www.bpmn.org) is an OMG standard notation for business process modelling. In order to facilitate analysis and understanding of BPMN models, an executable semantics for BPMN has been defined based on a Petri-net style formalism using tokens within a network. A model transformation can be defined to translate process specifications in BPMN 2.0 notation into their executable semantics, and in addition to simulate the execution of the process using this semantics. This second transformation is an update-in-place transformation, whose computation steps correspond to the process execution (or evolution) steps.

BPMN (Business Process Modeling Notation) [3] is an OMG standard for expressing workflows and business processes, using an elaborated version of UML Activity Diagram notation. The notation can express workflow patterns [1] and can help to systematise business process modelling. In order to avoid ambiguity in the meaning of BPMN diagrams, a formal semantics using Petri-net style token nets has been defined [2]. This gives a precise execution semantics to each valid BPMN diagram in terms of the permitted evolution of token markings of the nets, so that the correctness and behaviour of the process described by the diagram can be analysed.

Figure 13.4 shows the source and target metamodels and use cases of the UML-RSDS specification of the transformation. Note the use of the interface *FlowElementsContainer* and interface inheritance of this by *Process*, in order to permit a limited form of multiple inheritance for *Process*.

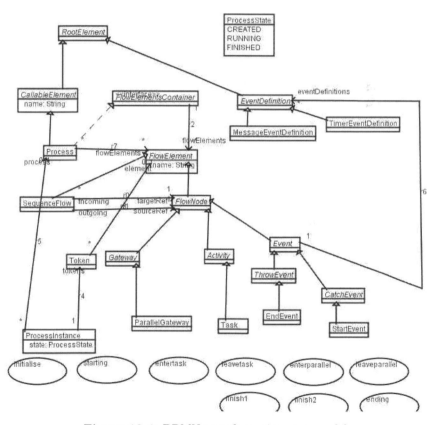

Figure 13.4: BPMN transformation metamodels

The transformation *initialise* maps the BPMN diagram model into its semantic representation in terms of process instances. Separate use cases are also defined for each of the separate situations of token movements, in order to provide interactive control of the execution semantics. The mapping from BPMN to the executable semantics is described by one rule, and the execution behaviour of the semantic representation is defined by several update-in-place rules defining how a process instance may evolve, and how its tokens may move around the process. Process instantiation is formalised by the use case *initialise*. Its postcondition has context *Process*:

```
sn : flowElements & sn : StartEvent &
sn.eventDefinitions->forAll( ed | ed :
 TimerEventDefinition ) =>
  ProcessInstance->exists( pi |
        pi.state = RUNNING &
        self : pi.process &
        Token->exists( t | t : pi.tokens & sn : t.element ) )
```

The effect of this rule can be understood as "If the process has a *StartEvent sn* which has only *TimerEventDefinition*s, create a process instance *pi* for the process, with one token at *sn*". This constraint is of type 1 because its write frame is disjoint from its read frame.

Normal termination of a process is expressed by the postconditions of use cases *finish1*, *finish2*, and these have context *ProcessInstance*:

```
state@pre = RUNNING &
process.flowElements->exists( e | e : EndEvent ) &
tokens@pre->forAll( t | t.element <: EndEvent )  =>
        state = FINISHED & tokens@pre->isDeleted()
```

```
state@pre = RUNNING &
process.flowElements->forAll( e | e /: EndEvent ) &
tokens@pre.element->forAll( n | n : FlowNode &
n.outgoing->size() = 0 )  =>
        state = FINISHED & tokens@pre->isDeleted()
```

Either (i) the process has an *EndEvent*, and all its tokens occupy *EndEvent* nodes, or (ii) the process has no *EndEvent*, and all its tokens occupy nodes with no outgoing flow. In either case the process is set to FINISHED and all its tokens deleted. We use `tokens@pre` and `state@pre` in the places where these features are read because we want to enforce a bounded loop implementation: we are only interested in a single process step. Any further steps enabled by this step will be simulated by the user invoking a use case for the step.

A process instance can start (use case *starting*) if it has a token *t* on a start event with at least one outgoing flow:

```
state = RUNNING & t : tokens &
```

```
fe : t.element@pre & fe : StartEvent &
fe.outgoing->size() > 0  =>
          fe.outgoing->exists( sf | t.element = Set{ sf } )
```

The succedent expresses that one of the outgoing flows *sf* of the start event is selected (*sf* is not created, because the argument *fe.outgoing* of the *exists* is not a concrete entity name) and the token *t* is moved to that flow.

If a process instance has a token on a *SequenceFlow* with target node an *EndEvent*, then the token can be moved to the *EndEvent* (use case *ending*):

```
state = RUNNING & t : tokens &
fe : t.element@pre &
fe : SequenceFlow &
fe.targetRef : EndEvent  =>
   t.element = Set{ fe.targetRef }
```

The same step applies if the target is a *Task* (use case *entertask*):

```
state = RUNNING & t : tokens &
fe : t.element@pre &
fe : SequenceFlow &
fe.targetRef : Task  =>
   t.element = Set{ fe.targetRef }
```

A process instance which has a token *t* on a *Task fe* can leave *fe* if *fe* has at least one outgoing flow (use case *leavetask*):

```
state = RUNNING & t : tokens@pre &
fe : t.element@pre &
fe : Task & fe.outgoing->size() > 0   =>
   t->isDeleted() &
   fe.outgoing->forAll( sf |
       Token->exists( t1 | sf : t1.element & t1 : tokens ) )
```

t is deleted, and new tokens are created for the process instance on each outgoing flow.

In order to enter a parallel gateway, there must be at most one token for a given process instance on each flow element. The process instance can enter parallel gateway *pg* if it has a token on every incoming flow of *pg*, and there is at least one such flow (use case *enterparallel*):

```
state = RUNNING &
pg : ParallelGateway &
v = tokens->select( t |
```

```
      pg.incoming->exists( sf | sf : t.element ) ) &
v.size > 0 &
v.size = pg.incoming->size()  =>
    Token->exists( t1 | pg : t1.element & t1 : tokens ) &
    v->isDeleted()
```

A single token $t1$ for the process instance on pg is then created, and the set v of the instance tokens on the incoming flows of pg is deleted. In this case the constraint requires fixed-point iteration, as it writes the same data (*Token :: element*) that it reads. The let variable v is used to store the pre-value of the expression it is assigned.

Leaving a parallel gateway is modelled by the following use case *leaveparallel* postcondition on *ProcessInstance*:

```
state = RUNNING & t : tokens@pre &
fe : t.element@pre &
fe : ParallelGateway &
fe.outgoing->size() > 0   =>
  t->isDeleted() &
  fe.outgoing->forAll( sf |
      Token->exists( t1 | sf : t1.element & t1 : tokens ) )
```

"If the process instance is running, and has a token t in a parallel gateway fe, with an outgoing flow, then delete t, and create a token for the process instance in each outgoing flow of fe."

A simple test case is that described in Fig. 13.5, with four tasks, two parallel gateways and a start and end node.

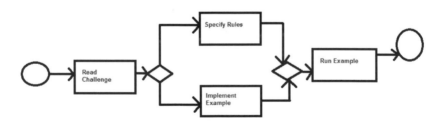

Figure 13.5: BPMN example

The representation of this in the BPMN metamodel is the instance model:

```
p1 : Process
p1.name = "test1"
pg1 : ParallelGateway
pg1.name = "pg1"
pg2 : ParallelGateway
```

```
pg2.name = "pg2"
pg1 : p1.flowElements
pg2 : p1.flowElements
se : StartEvent
se.name = "start event"
se : p1.flowElements
ee : EndEvent
ee.name = "end event"
ee : p1.flowElements
t1 : Task
t1.name = "Read Challenge"
t1 : p1.flowElements
t2 : Task
t2.name = "Specify Rules"
t2 : p1.flowElements
t3 : Task
t3.name = "Implement Example"
t3 : p1.flowElements
t4 : Task
t4.name = "Run Example"
t4 : p1.flowElements
sf1 : SequenceFlow
sf1.name = "startTotask1"
sf1 : p1.flowElements
sf1.sourceRef = se
sf1.targetRef = t1
sf2 : SequenceFlow
sf2.name = "task1Topg1"
sf2 : p1.flowElements
sf2.sourceRef = t1
sf2.targetRef = pg1
sf3 : SequenceFlow
sf3.name = "pg1Totask2"
sf3 : p1.flowElements
sf3.sourceRef = pg1
sf3.targetRef = t2
sf4 : SequenceFlow
sf4.name = "pg1Totask3"
sf4 : p1.flowElements
sf4.sourceRef = pg1
sf4.targetRef = t3
sf5 : SequenceFlow
sf5.name = "task2Topg2"
sf5 : p1.flowElements
sf5.sourceRef = t2
sf5.targetRef = pg2
sf6 : SequenceFlow
sf6.name = "task3Topg2"
sf6 : p1.flowElements
```

```
sf6.sourceRef = t3
sf6.targetRef = pg2
sf7 : SequenceFlow
sf7.name = "pg2Totask4"
sf7 : p1.flowElements
sf7.sourceRef = pg2
sf7.targetRef = t4
sf8 : SequenceFlow
sf8.name = "task4Toend"
sf8 : p1.flowElements
sf8.sourceRef = t4
sf8.targetRef = ee
```

The following shows a trace of the execution of the transformation on this model:

```
Model loaded
Entering startTotask1
Left startTotask1
Entered Read Challenge
Left task Read Challenge
Entered flow task1Topg1
Entered parallel pg1
Left pg1
Entering pg1Totask2
Left pg1
Entering pg1Totask3
Left pg1Totask2
Entered Specify Rules
Left pg1Totask3
Entered Implement Example
Left task Specify Rules
Entered flow task2Topg2
Left task Implement Example
Entered flow task3Topg2
Entered parallel pg2
Left pg2
Entering pg2Totask4
Left pg2Totask4
Entered Run Example
Left task Run Example
Entered flow task4Toend
Leaving task4Toend
Finished process instance
```

Summary

We have described examples of refactoring and update-in-place transformations, and shown how these can be specified in UML-RSDS. We have also given guidelines for the simplification of the specification and analysis of such transformations.

References

[1] W.M.P. van der Aalst, A.H.M. ter Hofstede, B. Kiepuszewski and A.P. Barros, *Workflow patterns*, in: *Distributed and Parallel Databases* 14(1), pp. 5–15, 2003.

[2] R. Dijkman and P.v. Gorp, *BPMN 2.0 Execution semantics formalized as graph rewrite rules*, Eindhoven University of Technology, 2013.

[3] OMG, *Business Process Model and Notation (BPMN) Version 2.0*, www.omg.org/spec/BPMN/2.0/PDF, 2013.

[4] A. Rensink and J.-H. Kuperus, *Repotting the Geraniums: on nested graph transformation rules*, proceedings of GT-VMT 2009, Electronic communications of the EASST vol. 18, 2009, http://dblp.uni-trier.de/db/journals/eceasst/eceasst18.html#RensinkK09.

[5] W. Smid and A. Rensink, *Class diagram restructuring with GROOVE*, TTC 2013.

[6] UML-RSDS toolset and manual, http://www.dcs.kcl.ac.uk/staff/kcl/uml2web/, 2014.

[7] YAWL, http://www.yawlfoundation.org, 2014.

Chapter 14

Bidirectional and Incremental Transformations

Bidirectional transformations (bx) are considered important in a number of transformation scenarios:

- Maintaining consistency between two models which may both change, for example, if a UML class diagram and corresponding synthesised Java code both need to be maintained consistently with each other, in order to implement *round-trip engineering* for model-driven development.

- Where a mapping between two languages may need to be operated in either direction for different purposes, for example, to represent behavioural models as either Petri Nets or as state machines [12].

- Where inter-conversion between two different representations is needed, such as two alternative formats of electronic health record [3].

In this chapter we describe specification techniques and patterns for defining bidirectional transformations in UML-RSDS.

14.1 Criteria for bidirectionality

Bidirectional transformations are characterised by a binary relation

$$R : SL \leftrightarrow TL$$

between a source language (metamodel) SL and a target language TL. $R(m, n)$ holds for a pair of models m of SL and n of TL when the models consist of data which corresponds under R.

It should be possible to automatically derive from the definition of R both forward and reverse transformations

$$R^{\rightarrow} : SL \times TL \rightarrow TL$$
$$R^{\leftarrow} : SL \times TL \rightarrow SL$$

which aim to establish R between their first (respectively second) and their result target (respectively source) models, given both existing source and target models.

Stevens [17] has identified two key conditions which bidirectional model transformations should satisfy:

1. *Correctness*: the forward and reverse transformations derived from a relation R do establish R:

   $$R(m, R^{\rightarrow}(m, n))$$
   $$R(R^{\leftarrow}(m, n), n)$$

   for each $m : SL$, $n : TL$.

2. *Hippocraticness*: if source and target models already satisfy R then the forward and reverse transformations do not modify the models:

   $$R(m, n) \ \Rightarrow \ R^{\rightarrow}(m, n) = n$$
   $$R(m, n) \ \Rightarrow \ R^{\leftarrow}(m, n) = m$$

   for each $m : SL$, $n : TL$.

Hippocraticness is a global property, in practice a stronger local property is desirable: if any part of a target (source) model is already consistent with the corresponding part of the source (target) model, then neither part should be modified. We refer to this as *local Hippocraticness*. In the following, we will consider only *separate-models* transformations, and not *update-in-place* transformations.

14.2　Patterns for bidirectional transformations

Inspection of published examples of bx shows that many rely upon the use of the following patterns:

Auxiliary Correspondence Model: maintain a detailed trace between source model and target model elements to facilitate change-propagation in source to target or target to source directions.

Cleanup before Construct: for $R^{\rightarrow}$, remove superfluous target model elements which are not in the transformation relation R with any source elements, before constructing target elements related to source elements. Similarly for $R^{\leftarrow}$.

Unique Instantiation: Do not recreate elements t in one model which already correspond to an element s in the other model, instead modify data of t to enforce the transformation relation. Use key attributes to identify when elements should be created or updated.

In addition, we have identified the following adaptions of transformation patterns from [15] which can assist in the construction of bx:

Phased Construction for bx: Define the relation between source and target models as a composition of relations between corresponding composition levels in the source and target languages.

Entity Merging/Splitting for bx: Define many-to-one and one-to-many relations between models using links to identify element groups in one model which are related to a single element in the other model.

Map Objects Before Links for bx: Separately relate the elements in the source and target models, and the values of their association ends.

In Section 14.4 we describe these patterns in detail.

14.3　Bidirectional transformation specification in UML-RSDS

As described in Chapter 7, model transformations are specified in UML-RSDS as UML use cases, defined declaratively by three main predicates, expressed in a subset of OCL:

1. Assumptions *Asm* which define when the transformation is applicable.

2. Postconditions *Post* which define the intended effect of the transformation at its termination. These are an ordered conjunction of OCL constraints (also termed *rules* in the following) and also serve to define a procedural implementation of the transformation.

3. Invariants *Inv* which define expected invariant properties which should hold during the transformation execution. These can be derived from *Post*, or specified explicitly by the developer.

The *Post* constraints are often universally quantified over particular source language entity types, i.e., their context entity. In this chapter we will write these quantifications explicitly (they are not written when writing a transformation specification in the UML-RSDS tools) because this helps to clarify the derivation of inverse constraints and transformations.

For example, an elementary transformation specification τ_{a2b} on the languages S consisting of entity type A and T consisting of entity type B (Fig. 14.1) could be:

■ (Asm) : $B{\to}forAll(b \mid b.y \geq 0)$

■ $(Post)$: $A{\to}forAll(a \mid B{\to}exists(b \mid b.y = a.x{\to}sqr()))$

■ (Inv) : $B{\to}forAll(b \mid A{\to}exists(a \mid a.x = b.y{\to}sqrt()))$

The postcondition is written in this case as a type 0 constraint instead of as the equivalent type 1 constraint:

A ::
$$B{\to}exists(b \mid b.y = x{\to}sqr())$$

The computation steps α of τ_{a2b} are applications of $B{\to}exists(b \mid b.y = a.x{\to}sqr())$ to individual $a : A$. These consist of creation of a new $b : B$ instance and setting its y value to $a.x * a.x$. These steps preserve *Inv*: $Inv \Rightarrow [\alpha]Inv$.

In the UML-RSDS tools, both *Post* and *Inv* are entered as constraints using the use case edit dialog. *Post* would be entered as

```
B->exists( b | b.y = x->sqr() )
```

on context entity A, and *Inv* as

```
A->exists( a | a.x = y->sqrt() )
```

on context entity B.

This example shows a typical situation, where the invariant is a dual to the postcondition, and expresses a form of minimality condition on the target model: that the only elements of this model should

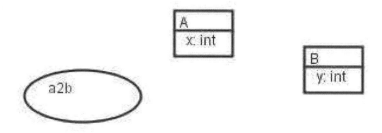

Figure 14.1: A to B transformation τ_{a2b}

be those derived from source elements by the transformation. In terms of the framework of [17], the source-target relation R_τ associated with a UML-RSDS transformation τ is *Post & Inv*. As in the above example, R_τ is not necessarily bijective. The forward direction of τ is normally computed as *stat(Post)*: the UML activity derived from *Post* when interpreted procedurally (Table 6.2). However, in order to achieve the correctness and hippocraticness properties, *Inv* must also be considered: before *stat(Post)* is applied to the source model m, the target model n must be cleared of elements which fail to satisfy *Inv*.

In the *a2b* example, the transformation $\tau^\times_{a2b}$ with postcondition constraints:

$(CleanTarget1):\quad B{\rightarrow}forAll(b \mid not(b.y \geq 0)\ \Rightarrow\ b{\rightarrow}isDeleted())$
$(CleanTarget2):$
$\qquad B{\rightarrow}forAll(b \mid not(A{\rightarrow}exists(a \mid a.x = b.y{\rightarrow}sqrt())))\ \Rightarrow$
$\qquad b{\rightarrow}isDeleted())$

is applied before τ_{a2b}, to remove all B elements which fail to be in R_{a2b} with some $a : A$, or which fail to satisfy *Asm*.

This is an example of the Cleanup before Construct pattern identified in Section 14.2 above. Additionally, the $E{\rightarrow}exists(e \mid P)$ quantifier in rule succedents should be procedurally interpreted as "create a new $e : E$ and establish P for e, unless there already exists an $e : E$ satisfying P". That is, the Unique Instantiation pattern should be used to implement 'check before enforce' semantics. The forward transformation $\tau^{\rightarrow}$ is then the sequential composition $\tau^\times$; τ of the cleanup transformation and the standard transformation (enhanced by Unique Instantiation).

In the reverse direction, the roles of *Post* and *Inv* are interchanged: elements of the source model which fail to satisfy *Asm*, or to satisfy *Post* with respect to some element of the target model should be deleted:

$(CleanSource2)$:
$$A{\rightarrow}forAll(a \mid not(B{\rightarrow}exists(b \mid b.y = a.x{\rightarrow}sqr()))) \Rightarrow$$
$$a{\rightarrow}isDeleted())$$

This cleanup transformation is denoted $\tau_{a2b}^{\sim\times}$. It is followed by an application of the normal inverse transformation $\tau^{\sim}$ which has postcondition constraints *Inv* ordered in the corresponding order to *Post*. Again, Unique Instantiation is used for source model element creation. The overall reverse transformation is denoted by $\tau^{\leftarrow}$ and is defined as $\tau^{\sim\times}; \tau^{\sim}$.

As the above simple example shows, UML-RSDS bx transformations need not be bijective: source models $(\{a1\}, \{a1 \mapsto -3\})$ and $(\{a2\}, \{a2 \mapsto 3\})$ both map to $(\{b1\}, \{b1 \mapsto 9\})$.

In many cases, *Inv* can be derived automatically from *Post* by syntactic transformation, the *CleanTarget* and *CleanSource* constraints can also be derived from *Post*, and from *Asm*. This is an example of a higher-order transformation (HOT) and is implemented in the UML-RSDS tools.

In general, in the following UML-RSDS examples, τ is a separate-models transformation with source language S and target language T, and postcondition *Post* as an ordered conjunction of constraints Cn of the form:

$$S_i{\rightarrow}forAll(s \mid SCond(s) \Rightarrow T_j{\rightarrow}exists(t \mid TCond(t)\ \&\ P_{i,j}(s,t)))$$

and *Inv* is a conjunction of dual constraints $Cn^{\sim}$ of the form

$$T_j{\rightarrow}forAll(t \mid TCond(t) \Rightarrow S_i{\rightarrow}exists(s \mid SCond(s)\ \&\ P_{i,j}^{\sim}(s,t)))$$

where the predicates $P_{i,j}(s,t)$ define the features of t from those of s, and are invertible: an equivalent form $P_{i,j}^{\sim}(s,t)$ should exist, which expresses the features of s in terms of those of t, and such that

$$S_i{\rightarrow}forAll(s \mid T_i{\rightarrow}forAll(t \mid P_{i,j}(s,t) = P_{i,j}^{\sim}(s,t)))$$

under the assumptions *Asm*. Tables 7.4, 7.5 and 7.6 show some examples of inverses $P^{\sim}$ of predicates P. The computation of these inverses are implemented in the UML-RSDS tools (the *reverse* option for use cases). More cases are given in [11]. The transformation developer can also specify inverses for particular Cn by defining a suitable $Cn^{\sim}$ constraint in *Inv*, for example, to express that a predicate $t.z = s.x + s.y$ should be inverted as $s.x = t.z - s.y$.

Each *CleanTarget* constraint based on *Post* then has the form $Cn^\times$:

$$T_j \rightarrow forAll(t \mid TCond(t) \ \&$$
$$not(S_i \rightarrow exists(s \mid SCond(s) \ \& \ P_{i,j}(s,t))) \ \Rightarrow$$
$$t \rightarrow isDeleted())$$

Similarly for *CleanSource*.

14.4 Patterns for bx

In this section we give a patterns catalogue for bx, and give pattern examples in UML-RSDS.

14.4.1 Auxiliary correspondence model

This pattern defines auxiliary entity types and associations which link corresponding source and target elements. These are used to record the mappings performed by a bx, and to propagate modifications from source to related target elements or vice-versa, when one model changes.

Figure 14.2 shows a typical schematic structure of the pattern.

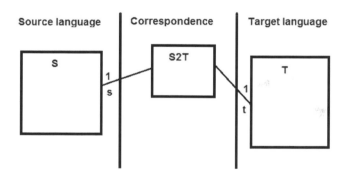

Figure 14.2: Auxiliary Correspondence Model pattern

Benefits:

The pattern is a significant aid in change-propagation between models, and helps to ensure the correctness of a bx. Feature value changes to a source element s can be propagated to changes to its corresponding target element, and vice-versa, via the links. Deletion of an element in one model may imply deletion of its corresponding element in the other model.

Disadvantages:

The correspondence metamodel must be maintained (by the transformation engineer) together with the source and target languages, and the necessary actions in creating and accessing correspondence elements adds complexity to the transformation and adds to its execution time and memory requirements.

Related patterns:

This pattern is a specialisation of the *Auxiliary Metamodel* pattern of [15].

Examples:

This mechanism is a key facility of Triple Graph Grammars (TGG) [1, 2], and correspondence traces are maintained explicitly or implicitly by other MT languages such as QVT-R [16]. The pattern could be used to retain intermediate models to facilitate composition of bx transformations [17].

In UML-RSDS the pattern is applied by introducing auxiliary attributes into source and target language entity types. These attributes are primary key/identity attributes for the entity types, and are used to record source-target element correspondences. Target element $t : T_j$ is considered to correspond to source element(s) $s_1 : S_1$, ..., $s_n : S_n$ if they all have the same primary key values: $t.idT_j = s_1.idS_1$, etc. The identity attributes are String-valued.

The existence of identity attributes facilitates element lookup by using the *Object Indexing* pattern (Chapter 9), which defines maps from *String* to each entity type, permitting elements to be retrieved by the value of their identity attribute: $T_j[v]$ denotes the T_j instance t with $t.idT_j = v$ if v is a single String value, or the collection of T_j instances t with $v \rightarrow includes(t.idT_j)$ if v is a collection. This approach is simpler than using a separate auxiliary correspondence model, and is adequate for many cases of bx, including non-bijective bx. Table 7.6 shows inverse predicates based on this approach to correspondence models. In the table S_i elements correspond to T_j elements, i.e., $S_i \rightarrow collect(idS) = T_j \rightarrow collect(idT)$, and likewise *SRef* corresponds to *TRef*.

The pattern can be used to define source-target propagation and incremental application of a transformation τ. For postconditions Cn of the form

$$S_i \rightarrow forAll(s \mid SCond(s) \Rightarrow T_j \rightarrow exists(t \mid TCond(t) \ \& \ P_{i,j}(s,t)))$$

the following derived constraints Cn^Δ are defined for the incremental application of Cn:

$$S_i \rightarrow forAll(s \mid s.sId : T_j \rightarrow collect(tId) \;\&\; t = T_j[s.sId] \;\&\;$$
$$not(SCond(s)) \;\Rightarrow\; t \rightarrow isDeleted())$$

This deletes those t which no longer correspond to a suitable s. It is iterated over the $s : S_i$ which have been modified. This constraint is omitted if $SCond$ is absent (i.e., it is the default *true*).

For deleted s, the following constraint is executed:

$$s.sId : T_j \rightarrow collect(tId) \;\&\; t = T_j[s.sId] \;\Rightarrow\; t \rightarrow isDeleted()$$

A further constraint maintains $P_{i,j}(s,t)$ for corresponding s and t by updating t:

$$S_i \rightarrow forAll(s \mid s.sId : T_j \rightarrow collect(tId) \;\&\; t = T_j[s.sId] \;\&\;$$
$$SCond(s) \;\&\; TCond(t) \;\Rightarrow\; P_{i,j}(s,t))$$

This only needs to be iterated over those $s : S_i$ which have been modified.

$$S_i \rightarrow forAll(s \mid T_j \rightarrow collect(tId) \rightarrow excludes(s.sId) \;\&\; SCond(s) \;\Rightarrow\;$$
$$T_j \rightarrow exists(t \mid TCond(t) \;\&\; P_{i,j}(s,t)))$$

This iterates over modified $s : S_i$ and newly-created $s : S_i$.

The incremental version τ^Δ of a transformation τ is defined to have postconditions formed from the above constraints Cn^Δ for each postcondition Cn of τ, and ordered according to the order of the Cn in the *Post* of τ. In a similar way, target-source change propagation can be defined.

14.4.2 Cleanup before construct

This pattern defines a two-phase approach in both forward and reverse transformations associated with a bx with relation R: the forward transformation $R^\rightarrow$ first removes all elements from the target model n which fail to satisfy R for any element of the modified source model m', and then modifies or constructs elements of n to satisfy R with respect to m' (Fig. 14.3). The reverse transformation $R^\leftarrow$ operates on m in the same manner.

Benefits:

The pattern is an effective way to ensure the correctness of separate-models bx.

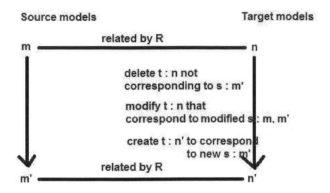

Figure 14.3: Cleanup before Construct pattern

Disadvantages:

There may be efficiency problems because for each target model element, a search through the source model for possibly corresponding source elements may be needed. Elements may be deleted in the Cleanup phase only to be reconstructed in the Construct phase: Auxiliary Correspondence Model may be an alternative strategy to avoid this problem, by enforcing that feature values should change in response to a feature value change in a corresponding element, rather than deletion of elements.

Related patterns:

This pattern is a variant of the *Construction and Cleanup* pattern of [15].

Examples:

An example is the Composers bx [4]. Implicit deletion in QVT operates in a similar manner, but can only modify models (domains) marked as *enforced* [16]. In UML-RSDS, explicit cleanup rules $Cn^{\times}$ can be deduced from the construction rules Cn, for mapping transformations, as described in Section 14.3 above. If identity attributes are used to define the source-target correspondence, then $Cn^{\times}$ can be simplified to:

$$T_j \rightarrow forAll(t \mid TCond(t) \text{ \& } t.tId \notin S_i \rightarrow collect(sId) \Rightarrow$$
$$t \rightarrow isDeleted())$$

and

$$T_j \rightarrow forAll(t \mid TCond(t) \text{ \& } t.tId : S_i \rightarrow collect(sId) \text{ \& } s = S_i[t.tId]$$
$$\text{\& } not(SCond(s)) \Rightarrow t \rightarrow isDeleted())$$

The second constraint is omitted if *SCond* is the default *true* predicate.

In the case that $TCond(t)$ and $SCond(s)$ hold for corresponding s, t, but $P_{i,j}(s,t)$ does not hold, t should not be deleted, but $P_{i,j}(s,t)$ should be established by updating t:

$$S_i \rightarrow forAll(s \mid s.sId : T_j \rightarrow collect(tId) \ \& \ t = T_j[sId] \ \&$$
$$SCond(s) \ \& \ TCond(t) \ \Rightarrow \ P_{i,j}(s,t))$$

For a transformation τ, the cleanup transformation $\tau^\times$ has the above $Cn^\times$ constraints as its postconditions, in the same order as the Cn occur in the *Post* of τ. Note that $\tau^\rightarrow$ is $\tau^\times$; τ, and τ^Δ is $\tau^\times$; τ incrementally applied.

14.4.3 *Unique instantiation*

This pattern avoids the creation of unnecessary elements of models and helps to resolve possible choices in reverse mappings. It uses various techniques such as traces and unique keys to identify when elements should be modified and reused instead of being created. In particular, unique keys can be used to simplify checking for existing elements.

Benefits:

The pattern helps to ensure the Hippocraticness property of a bx by avoiding changes to a target model if it is already in the transformation relation with the source model.

Disadvantages:

The need to test for existence of elements adds to the execution cost. This can be ameliorated by the use of the Object Indexing pattern [15] to provide fast lookup of elements by their primary key value.

Examples:

The *key* attributes and check-before-enforce semantics of QVT-R follow this pattern, whereby new elements of source or target models are not created if there are already elements which satisfy the specified relations of the transformation [17]. The $E \rightarrow exists1(e \mid P)$ quantifier in UML-RSDS is used in a similar way. It is procedurally interpreted as "create a new $e : E$ and establish P for e, unless there already exists an $e : E$ satisfying P" [11]. For bx, the quantifier *exists* should also be treated in this way. If a transformation uses identity attributes (to implement Auxiliary Correspondence Model), the quantifier $E \rightarrow exists(e \mid e.eId = v \ \& \ P)$ can be interpreted as: "if $E[v]$ exists, apply $stat(P)$ to this element, otherwise create a new E instance with $eId = v$ and apply $stat(P)$ to it". This ensures local Hippocraticness.

14.4.4 Phased construction for bx

This pattern defines a bx τ by organising R_τ as a composition of relations $R_{Si,Tj}$, which relate instances of entities Si and Tj in corresponding levels of the composition hierarchies of the source and target languages. Figure 14.4 shows the typical schematic structure of the pattern. At each composition level there is a 0..1 to 0..1 relation (or more specialised relation) between the corresponding source and target entity types.

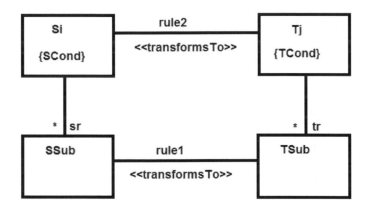

Figure 14.4: Phased Construction pattern

Benefits:

The pattern provides a modular and extensible means to structure a bx.

Disadvantages:

It is sometimes not possible to organise a transformation in this way, if an element in one model corresponds to multiple elements at different composition levels in the other model. In such cases *Entity Merging/Splitting for bx* should be used.

Related patterns:

The pattern is based on the general transformation pattern *Phased Construction* [15].

Examples:

The UML to relational database example of [16] is a typical case, where *Package* and *Schema* correspond at the top of the source/target language hierarchies, as do *Class* and *Table* (in the absence of inheritance), and *Column* and *Attribute* at the lowest level.

In UML-RSDS a transformation defined according to this pattern has its *Post* consisting of constraints *Cn* of the form

$$S_i \rightarrow forAll(s \mid SCond(s) \Rightarrow T_j \rightarrow exists(t \mid TCond(t) \ \& \ P_{i,j}(s,t)))$$

where S_i and T_j are at corresponding hierarchy levels, and *Inv* consists of constraints $Cn^\sim$ of the form

$$T_j \rightarrow forAll(t \mid TCond(t) \Rightarrow S_i \rightarrow exists(s \mid SCond(s) \ \& \ P^\sim_{i,j}(s,t)))$$

No nested quantifiers or deletion expressions $x \rightarrow isDeleted()$ are permitted in *SCond*, *TCond* or $P_{i,j}$, and $P_{i,j}$ is restricted to be formed of invertible expressions.

Each rule creates instances t of some target entity type T_j, and may lookup target elements produced by preceding rules to define the values of association end features of t: $t.tr = TSub[s.sr.idSSub]$ for example, where *TSub* is lower than T_j in the target language composition hierarchy (as in Fig. 14.4) and there are identity attributes in the entity types to implement a source-target correspondence at each level. Both forward and reverse transformations will conform to the pattern if one direction does. The assignment to $t.tr$ has inverse: $s.sr = SSub[t.tr.idTSub]$.

The example of Fig. 14.1 can be elaborated by the addition of another composition level to the languages, and the addition of primary keys to all entity types (Fig. 14.5).

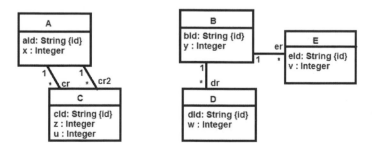

Figure 14.5: Extended a2b example: τ_{ac2bde}

The specification can be organised as a Phased Construction by relating the entity types C and D at one level, and then A and B at the next (higher) level:

$$C \rightarrow forAll(c \mid D \rightarrow exists(d \mid d.dId = c.cId \ \& \ d.w = c.z + 5))$$
$$A \rightarrow forAll(a \mid B \rightarrow exists(b \mid b.bId = a.aId \ \& \ b.y = a.x \rightarrow sqr() \ \&$$
$$b.dr = D[a.cr.cId]))$$

These constraints can be automatically inverted to produce the transformation invariants:

$$D \rightarrow forAll(d \mid C \rightarrow exists(c \mid c.cId = d.dId \ \& \ c.z = d.w - 5))$$
$$B \rightarrow forAll(b \mid A \rightarrow exists(a \mid a.aId = b.bId \ \& \ a.x = b.y \rightarrow sqrt() \ \&$$
$$a.cr = C[b.dr.dId]))$$

These can be used to define the *Post* constraints of the reverse transformation.

Two UML-RSDS bx $\tau : S \rightarrow T$, $\sigma : T \rightarrow U$ using this pattern can be sequentially composed to form another bx between S and U: the language T becomes auxiliary in this new transformation. The forward direction of the composed transformation is $\tau^{\rightarrow}$; $\sigma^{\rightarrow}$, the reverse direction is $\sigma^{\leftarrow}$; $\tau^{\leftarrow}$.

14.4.5   Entity merging/splitting for bx

In this variation of Phased Construction, data from multiple source model elements may be combined into single target model elements, or vice-versa, so that there is a many-one relation from one model to the other. The pattern supports the definition of such bx by including correspondence links between the multiple elements in one model which are related to one element in the other.

Benefits:

The additional links enable the transformation to be correctly reversed.

Disadvantages:

Additional auxiliary data needs to be added to record the links. The validity of the links between elements needs to be maintained. There may be potential conflict between different rules which update the same element.

Related patterns:

This pattern uses a variant of Auxiliary Correspondence Model in which there are correspondences between elements in one model in addition to cross-model correspondences. The attributes used to record intra-model correspondences may not necessarily be primary keys.

Examples:

An example of Entity Merging is the Collapse/Expand State Diagrams benchmark of [6]. The UML to RDB transformation is also an example in the case that all subclasses of a given root class are mapped to a single table that represents this class. The Pivot/Unpivot transformation of [3] is an example of Entity Splitting. The forward transformation represents a 2-dimensional table of data as an indexed collection of maps (Fig. 14.6).

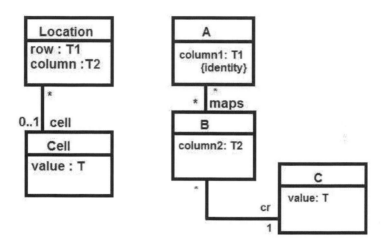

Figure 14.6: Pivoting/unpivoting transformation

The forward transformation has postcondition

$Location{\rightarrow}forAll(l \mid$
   $Cell{\rightarrow}forAll(cl \mid l.cell{\rightarrow}includes(cl) \Rightarrow$
      $A{\rightarrow}exists(a \mid a.column1 = l.row \ \&$
         $B{\rightarrow}exists(b \mid b : a.maps \ \& \ b.column2 = l.column \ \&$
            $C{\rightarrow}exists(c \mid b.cr = c \ \& \ c.value = cl.value))))$

From this the corresponding invariant can be syntactically derived:

$A{\rightarrow}forAll(a \mid$
   $B{\rightarrow}forAll(b \mid b : a.maps \Rightarrow$
      $C{\rightarrow}forAll(c \mid b.cr = c \Rightarrow$
         $Location{\rightarrow}exists(l \mid l.column = b.column2 \ \& \ l.row = a.column1 \ \&$
         $Cell{\rightarrow}exists(cl \mid cl : l.cell \ \& \ cl.value = c.value))))$

This illustrates the general case of merging/splitting, where the inverse of Cn:

$$S_{i1} \rightarrow forAll(s1 \mid \ldots S_{in} \rightarrow forAll(sn \mid SCond(s1, \ldots, sn) \Rightarrow$$
$$T_{j1} \rightarrow exists(t1 \mid \ldots$$
$$T_{jm} \rightarrow exists(tm \mid TCond(t1, \ldots, tm) \& P(s1, \ldots, sn, t1, \ldots,$$
$$tm))\ldots)) \ldots)$$

is $Cn^{\sim}$:

$$T_{j1} \rightarrow forAll(t1 \mid \ldots T_{jm} \rightarrow forAll(tm \mid TCond(t1, \ldots, tm) \Rightarrow$$
$$S_{i1} \rightarrow exists(s1 \mid \ldots$$
$$S_{in} \rightarrow exists(sn \mid SCond(s1, \ldots, sn) \& P^{\sim}(s1, \ldots, sn, t1, \ldots,$$
$$tm))\ldots))\ldots)$$

In UML-RSDS, correspondence links between elements in the same model are maintained using additional attributes. All elements corresponding to a single element will have the same value for the auxiliary attribute (or a value derived by a 1-1 function from that value). In our running example, the entity type C could be split into entity types D and E in the other language:

$$C \rightarrow forAll(c \mid D \rightarrow exists(d \mid d.dId = c.cId \& d.w = c.z + 5))$$
$$C \rightarrow forAll(c \mid E \rightarrow exists(e \mid e.eId = c.cId \& e.v = c.u))$$
$$A \rightarrow forAll(a \mid B \rightarrow exists(b \mid b.bId = a.aId \& b.y = a.x \rightarrow sqr() \&$$
$$b.dr = D[a.cr.cId] \& b.er =$$
$$E[a.cr2.cId]))$$

Again, these constraints can be automatically inverted to produce transformation invariants and an entity merging reverse transformation:

$$D \rightarrow forAll(d \mid C \rightarrow exists(c \mid c.cId = d.dId \& c.z = d.w - 5))$$
$$E \rightarrow forAll(e \mid C \rightarrow exists(c \mid c.cId = e.eId \& c.u = e.v))$$
$$B \rightarrow forAll(b \mid A \rightarrow exists(a \mid a.aId = b.bId \& a.x = b.y \rightarrow sqrt() \&$$
$$a.cr = C[b.dr.dId] \& a.cr2 =$$
$$C[b.er.eId]))$$

14.4.6 *Map objects before links for bx*

If there are self-associations on source entity types, or other circular dependency structures in the source model, then this variation on Phased Construction for bx can be used. This pattern separates the relation between elements in target and source models from the relation between links in the models.

Benefits:

The specification is made more modular and extensible. For example, if a new association is added to one language, and a corresponding association to the other language, then a new relation relating the values of these features can be added to the transformation without affecting the existing relations.

Disadvantages:

Separate rules (constraints) operate on different features of a single entity type.

Examples:

In UML-RSDS a first phase of such a transformation relates source elements to target elements, then in a second phase source links are related to corresponding target links. The second phase typically has postcondition constraints of the form $S_i \rightarrow forAll(s \mid T_j[s.idS].rr = TRef[s.r.idSRef])$ to define target model association ends rr from source model association ends r, looking-up target model elements $T_j[s.idS]$ and $TRef[s.r.idSRef]$ which have already been created in a first phase. Such constraints can be inverted to define source data from target data as: $T_j \rightarrow forAll(t \mid S_i[t.idT].r = SRef[t.rr.idTRef])$. The reverse transformation also conforms to the Map Objects Before Links pattern.

An example of this pattern is the tree to graph transformation [9], Fig. 14.7.

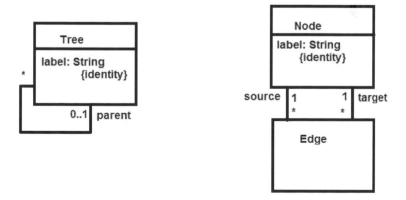

Figure 14.7: Tree to graph metamodels

A first rule creates a node for each tree:

$$(C1): \quad Tree {\rightarrow} forAll(t \mid Node {\rightarrow} exists(n \mid n.label = t.label))$$

A second rule then creates edges for each link between parent and child trees:

$$(C2): \quad Tree {\rightarrow} forAll(t \mid Tree {\rightarrow} forAll(p \mid p : t.parent \Rightarrow$$
$$Edge {\rightarrow} exists(e \mid e.source = Node[t.label] \ \& \ e.target =$$
$$Node[p.label])))$$

The corresponding invariant predicates, defining the reverse transformation, are:

$$(I1): \quad Node {\rightarrow} forAll(n \mid Tree {\rightarrow} exists(t \mid t.label = n.label))$$

and

$$(I2): \quad Edge {\rightarrow} forAll(e \mid Tree {\rightarrow} exists(t \mid Tree {\rightarrow} exists(p \mid p :$$
$$t.parent \ \&$$
$$t.label = e.source.label \ \& \ p.label =$$
$$e.target.label)))$$

Inv is derived mechanically from *Post* using Tables 7.4, 7.5 and 7.6, and provides an implementable reverse transformation, since $stat(Inv)$ is defined.

The running example can also be rewritten into this form:

$$C {\rightarrow} forAll(c \mid D {\rightarrow} exists(d \mid d.dId = c.cId \ \& \ d.w = c.z + 5) \ )$$
$$C {\rightarrow} forAll(c \mid E {\rightarrow} exists(e \mid e.eId = c.cId \ \& \ e.v = c.u) \ )$$
$$A {\rightarrow} forAll(a \mid B {\rightarrow} exists(b \mid b.bId = a.aId \ \& \ b.y = a.x {\rightarrow} sqr()) \ )$$
$$A {\rightarrow} forAll(a \mid B[a.aId].dr = D[a.cr.cId] \ \& \ B[a.aId].er =$$
$$E[a.cr2.cId] \ )$$

Again, these constraints can be automatically inverted:

$$D {\rightarrow} forAll(d \mid C {\rightarrow} exists(c \mid c.cId = d.dId \ \& \ c.z = d.w - 5) \ )$$
$$E {\rightarrow} forAll(e \mid C {\rightarrow} exists(c \mid c.cId = e.eId \ \& \ c.u = e.v) \ )$$
$$B {\rightarrow} forAll(b \mid A {\rightarrow} exists(a \mid a.aId = b.bId \ \& \ a.x = b.y {\rightarrow} sqrt()) \ )$$
$$B {\rightarrow} forAll(b \mid A[b.bId].cr = C[b.dr.dId] \ \& \ A[b.bId].cr2 =$$
$$C[b.er.eId] \ )$$

14.5   View updates

If a predicate such as $t.g = s.f {\rightarrow} last()$ or $t.g = s.f {\rightarrow} select(P1)$ is inverted, the result is a predicate $s.f {\rightarrow} last() = t.g$ or $s.f {\rightarrow} select(P1) =$

t.g. These are termed *view updates*, because they specify an update to *s.f* based on the required value of some view, function or selection of its data. The procedural interpretation *stat*(P) of such a predicate is a statement which makes P true by making the minimal necessary changes to *s.f*. It can be used to implement target-to-source change propagation for a bx where the target model is constructed from views of the source model.

Table 14.1 shows the view update interpretation for some common view predicates.

In the cases for *tail* and *front*, d is the default element of the element type of f. In the case for *collect*, $e^{\sim}$ is an inverse to e, defined, for example, according to Table 7.4. $s \cap t$ is treated as for $s \rightarrow select(x \mid x : t)$. The operator $f \rightarrow merge(col)$ makes minimal changes to f to add the elements of *col*. It is the same as *union* if f is a set. On sequences it is:

$$sq \rightarrow merge(col) \ = \ col \rightarrow asSequence() \frown (sq - col)$$

It has the same ordering and multiplicity of elements as in *col*, for the elements of *col*.

The inverse of an assignment $t.g = D[s.f \rightarrow select(P) \rightarrow collect(bId)]$ is $s.f \rightarrow select(P) = B[t.g.dId]$ if D is the corresponding target entity type for source entity B. The view update definitions can therefore also be used for bx that involve source-target correspondences using identity attributes.

Table 14.1: View update interpretations

P	$stat(P)$
$f \rightarrow last() = x$	if $f.size = 0$ then $f := Sequence\{x\}$ else $f[f.size] := x$
$f \rightarrow front() = g$	if $f.size > 0$ then $f := g \frown Sequence\{f.last\}$ else $f := g \frown Sequence\{d\}$
$f \rightarrow first() = x$	if $f.size = 0$ then $f := Sequence\{x\}$ else $f[1] := x$
$f \rightarrow tail() = g$	if $f.size > 0$ then $f := Sequence\{f.first\} \frown g$ else $f := Sequence\{d\} \frown g$
$f \rightarrow select(P) = g$	$f := f - (f \rightarrow select(P) - g)$; $f := f \rightarrow merge(g \rightarrow select(P))$
$f \rightarrow reject(P) = g$	Same as $f \rightarrow select(not(P)) = g$
$f \rightarrow selectMaximals(e) = g$	$f := f \rightarrow reject(x \mid x.e \geq g.e \rightarrow max() \ \& \ x \notin g)$; $f := f \rightarrow merge(g)$
$f \rightarrow selectMinimals(e) = g$	$f := f \rightarrow reject(x \mid x.e \leq g.e \rightarrow min() \ \& \ x \notin g)$; $f := f \rightarrow merge(g)$
$f \rightarrow collect(e) = g$	$f := f \rightarrow reject(x \mid x.e \ / : g)$; $f := f \rightarrow merge(g \rightarrow collect(e^{\sim}))$
$f \rightarrow any() = x$	$f := f \rightarrow merge(Set\{x\})$
$f.subrange(a, b) = g$	$f := f.subrange(1, a - 1) \frown g \frown$ $f.subrange(b + 1, f.size)$
$f \rightarrow including(x) = g$ set-valued f	$f := f \rightarrow intersection(g)$; $f := f \cup (g - Set\{x\})$
$f \rightarrow including(x) = g$ sequence-valued f	$f := g \rightarrow front()$
$f \rightarrow union(s) = g$ set-valued f	$f := f \rightarrow intersection(g)$; $f := f \cup (g - s)$
$f \rightarrow union(s) = g$ sequence-valued f	$f := g.subrange(1, g.size - s.size)$
$f \rightarrow excluding(x) = g$ set-valued f	$f := f \rightarrow intersection(g \cup Set\{x\})$; $f := f \cup g$
$f \rightarrow excluding(x) = g$ sequence-valued f	$f := f \rightarrow reject(y \mid y \neq x \ \& \ y \notin g)$; $f := f \rightarrow merge(g)$
$f - s = g$ set-valued f	$f := f \rightarrow intersection(s \cup g)$; $f := f \cup g$
$f - s = g$ sequence-valued f	$f := f \rightarrow reject(y \mid y \notin s \ \& \ y \notin g)$; $f := f \rightarrow merge(g)$

14.6 Verification techniques for bidirectional transformations

The properties of correctness and hippocraticness for bidirectional transformations follow by construction for UML-RSDS transformations defined according to the patterns and restrictions given in Sections 14.3, 14.4. Such bx τ should use all of the patterns Auxiliary Correspondence Model, Cleanup before Construct, Unique Instantiation, and at least one of the three patterns Phased Construction for bx, Entity Merging/Splitting for bx, and Map Objects Before Links for bx. The correctness property is ensured by the fact that $\tau^{\rightarrow}$ defined as $\tau^{\times}$; τ establishes the *Post* predicate of τ. The reverse transformation $\tau^{\leftarrow}$ defined as $\tau^{\sim\times}$; $\tau^{\sim}$ likewise establishes *Inv*. Hippocraticness is ensured by the use of Unique Instantiation.

A Phased Construction transformation should satisfy the condition that if a postcondition constraint $R1$ refers to instances of a target entity type $T2$, then any other rule $R2$ which creates $T2$ instances must precede $R1$. This is ensured by the condition of *syntactic non-interference* for a use case: a transformation with rules ordered as $R_1, \ldots, R_n$ should satisfy:

1. If $R_i < R_j$ and $i \neq j$, then $i < j$.

2. If $i \neq j$ then $wr(R_i) \cap wr(R_j) = \{\}$.

Together, these conditions ensure semantic non-interference of the rules: that subsequent rules R_j cannot invalidate earlier rules R_i, for $i < j$. Thus the implementation $stat(Post)$ will establish the conjunction of the postconditions [10]. If a rule r has $rd(r)$ disjoint from $wr(r)$ then it can usually be implemented by a bounded iteration (such as a *for*-loop over a fixed set of elements). Otherwise a fixed-point iteration may be required, in which the rule is applied until no more input elements exist that match its application conditions. If the constraint is *localised* [13], then its implementation is confluent.

For bidirectional transformations, we also require that the reverse transformation based on *Inv* satisfies syntactic non-interference. For Entity Merging transformations, the same target element may be looked-up and updated by different rules of *Post*, so that $wr(C_i) \cap wr(C_j)$ may be non-empty for some $i < j$. However these rules should be semantically non-interfering:

$$C_i \;\Rightarrow\; [stat(C_j)]\,C_i$$

This can be ensured if the rules modify common data in consistent ways, such as both creating instances of a target entity type TE but not deleting instances.

The bx relation *Post and Inv* can encode the semantic equivalence of source and target models, and hence can be used to derive *model-level semantic correctness* [13]. Additional correctness conditions of termination and confluence can be derived by construction, subject to restrictions on the transformation syntax. If each *Post* constraint of τ satisfies the localisation and non-interference conditions of [13], then $stat(Post)$ is terminating and confluent by construction.

Sequential composition is supported for UML-RSDS bx using the Auxiliary Correspondence Model, Cleanup before Construct, Unique Instantiation and one of the other patterns, as shown in Table 14.2.

Table 14.2: Composition rules for UML-RSDS bx

bx Transformation τ	*bx Transformation* σ	*Composed bx* τ; σ
Phased Construction	Phased Construction	Phased Construction
Phased Construction	Entity Merging	Entity Merging
Entity Merging	Phased Construction	Entity Merging
Phased Construction	Entity Splitting	Entity Splitting
Entity Splitting	Phased Construction	Entity Splitting
Entity Merging	Entity Merging	Entity Merging
Entity Splitting	Entity Splitting	Entity Splitting

14.7 Incremental transformations

Transformations may need to operate upon data which is presented in a series of increments or model deltas. Transformations of this type are termed *streaming* or *incremental* transformations. A single source model may not exist, because of size limitations, or it may be continually updated (for example, a transformation may need to process tweets in a twitter feed). Bidirectional transformations may need to operate in an incremental manner if their purpose is to maintain consistency between two different models: incremental changes in one model should be propagated to the other without re-executing the transformation on the entire updated model.

In UML-RSDS incremental transformations can be written as use cases defined by postconditions, as for other forms of transformation. The difference in their operation is that models may be loaded for processing at any number of points in their execution, instead of only at the start of execution.

Figure 14.8 shows a typical example of a bidirectional incremental transformation, relating a source entity A to target entity B, where each model holds data which is not represented in the other, but there is related data which must be kept consistent between the models. The postcondition of $bxab$ is:

A ::
$$B \rightarrow exists(b \mid b.z = 2 * x)$$

To implement this transformation as an incremental transformation in UML-RSDS, we need to introduce primary keys $id : String$ into A and B for the Auxiliary Correspondence Model pattern. The postcondition then becomes:

A ::
$$B \rightarrow exists(b \mid b.id = id \ \& \ b.z = 2 * x)$$

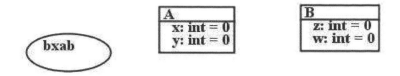

Figure 14.8: Incremental transformation example

The incremental version of *bxab* has the following postconditions (using the Cleanup before Construct pattern from Section 14.4.2) to propagate changes from *A* to *B*:

> B ::
> > $id \notin A.id \;\Rightarrow\; self \rightarrow isDeleted()$
>
> A ::
> > $id : B.id \;\&\; b = B[id] \;\Rightarrow\; b.z = 2 * x$
>
> A ::
> > $id \notin B.id \;\Rightarrow\; B \rightarrow exists(b \mid b.id = id \;\&\; b.z = 2 * x)$

This transformation leaves attributes *y* and *w* unchanged, and only updates the target model in response to source model changes. The first constraint only needs to be invoked for *B* instances corresponding to *A* instances that are deleted in the model increment, the second is only needed for modified *A* instances, and the third only for new *A* instances.

A separate-models transformation consisting of type 1 constraints can be given an incremental implementation (for Java 4) by selecting *incremental* as the execution mode option on the use case edit dialog. The *load model* GUI option then loads in.txt incrementally.

The transformation should conform to the Phased Composition or Map Objects before Links patterns, and use identity attributes to implement Auxiliary Correspondence Model. That is, every postcondition constraint should be of the forms

> Si ::
> > $Ante \;\Rightarrow\; Tj \rightarrow exists(t \mid t.id = id \;\&\; P)$

or

> Si ::
> > $Ante \;\Rightarrow\; Tj[id].tr = TSub[sr.id]$

The transformation should satisfy syntactic non-interference. Changes to the id values of objects are not possible.

14.8 Related work

The patterns we have described here have been used in a number of different bx examples in different transformation languages. Auxiliary correspondence model is used in TGG (explicitly) and QVT-R (implicitly) by means of correspondence/trace model elements. Unique Instantiation is an important mechanism in QVT-R, and implicit deletion in QVT-R provides a version of Cleanup before Construct. Currently no language provides built-in support for Entity merging/splitting, however correspondence model elements in TGG can be used to implement such one-to-many correspondences.

There are a wide range of approaches to bx [8]. Currently the most advanced approaches [5, 2] use constraint-based programming techniques to interpret relations $P(s, t)$ between source and target elements as specifications in both forward and reverse directions. These techniques would be a potentially useful extension to the syntactic inverses defined in Tables 7.4, 7.5, 7.6 and 14.1, however the efficiency of constraint programming will generally be lower than the statically-computed inverses. The approach also requires the use of additional operators extending standard OCL. Further techniques include the inversion of recursively-defined functions [18], which would also be useful to incorporate into the UML-RSDS approach.

Optimisation patterns such as Restrict Input Ranges [15] are not specific to bx, however they could be used in the design process to make forward and reverse transformations more efficient. Omit Negative Application Conditions applies to the cleanup constraints of the transformations.

Summary

In this chapter we have shown how bidirectional transformations can be implemented in UML-RSDS, based on the derivation of forward and reverse transformations from a specification of dual postcondition and invariant relations between source and target models. We have described transformation patterns which may be used to structure bx, and verification techniques which can be used to show correctness properties for the forward and reverse transformations.

References

[1] A. Anjorin and A. Rensink, *SDF to Sense transformation*, TU Darmstadt, Germany, 2014.

[2] A. Anjorin, G. Varro and A. Schurr, *Complex attribute manipulation in TGGs with constraint-based programming techniques*, BX 2012, Electronic Communications of the EASST vol. 49, 2012.

[3] M. Beine, N. Hames, J. Weber and A. Cleve, *Bidirectional transformations in database evolution: a case study 'at scale'*, EDBT/ICDT 2014, CEUR-WS.org, 2014.

[4] J. Cheney, J. McKinna, P. Stevens and J. Gibbons, *Towards a repository of bx examples*, EDBT/ICDT 2014, 2014, pp. 87–91.

[5] A. Cicchetti, D. Di Ruscio, R. Eramo and A. Pierantonio, *JTL: a bidirectional and change propagating transformation language*, SLE 2010, LNCS vol. 6563, 2011, pp. 183–202.

[6] K. Czarnecki, J. Nathan Foster, Z. Hu, R. Lammel, A. Schurr and J. Terwilliger, *Bidirectional transformations: a cross-discipline perspective*, GRACE workshop, 2008.

[7] E. Gamma, R. Helm, R. Johnson and J. Vlissides, *Design Patterns: Elements of Reusable Object-Oriented Software*, Addison-Wesley, 1994.

[8] Z. Hu, A. Schurr, P. Stevens and J. Terwilliger (eds.), *Report from Dagstuhl Seminar 11031*, January 2011, www.dagstuhl.de/11031.

[9] D.S. Kolovos, R.F. Paige and F. Polack, *The Epsilon Transformation Language*, ICMT, 2008, pp. 46–60.

[10] K. Lano and S. Kolahdouz-Rahimi, *Constraint-based specification of model transformations*, Journal of Systems and Software, vol. 88, no. 2, February 2013, pp. 412–436.

[11] K. Lano, *The UML-RSDS Manual*, www.dcs.kcl.ac.uk/staff/kcl/uml2web/umlrsds.pdf, 2015.

[12] K. Lano, S. Kolahdouz-Rahimi and K. Maroukian, *Solving the Petri-Nets to Statecharts Transformation Case with UML-RSDS*, TTC 2013, EPTCS, 2013.

[13] K. Lano, S. Kolahdouz-Rahimi and T. Clark, *A Framework for Model Transformation Verification*, BCS FACS journal, 2014.

[14] K. Lano and S. Kolahdouz-Rahimi, *Towards more abstract specification of model transformations*, ICTT 2014.

[15] K. Lano and S. Kolahdouz-Rahimi, *Model-transformation Design Patterns*, IEEE Transactions in Software Engineering, Vol. 40, 2014.

[16] OMG, *MOF 2.0 Query/View/Transformation Specification v1.1*, 2011.

[17] P. Stevens, *Bidirectional model transformations in QVT: semantic issues and open questions*, SoSyM, vol. 9, no. 1, January 2010, pp. 7–20.

[18] J. Voigtlander, Z. Hu, K. Matsuda and M. Wang, *Combining syntactic and semantic bidirectionalization*, ICFP '10, ACM Press, 2010.

Chapter 15

Backtracking and Exploratory Transformations

In this chapter we consider examples of backtracking and exploratory transformations, and describe how such transformations can be implemented in UML-RSDS.

15.1 Introduction

In some transformation problems it is difficult to formulate precisely how the transformation (considered as a collection of possibly non-deterministic rewrite rules) should behave. Instead, it is simpler to identify the characteristics of acceptable result models that should be produced by the transformation. This entails that the transformation should not terminate unless a satisfactory model is produced. For example, a program or class diagram refactoring transformation could apply automatically some rewrite rules to the program/model, and it is possible that the applications could lead to a model which is of unacceptably poor quality and the choices which led to this model must therefore be undone, and alternative rewrites applied. Other situations could be multi-objective optimisation problems, or exploratory program design. Figure 15.1 shows the execution behaviour which may occur, with some transformation executions having choice points which may lead to either an acceptable or unacceptable final model being produced, depending on the choice made at the point.

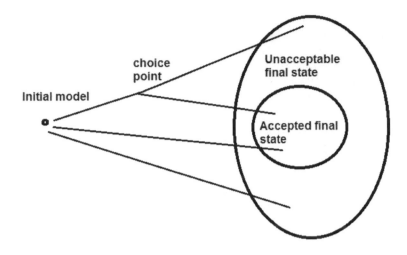

Figure 15.1: Transformation executions with choice points

The ability for a transformation (particularly an update-in-place transformation) to explore alternatives in rule applications, and to undo and redo choices in rule applications is therefore of potential use. In this chapter we consider two simple problems which involve such behaviour: the Sudoku solver, and a maze-solver.

15.2 Implementation of backtracking transformations

In UML-RSDS a backtracking transformation can be specified and implemented using an extension of the development process for standard transformations. Let τ be a transformation for which a backtracking implementation is needed. For simplicity, assume that all of τ's constraints iterate over the same entity type E. The possible executions of τ can be viewed as finite sequences

$$[step_1(ex_1, p1), ..., step_m(ex_m, pm)]$$

of steps, and each step is an application of some postcondition constraint of τ to some instance of E, together with some other parameters – the values of quantified additional variables in the constraint antecedent – the choices of the values for these variables will be backtracked over.

If this sequence of rule applications leads to an unacceptable end state after performing $step_m$, then the rule of this step must be either

(i) *redone* with a different *pm* value, if more choices for the rule parameter(s) still remain untried at this point in the search, or (ii) *undone* and the search for alternative possibilities attempted at the preceding step $(m-1)$ instead. If $m = 1$ then the overall search fails. Alternative rules could be attempted at stage (ii) if such are available: the constraint ordering of the postconditions of τ indicates the priority order in which different rules should be attempted.

To organise such an execution model, two auxiliary variables are needed: (i) a variable $\$chosen_r$: $Set(Value)$ of E for each rule r, which holds for each ex : E the already considered choices for r's other parameter values at this point in the search, and (ii) a variable $\$history$: $Sequence(Rule * E * Value)$ which records the sequence of completed rule applications. When $r(ex, p)$ completes, p is added to $ex.\$chosen_r$ and (r, ex, p) is added to $\$history$. For each r there will be an expression $ex.possible_r$ which identifies the set of possible parameter values p for which r could be applied with arguments ex, p. Redoing and undoing a step can then be described schematically as:

$redo_r(ex$: $E,\ p$: $Value)$
pre: $\$history.size > 0$ & $(ex.possible_r - ex.\$chosen_r) \rightarrow size() > 0$
activity:
  $\$history := \$history \rightarrow front()$;
  undo updates performed by $r(ex, p)$;
  apply r *to* ex *and an element* p1 *of* $ex.possible_r - ex.\$chosen_r$

and:

$undo_r(ex$: $E,\ p$: $Value)$
pre: $\$history.size > 0$ & $(ex.possible_r - ex.\$chosen_r) \rightarrow size() = 0$
activity:
  $\$history := \$history \rightarrow front()$;
  undo updates performed by $r(ex, p)$;
  clear $ex.\$chosen_r$

An undo action for $v : s$ or $s \rightarrow includes(v)$ for a set s is $s \rightarrow excludes(v)$. Assignments $f = v$ can be undone by assigning the previous (overwritten) value to f, if this is known. Table 15.1 shows some common undo actions for constraint succedent predicates P.

The *redo* and *undo* operations may need to be manually customised for particular constraints. Since the steps

  $\$history := \$history \rightarrow front()$;
  undo updates performed by $r(ex, p)$

are in common to *redo* and *undo*, these can be factored out and placed into *backtrack*. An operation *getPossibleValues()* of E returns the remaining unchosen possible values:

Table 15.1: Undo actions

P	$undo(P)$	condition
$e \to display()$	$true$	
$e \to includes(v)$	$e \to excludes(v)$	Set-valued e,
		v not originally in e
$e \to includesAll(v)$	$e \to excludesAll(v)$	Set-valued e, none of
		v elements originally in e
$e \to includes(v)$	$e = e@pre \to front()$	Sequence-valued e
$E \to exists(e \mid e.id =$	$undo(P1[E[v]/e])$ &	
v & $P1)$		
	$E[v] \to isDeleted()$	
$v = e$	$v = p$	p is prior value of v,
		because of antecedent
		conjunct $v = p$

$query\ getPossibleValues()\ :\ Set(Value)$
post: $result\ =\ possible_r\ -\ \$chosen$

The backtracking operation is then:

```
E::
static backtrack() : Boolean
( while $history.size > 0
  do
  ( sqx : Sequence := $history.last ;
    r : String := sqx.first ;
    ex : E := sqx[2] ;
    p : Value := sqx.last ;
    $history := $history->front() ;
    undo updates performed by r(ex,p) ;

    if ex.getPossibleValues()->size() > 0
    then
    ( ex.redor(p) ;
      return true
    )
    else
    ( ex.undor(p) )
  ) ;
  return false
)
```

Backtracking can fail (the final *return false* statement) if there are no
further choices available at any point in the history of the transformation execution. There are two conditions on the state of the search which
need to be tested at each step: *Success* indicates that the transformation
has reached an acceptable state and the search can terminate, whilst

Backtrack indicates that an unacceptable state has been reached, and that the search must backtrack. Together, all these aspects of a backtracking problem form a DSL (Section 3.4) which could be used as a specification input to the design generation step of UML-RSDS. Figure 15.2 shows the backtracking DSL metamodel.

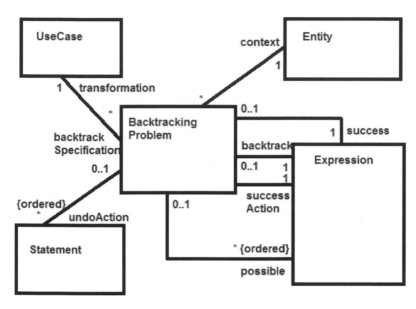

Figure 15.2: Backtracking DSL metamodel

These features are entered using a dialog to specify backtracking execution mode for a use case τ (Fig. 15.3).

If r is the first postcondition of τ, r should have the general form:

$$value : possibler \ \& \ Ante \ \Rightarrow \ Succ$$

with context entity E, where *value* does not occur in *Ante*. Backtracking will be performed over the choices of *value* in *possibler*. The fields of the backtracking mode dialog are filled in based on the use case and r, except for the undo actions and success test, which the developer needs to define. The design generation step augments the transformation with a new static variable: $\$history : Sequence(Sequence(Any))$ of E, and a new instance variable $\$chosen : Set(Any)$ of E. The constraint itself is transformed to:

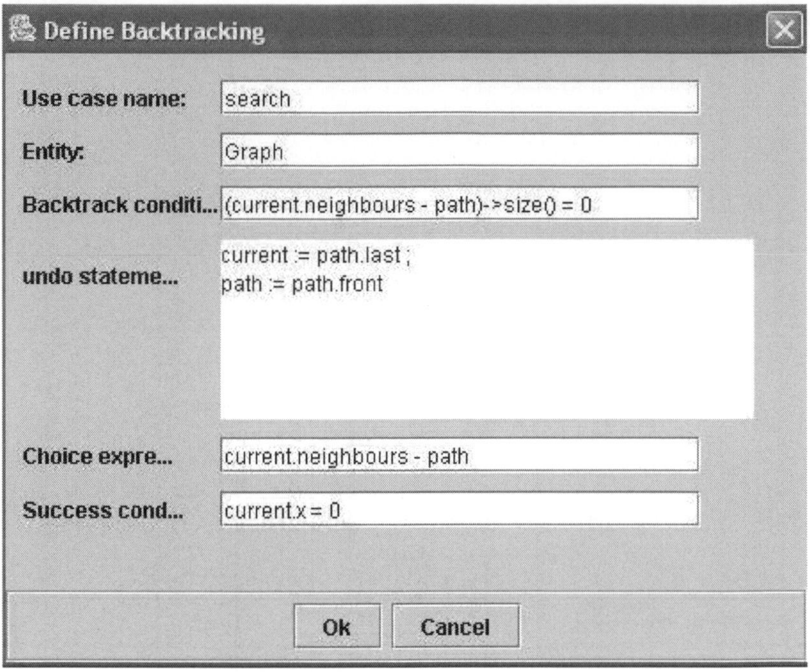

Figure 15.3: Backtracking mode dialog

$$value : getPossibleValues() \ \& \ Ante \ \Rightarrow$$
$$Succ \ \& \ value : \$chosen_r \ \& \ Sequence\{r, self, value\} : \$history$$

The generated design for a transformation τ with backtracking behaviour modifies the type 3 search and return loop which iterates through all elements of E:

```
E::
static search() : Boolean
(result : Boolean ;

 for (ex : E)
 do
 ( if ex.rtest() then ex.r()
   else
     ... cases for other rules, in descending priority order ... ;


   if ex.Success then
   ( successAction ; return false ) ;

   if ex.Backtrack then
   ( result = ex.backtrack() ;
```

```
        return result ) ;
     return true
  ) ;
 return false
)
```

This is a static operation of *E*.

15.3   Case study: maze route finder

This transformation attempts to find a loop-free route (e.g., for a rat) through a maze from a start node to an exit node, moving at each step from the current node to a neighbouring node. Figure 15.4 shows a possible metamodel for the maze problem.

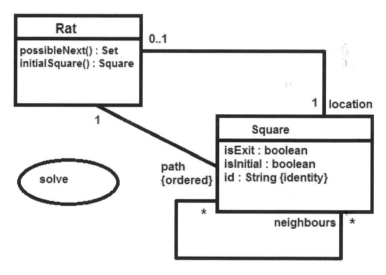

Figure 15.4: Maze solver metamodel

The solution transformation should be broken down into the following subtransformations:

1. Generating a non-trivial maze with alternative paths and deadends. Squares are either empty and can be occupied by the solver, or they are filled and cannot be occupied. The allocation of squares as filled or unfilled is fixed at the start of the solution process.

   The maze dimension is fixed at 10 squares in each direction in the test cases, but ideally the transformation should be able to generate problems of any size.

2. An option to display the maze and the location of the solver.

3. A maze solver which explores, step by step, possible paths from the starting square to an exit square. The solver may move one square in any direction to an unoccupied square. The transformation should terminate successfully if it finds a path from start to exit, and should display the path followed.

   If the solver reaches a dead-end with no unvisited squares possible to explore, it should backtrack to the most recent choice point, and attempt an alternative choice.

   If backtracking returns to the initial square, with no further choices available, then the transformation should terminate with a failure message.

The current state of the maze and location of the solver should be displayed upon each change in state/location.

The solution to part 3 of this problem can be implemented using backtracking on the choice of possible next square at each step. An operation *possibleNext* of *Rat* returns the set of possible next squares from a square *sq*: neighbours of *sq* not included in the current path:

```
Rat::
query possibleNext(sq : Square) : Set(Square)
pre: true
post:
  result = sq.neighbours - path
```

The maze solver use case *solve* has the postcondition (*Go*):

```
Rat::
  location.isExit = false & p : possibleNext(location)  =>
                    location = p & p : path & path->display()
```

This defines a single step from the current non-exit location to a neighbour that is not already in the path.

This problem fits the backtracking DSL with the following assignment of DSL features (Table 15.2). The *redoGo(p : Square)* operation of *Rat* is:

```
redoGo(p : Square)
(Square p1 = (possibleNext(location) - $chosen)->any() ;
 location := p1 ;
 path->includes(p1) ;
 path->display() ;
 $chosen->includes(p1) ;
 $history->includes(Sequence{"Go", self, p1})
)
```

Table 15.2: Maze problem features

transformation	solve
context	Rat
r	Go
possible$_r$	possibleNext(location)
Success	location.isExit = true
Backtrack	location.isExit = false & possibleNext(location)→size() = 0
successAction	("Found exit at " + self)→display()
undorAction	if path.size > 0 then location := path.last ; path := path.front else location := initialSquare()

An example maze is shown in Fig. 15.5. The data of this maze layout is defined in an instance model file *in.txt*.

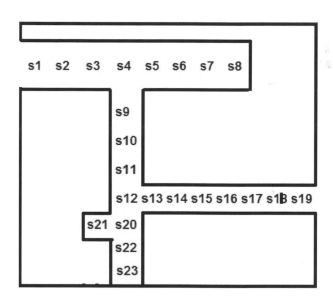

Figure 15.5: Maze example

The maze solver follows the route to s8, then backtracks, starting again from s9, and finally succeeding at s19:

```
. . . .
[(Square) false,0,s1, (Square) false,0,s2, (Square) false,0,s3,
(Square) false,0,s4,
(Square) false,0,s5, (Square) false,0,s6, (Square) false,0,s7,
(Square) false,0,s8]
Backtracking
[(Square) false,0,s1, (Square) false,0,s2, (Square) false,0,s3,
```

```
(Square) false,0,s4,
(Square) false,0,s9]
....
[(Square) false,0,s1, (Square) false,0,s2, (Square) false,0,s3,
(Square) false,0,s4,
(Square) false,0,s9, (Square) false,0,s10, (Square) false,0,s11,
(Square) false,0,s12,
(Square) false,0,s13, (Square) false,0,s14, (Square) false,0,s15,
(Square) false,0,s16,
(Square) false,0,s17, (Square) false,0,s18, (Square) true,0,s19]
Found exit at: (Square) true,0,s19
```

The search hits a dead end at square s8, and backtracks to s4 before finding a route through s9 to the exit.

15.4 Case study: Sudoku solver

The Sudoku solver described in Chapter 2 can be extended to use backtracking to complete 9-by-9 puzzles. For convenience, we add use cases to initialise 4-by-4 and 9-by-9 boards (Fig. 15.6).

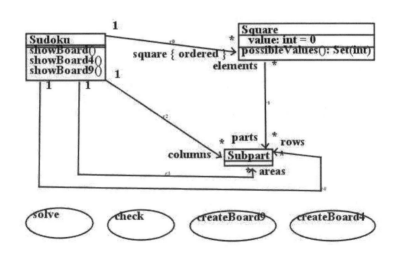

Figure 15.6: Extended Sudoku solver

Initialisation of 4-by-4 boards involves (i) creation of the *Sudoku* game instance; (ii) creating the four rows and the individual squares in them; (iii) creating the four columns and populating them with the appropriate squares; (iv) creating the four 2-by-2 areas and populating them with the appropriate squares. These steps are specified by the following constraints of *createBoard4*:

```
Sudoku->exists( s | true )

Sudoku::
Integer.subrange(1,4)->forAll( i |
    Subpart->exists( p | p : rows &
        Integer.subrange(1,4)->forAll( j |
            Square->exists( sq | sq : p.elements & sq : square ) ) ) )

Sudoku::
Integer.subrange(1,4)->forAll( i |
    Subpart->exists( p | p : columns &
        Integer.subrange(1,4)->forAll( j |
            square[i + ( j - 1 ) * 4] : p.elements ) ) )

Sudoku::
Subpart->exists( ar1 | ar1 : areas &
    square[1] : ar1.elements & square[2] : ar1.elements &
    square[5] : ar1.elements & square[6] : ar1.elements ) &
Subpart->exists( ar2 | ar2 : areas &
    square[3] : ar2.elements & square[4] : ar2.elements &
    square[7] : ar2.elements & square[8] : ar2.elements )

Sudoku::
Subpart->exists( ar3 | ar3 : areas &
    square[9] : ar3.elements & square[10] : ar3.elements &
    square[13] : ar3.elements & square[14] : ar3.elements ) &
Subpart->exists( ar4 | ar4 : areas &
    square[11] : ar4.elements & square[12] : ar4.elements &
    square[15] : ar4.elements & square[16] : ar4.elements )
```

The first constraint is of type 0, the others are of type 1 and iterate over *Sudoku*.

Initialisation of 9-by-9 boards involves (i) creation of the *Sudoku* game instance; (ii) creating the nine rows and the individual squares in them; (iii) creating the nine columns and populating them with the appropriate squares; (iv) creating the nine 3-by-3 areas and populating them with the appropriate squares. These steps are specified by the following constraints of *createBoard9*:

```
Sudoku->exists( s | true )

Sudoku::
Integer.subrange(1,9)->forAll( i |
    Subpart->exists( p | p : rows &
        Integer.subrange(1,9)->forAll( j |
            Square->exists( sq | sq : p.elements & sq : square ) ) ) )

Sudoku::
Integer.subrange(1,9)->forAll( i |
    Subpart->exists( p | p : columns &
```

```
    Integer.subrange(1,9)->forAll( j | square[i + ( j - 1 ) * 9] :
    p.elements ) ) )
```

```
Sudoku::
Integer.subrange(0,2)->forAll( j |
    Subpart->exists( ar | ar : areas &
        Integer.subrange(1,3)->forAll( i |
            square[i + j * 3] : ar.elements &
            square[i + 9 + j * 3] : ar.elements &
            square[i + 18 + j * 3] : ar.elements ) ) )
```

```
Sudoku::
Integer.subrange(0,2)->forAll( j |
    Subpart->exists( ar | ar : areas &
        Integer.subrange(1,3)->forAll( i |
            square[i + 27 + j * 3] : ar.elements &
            square[i + 36 + j * 3] : ar.elements &
            square[i + 45 + j * 3] : ar.elements ) ) )
```

```
Sudoku::
Integer.subrange(0,2)->forAll( j |
    Subpart->exists( ar | ar : areas &
        Integer.subrange(1,3)->forAll( i |
            square[i + 54 + j * 3] : ar.elements &
            square[i + 63 + j * 3] : ar.elements &
            square[i + 72 + j * 3] : ar.elements ) ) )
```

Again, the first constraint is of type 0, the others are of type 1, iterating over *Sudoku*.

The *possibleValues* operation needs to be modified for the case of 9-by-9 games:

```
Square::
query possibleValues() : Set(int)
pre: true
post:
  result = Integer.subrange(1,9) - parts.elements.value
```

The *solve* use case is modified from the version described in Chapter 2 to have a single post-condition *r*, with context class *Square*:

```
value = 0 & v : possibleValues()    =>    value = v & Sudoku.showBoard()
```

The constraint is given backtracking behaviour, with the *Backtrack* condition on *Square* defined as:

$$value = 0 \ \& \ possibleValues() \rightarrow size() = 0$$

That is, the square is blank and no possible value can be used to fill it. Table 15.3 shows the features of the Sudoku solver transformation in terms of the backtracking DSL.

The *redor*(*v* : *int*) operation of *Square* is:

Table 15.3: Sudoku problem features

transformation	solve
context	Square
r	r
$possible_r$	$possible\,Values()$
Success	$Square \rightarrow collect(value) \rightarrow excludes(0)$
Backtrack	$value = 0\ \&\ possible\,Values() \rightarrow size() = 0$
successAction	"Game is solved"$\rightarrow display()$
undorAction	$value := 0$

```
redor(v : int)
(int p1 = (possibleValues() - $chosen)->any();
 value := p1;
 Sudoku.showBoard();
 $chosen->includes(p1);
 $history->includes(Sequence{"r", self, p1})
)
```

$undor(v : int)$ is:

```
undor(v : int)
($chosen->clear()
)
```

The display operation needs to be adapted to display boards of either size 4 or size 9:

```
Sudoku::
showBoard()
pre: true
post:
    ( square.size = 16  => showBoard4() ) &
    ( square.size = 81  => showBoard9() )

Sudoku::
showBoard4()
pre: true
post:
    ( square[1].value + " " + square[2].value + " " +
      square[3].value + " " + square[4].value )->display() &
    ( square[5].value + " " + square[6].value + " " +
      square[7].value + " " + square[8].value )->display() &
    ( square[9].value + " " + square[10].value + " " +
      square[11].value + " " + square[12].value )->display() &
    ( square[13].value + " " + square[14].value + " " +
      square[15].value + " " + square[16].value )->display() &
    ""->display()
```

```
Sudoku::
showBoard9()
pre: true
post:
  ( square.subrange(1,9)->collect(value) )->display() &
  ( square.subrange(10,18)->collect(value) )->display() &
  ( square.subrange(19,27)->collect(value) )->display() &
  ( square.subrange(28,36)->collect(value) )->display() &
  ( square.subrange(37,45)->collect(value) )->display() &
  ( square.subrange(46,54)->collect(value) )->display() &
  ( square.subrange(55,63)->collect(value) )->display() &
  ( square.subrange(64,72)->collect(value) )->display() &
  ( square.subrange(73,81)->collect(value) )->display() &
  ""->display()
```

An example execution is as follows, starting from the partially completed board:

```
[8, 1, 0, 0, 0, 0, 0, 6, 0]
[0, 0, 0, 0, 0, 0, 3, 0, 0]
[0, 0, 0, 0, 0, 0, 0, 0, 0]
[0, 0, 1, 0, 0, 0, 0, 0, 0]
[0, 0, 0, 0, 0, 2, 0, 0, 0]
[0, 0, 0, 0, 0, 0, 0, 0, 0]
[0, 0, 0, 0, 0, 0, 0, 0, 0]
[0, 0, 0, 0, 0, 0, 0, 0, 0]
[0, 0, 0, 0, 0, 0, 0, 0, 0]
```

Backtracking behaviour is needed at several points in the solution process, for example:

```
[8, 1, 2, 3, 4, 5, 7, 6, 9]
[4, 5, 6, 1, 2, 0, 3, 8, 0]
[0, 0, 0, 0, 0, 0, 0, 0, 0]
[0, 0, 1, 0, 0, 0, 0, 0, 0]
[0, 0, 0, 0, 0, 2, 0, 0, 0]
[0, 0, 0, 0, 0, 0, 0, 0, 0]
[0, 0, 0, 0, 0, 0, 0, 0, 0]
[0, 0, 0, 0, 0, 0, 0, 0, 0]
[0, 0, 0, 0, 0, 0, 0, 0, 0]
```

```
Backtracking, undoing [solve1, (Square) 8, 8]
Backtracking, undoing [solve2, (Square) 2, 2]
[8, 1, 2, 3, 4, 5, 7, 6, 9]
[4, 5, 6, 1, 7, 8, 3, 0, 0]
[0, 0, 0, 0, 0, 0, 0, 0, 0]
```

```
[0, 0, 1, 0, 0, 0, 0, 0, 0]
[0, 0, 0, 0, 0, 2, 0, 0, 0]
[0, 0, 0, 0, 0, 0, 0, 0, 0]
[0, 0, 0, 0, 0, 0, 0, 0, 0]
[0, 0, 0, 0, 0, 0, 0, 0, 0]
[0, 0, 0, 0, 0, 0, 0, 0, 0]

[8, 1, 2, 3, 4, 5, 7, 6, 9]
[4, 5, 6, 1, 7, 8, 3, 2, 0]
[0, 0, 0, 0, 0, 0, 0, 0, 0]
[0, 0, 1, 0, 0, 0, 0, 0, 0]
[0, 0, 0, 0, 0, 2, 0, 0, 0]
[0, 0, 0, 0, 0, 0, 0, 0, 0]
[0, 0, 0, 0, 0, 0, 0, 0, 0]
[0, 0, 0, 0, 0, 0, 0, 0, 0]
[0, 0, 0, 0, 0, 0, 0, 0, 0]

Backtracking, undoing [solve1, (Square) 2, 2]
Backtracking, undoing [solve2, (Square) 8, 8]
[8, 1, 2, 3, 4, 5, 7, 6, 9]
[4, 5, 6, 1, 7, 9, 3, 2, 0]
[0, 0, 0, 0, 0, 0, 0, 0, 0]
[0, 0, 1, 0, 0, 0, 0, 0, 0]
[0, 0, 0, 0, 0, 2, 0, 0, 0]
[0, 0, 0, 0, 0, 0, 0, 0, 0]
[0, 0, 0, 0, 0, 0, 0, 0, 0]
[0, 0, 0, 0, 0, 0, 0, 0, 0]
[0, 0, 0, 0, 0, 0, 0, 0, 0]
```

The first backtracking process is triggered by the last square on the second row becoming unfillable. The *solve*1 step filling the adjacent square with 8 is undone, and the *solve*2 step filling the middle square in the row with 2 is redone, with the value 7 attempted there instead. The second backtracking is also triggered by the last square on row two being unfillable, and the filling of the 6th square on the row with 8 is redone to use 9 instead.

Finally a complete solution is produced:

```
[8, 1, 2, 3, 4, 5, 7, 6, 9]
[4, 5, 6, 1, 7, 9, 3, 2, 8]
[3, 7, 9, 2, 6, 8, 1, 4, 5]
[2, 3, 1, 4, 5, 6, 8, 9, 7]
[5, 4, 7, 8, 9, 2, 6, 1, 3]
[6, 9, 8, 7, 1, 3, 2, 5, 4]
```

```
[1, 2, 3, 5, 8, 4, 9, 7, 6]
[7, 6, 4, 9, 3, 1, 5, 8, 2]
[9, 8, 5, 6, 2, 7, 4, 3, 1]
```

Summary

In this chapter we have described specification and implementation techniques for search-based transformations using UML-RSDS, and we have shown how such transformations can be defined.

Chapter 16

Agile Development and Model-based Development

UML-RSDS may be used with a wide range of development approaches, including traditional plan-based development with strict stages, or with techniques such as pair programming (adapted to become pair modelling). However, we have found in practice that some form of agile development process best suits the approach. In this chapter we describe the concepts of agile development, and identify how agile development can be combined with model-based development to form the concept of agile model-based development (AMBD). Finally, we also describe specific AMBD approaches that can be used with UML-RSDS.

16.1 Agile development

The idea of agile development originated in the recognition that traditional plan-based development, with strict phasing of requirements analysis, specification, design and implementation phases, was unrealistic and counter-productive in situations where requirements may change rapidly and new revisions of a system are required within short periods of time [1].

Even in the early days of software engineering it was recognised that an artificial separation between different software engineering activities was unnecessary, as seen in the following quote from IBM's Watson Research Center in 1969:

"The basic approach recognises the futility of separating design, evaluation and documentation processes in software design. The design process is structured by an expanding model [...] It is tested and further expanded through a sequence of models that develop an increasing amount of function and detail. Ultimately, the model becomes the system." [8]

Traditional software development processes are plan-based: focussed on prescriptive activities and on a fixed sequence of stages (e.g., Analysis; Design; Coding; Testing in the Waterfall process). Agile processes in contrast attempt to be as lightweight as possible in terms of development process: their primary goal is to deliver a system to the customer that meets their needs, in the shortest possible time, taking account of changes in requirements.

The following principles are key characteristics of agile development [1]:

■ Responding to change is more important than following a plan.

■ Producing working software is more important than comprehensive documentation.

■ Individuals and interactions are emphasised over processes and tools.

■ Customer collaboration is emphasised over contract negotiation.

Development cycles are iterative, and build small parts of systems, with continuous testing and integration. Agile development methods include XP [2] and Scrum [13].

Other characteristics of agile development include:

■ "Self-selecting teams" – it is argued by agile development proponents that the best architectures, requirements, designs emerge from such teams.

■ Agile methodologies are more suitable for smaller organisations and projects.

■ eXtreme programming (XP) is more suitable for single projects developed and maintained by a single person or by a small team.

Table 16.1 contrasts agile versus plan-based development. Agile development techniques include:

■ *Sprints*: development work which implements specific user requirements, in a short time frame as a step in the production of a new release (Fig. 16.1).

■ *Refactoring*: regular restructuring of code to improve its quality, to remove redundancy and other flaws, etc. [3].

Table 16.1: Agile versus plan-based development

Agile development	*Plan-based development*
Small/medium-scale	Large scale (10+ people)
In-house project, co-located team	Distributed/outsourced team
Experienced/self-directed developers	Varied experience levels
Requirements/environment volatile	Requirements fixed in advance
Close interaction with customer	Distant customer/ stakeholders
Rapid value, high-responsiveness required	High reliability/correctness required

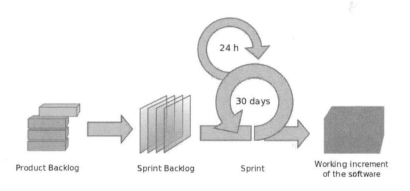

Figure 16.1: Sprints in the Scrum process [13]

16.1.1   Agile development: sprints

Sprints are regular re-occurring development iterations in which a subset of the project backlog work items are completed. This subset is termed the *sprint backlog*. Sprints produce deliverables that contribute to the overall project. Each iteration of a system involves a set of new use cases (termed 'stories' in Scrum) to be implemented, or other required improvements/corrections in the system. The work items to be carried out can be classified by their business value to a customer (high, medium, low), and by the risk/effort required by the developer. High priority and high risk work items should usually be dealt with first. The project *velocity* is the amount of developer-time available per iteration.

16.1.2 Defining a release plan

Taking the factors of work item priority and staff availability into account, the development team can define a *release plan*: a schedule of which work items will be delivered by which iteration and by which developers. A release consists of a set of iterations (e.g., sprints) and produces a deliverable which can be released to the client. The release plan is subject to several constraints:

■ If use case $uc1$ depends on $uc2$ via ≪ *extend* ≫, ≪ *include* ≫ or an inheritance arrow from $uc1$ to $uc2$, then $uc1$ must be in the same or a later iteration to $uc2$.

■ If a functionality $f1$ depends upon a functionality $f2$, then $f1$ must be in the same or a later iteration to $f2$.

■ Iterations also depend on the availability of developers with the required skills for development of the use cases/carrying out the work items in an iteration: a work item can only be allocated to an iteration if a developer with the skills required by the work item is available in that iteration.

■ Some use cases/work items may be prioritised over others.

Typically the release plan and project backlog is reviewed and reconsidered after completion of each sprint, and may be revised in the light of progress made and any new requirements which have arisen.

Figure 16.2 shows a situation where five new use cases are to be completed in a release, and their development must be scheduled into iterations. There are three developers available, but a high-skilled developer (number 1) is only available for at most 20 days in our project and their time must be blocked in a continuous period. The plan in the lower half of the figure shows a possible schedule meeting all the use case dependency constraints, and the skill and availability constraints of the developers.

16.1.3 Agile development: refactoring

Refactorings are small changes in a system, which aim to rationalise/generalise or improve the structure of the existing system. For example, if we discover that there are common attributes in all subclasses of a class then we can move all the common attributes up to the superclass (Fig. 16.3). Refactoring should not change existing functionality: tests should be rerun to check this. Regular refactoring should be carried out when time is available.

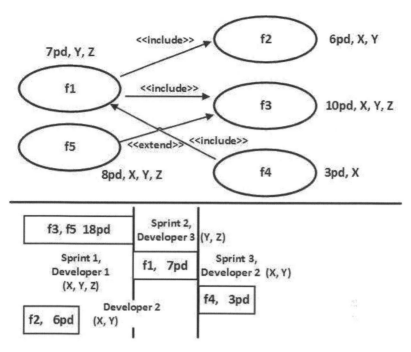

Figure 16.2: Release plan example

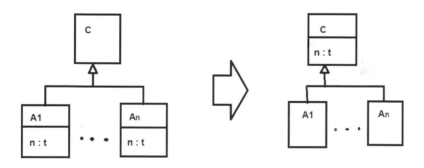

Figure 16.3: Pull-up attribute refactoring

Refactoring improves the maintainability of code by reducing redundancy and rationalising system structure. In the example of Fig. 16.3, changes to the type of attribute n only need to be made in one place after the refactoring, compared with changes to multiple occurrences before the refactoring.

Other agile development techniques include:

- *Test driven development (TDD)*: write unit tests first, then successively extend and refine the code until it passes all tests.

- *Pair programming*: two developers work at the same terminal, with one acting as an observer who has the role to identify problems with and possible improvements to the programmer's code.

TDD is appropriate if there is no clear initial understanding of how to solve the problem. Pair programming can improve quality, and reduce time, whilst increasing cost. Both of these techniques can be used with agile MBD, by using executable models in place of code.

16.1.4   Agile methods: eXtreme Programming (XP)

XP was devised by Beck [2] and other industrial practitioners with the aim of combining best practices in development projects and to focus on agility and code production. It is based on short development cycles and uses the following development practices: pair programming; code reviews; frequent integration and testing; close collaboration with customers; daily review meetings.

XP defines five development phases:

- *Exploration*: determine feasibility, understand the requirements, develop exploratory prototypes.

- *Planning*: agree timing and the use cases for the first release.

- *Iterations*: implement/test use cases in a series of iterations.

- *Productionizing*: prepare documentation, training, etc. and deploy the system.

- *Maintenance*: fix and enhance the deployed system.

XP recommends that iterations are one to two weeks long. The approach is oriented to smaller systems with small development teams, including the case of a single developer. The emphasis is on coding as the key development activity, and as a means of communicating ideas between developers and of demonstrating ideas to customers. Unit testing is used to check the correct implementation of individual features, and acceptance testing is used to check that what has been implemented meets the customer expectations. Integration testing checks that separately developed features operate correctly as part of the complete system.

16.1.5 Agile methods: Scrum

In the Scrum development process [13], a development team maintains a list (the *product backlog*) of product requirements. These consist of new use cases, use case extensions or corrections, or other required work items related to the product. A priority ordering is placed on the product backlog – normally the highest-priority items will be worked on first. Selected work items are removed from the product backlog and placed in the *sprint backlog* for completion in the first sprint (Fig. 16.1). This process is repeated for successive sprints. The product backlog will change from sprint to sprint as work items are moved to sprint backlogs, and also because of new requirements that arise from sprints or externally. A *Scrum board* shows the current list of items in the product backlog, the current sprint backlog and the status of items being worked on or completed in the current sprint (Fig. 16.4).

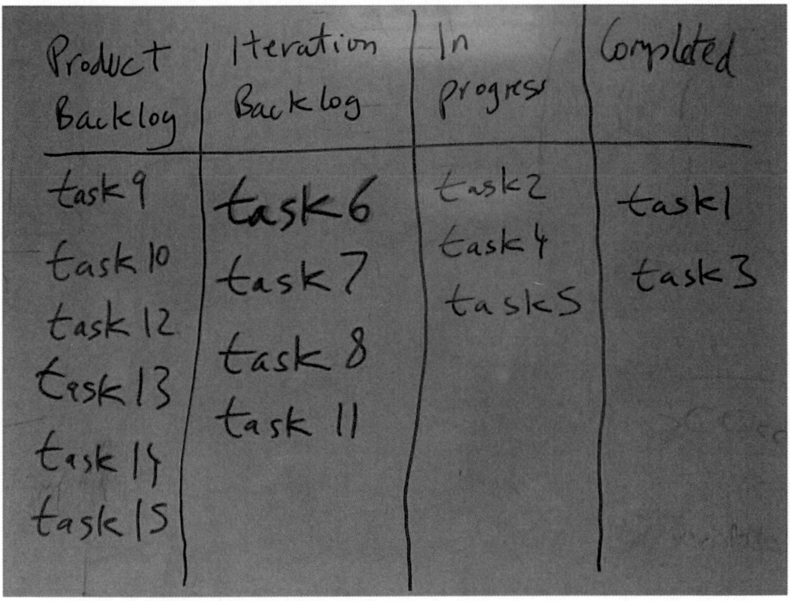

Figure 16.4: Scrum board example

Scrum defines three key roles for members of a software development team using the Scrum method:

- **Product owner**: the customer representative in the team, this role is responsible for liaising between the technical staff and the stakeholders. The product owner identifies required work items, identifies their priority, and adds these to the product backlog.

- **Development team**: the workers who perform the technical work. The team should have all needed skills and be self-organising. Typically there will be between 3 to 9 team members in this role.

- **Scrum master**: the Scrum master facilitates the Scrum process and events, and the self-organisation of the team. This role is not a project manager role and does not have personnel management responsibilities.

Four development phases are defined in Scrum:

- *Planning*: establish the vision, set expectations, develop exploratory prototypes. Identify the product backlog and apply requirements engineering techniques to clarify and refine the requirements.

- *Staging*: prioritise work items and plan the overall release, identify items (the sprint backlog) for the first iteration (sprint), develop exploratory prototypes.

- *Development*: implement the product backlog items in a series of sprints, and refine the release plan. Daily Scrum meetings take place, often at the start of a day, to check progress.

- *Release*: prepare documentation, training, etc. and deploy the system.

Scrum recommends that iterations (sprints) are 1 week to 1 month long. The main artifacts of the Scrum process are:

- *Story*: a generalised task or work item (e.g., a new or modified use case). It can consist of a set of subtasks.

- *Product backlog*: an ordered (in terms of priority) list of work items required for the product.

- *Sprint backlog*: an ordered list of work items to be completed in a sprint.

The team uses a Scrum board showing the tasks to do, in progress and completed. A *Burndown chart* shows a graph of the remaining work against time.

The key events in Scrum are:

- *Sprint planning*: performed by the Scrum team before the sprint, the team agrees upon the use cases to be worked on in the sprint (the sprint backlog).

- *Daily Scrum*: this organises the activities of the team, reviews sprint progress and deals with any issues. It is time-limited (e.g., 15 mins). The key questions for developers at this meeting are: (i) what did I achieve yesterday? (ii) what will I achieve today? (iii) is there anything blocking me from achieving my work?

- *Sprint review*: at the end of the sprint, this reviews the sprint outcomes, and presents completed work to the stakeholders.

- *Sprint retrospective*: this is performed after the sprint review, and before planning of the next sprint. This is facilitated by the Scrum master and analyses the achievements of the sprint, and ideas for improvement of the process.

It can be seen that Scrum does not necessarily need to be applied at the source code level, and (provided that all required product extensions/changes in the product backlog can be carried out at the specification level) it could instead be applied at the specification model level. For UML-RSDS this means that the Scrum team works on class diagram and use case specifications, instead of on source code. Scrum has become the most widely-used agile method in industry [14].

16.2   Agile model-based development approaches

Various attempts have been made to combine agile development and model-based development [5, 10]. In some ways these development approaches are compatible and complementary:

- Both agile development and MBD aim to reduce the gap between requirements analysis and implementation, and hence to reduce the errors that arise from incorrect interpretation or formulation of requirements. Agile development reduces the gap by using short incremental cycles of development, and by direct involvement of the customer during development, whilst MBD reduces the gap by automating development steps.

- Executable application models (or models from which code can be automatically generated) of MBD serve as a good communication medium between developers and stakeholders, supporting the collaboration which is a key element of agile development.

- Automated code generation accelerates development, in principle, by avoiding the need for much detailed manual low-level coding.

- The need for producing separate documentation is reduced or eliminated, since the executable model is its own documentation.

On the other hand, the culture of agile development is heavily code-centric, and time pressures may result in fixes and corrections being applied directly to generated code, rather than via a reworking of the models, so that models and code become divergent. A possible corrective to this tendency is to view the reworking of the model to align it to the code as a necessary 'refactoring' activity to be performed as soon as time permits. We have followed this approach in some time-critical UML-RSDS applications.

Tables 16.2 and 16.3 summarise the parallels and conflicts between MBD and Agile development.

Table 16.2: Adaptions of Agile development for MBD

Agile practice	*Practice in Agile MBD*
Refactoring for quality improvement	Use application model refactoring, not code refactoring
Test-based validation	(i) Generate tests from application models (ii) Correct-by-construction code generation
Rapid iterations of development	Rapid iterations of modeling + Automated code generation
No documentation separate from code	Application models are both code and documentation

Table 16.3: Conflicts between Agile development and MBD

Conflict	*Resolutions in Agile MBD*
Agile is oriented to source code, not models	(i) Models as code (ii) Round-trip engineering (iii) Manual re-alignment
Agile focus on writing software, not documentation	Application models are both documentation and software
Agile's focus on users involvement in development, versus MBD focus on automation	Active involvement of users in conceptual and system modelling

Agile development has been criticised for its dependence upon highly-skilled developers and its failure to consider non-functional requirements. It also focusses upon the development of a specific product in each process, and does not consider long-term support for the development of product families. An agile MBD approach could help to address these problems as shown in Table 16.4.

Table 16.4: Problems of Agile development

Problem	Resolutions in Agile MBD
Cost of customer meetings	Models are more abstract than code, hence easier and faster to review
Lack of design and documentation	Models provide documentation
Requires high-skilled developers	Modelling requires fewer resources than coding
Does not address non-functional requirements	Introduce explicit requirements engineering stage in each iteration
Does not address product-line development	Build libraries and components for reuse within other related products

The key elements of an agile MBD approach are therefore:

■ Combines Agile development and MBD.

■ The system specification is expressed as an *executable application model* (a PIM or PSM), which can be delivered as a running system, or used to automatically generate a running system, and can be discussed with and demonstrated to customers.

■ Incremental development of the system now uses executable models, rather than code. The models serve as documentation, also.

■ Alignment of models with code (because of manual modification of generated code) is considered as a high-priority refactoring activity.

■ Reuse is considered by creating reusable subcomponents during product developments.

16.2.1 Agile MBD methods

A small number of agile MBD approaches have been formulated and applied:

■ Executable UML (xUML) [11].

■ UML-RSDS [7].

- Sage [6].

- MDD-SLAP [15].

- Hybrid MDD [4].

Table 16.5 compares these approaches with regard to their support for agility, model-based development, and their domains of use. $\sqrt{}$ indicates support, ? indicates partial support, × no support.

Table 16.5: Comparison of Agile MBD approaches

	xUML	*UML-RSDS*	*Sage*	*MDD-SLAP*	*Hybrid MDD*
Incremental	?	$\sqrt{}$	?	$\sqrt{}$	$\sqrt{}$
Interoperable	?	?	?	$\sqrt{}$	$\sqrt{}$
Verification	$\sqrt{}$	$\sqrt{}$	×	×	×
Round-trip engineering	×	×	×	×	×
Model-based testing	×	×	×	?	×
Reuse	$\sqrt{}$	$\sqrt{}$	?	?	×
Based upon	UML, MDA	UML, MDA	Reactive systems modelling	Scrum + MDD	Parallel agile and MDD
Principal domains of use	High-assurance, embedded	Transfor-mations	Reactive multi--agent systems	Real-time telecoms	Small medium sized

Both xUML and UML-RSDS use the principle that "The model is the code", and support incremental system changes via changes to the specification. There is a clearly-defined process for incremental revision in UML-RSDS, MDD-SLAP and Hybrid MDD. Interoperability refers to the capability to integrate automatically generated code and subsystems with manually-produced code/systems, and for interoperation of the tools with external tools such as Eclipse. UML-RSDS provides partial support for system integration via the use of proxy/facade classes which can be declared to represent external subsystems, including hand-crafted code modules (Chapter 10). It supports import and export of metamodels and models from and to Eclipse. MDD-SLAP and Hybrid MDD define explicit integration processes for combining synthesised and hand-crafted code.

Explicit verification processes are omitted from Sage, MDD-SLAP and Hybrid MDD. Some support is provided by xUML and UML-RSDS: xUML provides specification simulation and testing facilities, and UML-RSDS supports correctness analysis via a translation to the B formal method. Model checking and counter-example synthesis is also supported via translations to SMV and Z3. By automating code generation, agile MBD approaches should however improve the reliability and correctness of code compared to manual-coding development. None of the approaches support round-trip engineering (the automated inter-conversion of code and models), which means that synchronisation of divergent code and models is a manual process. MDD-SLAP partially supports model-based test case generation, using sequence diagrams. The Agile MDD approaches provide only limited support for reuse and for product line development, and the issue is not considered in [15] or [4]. xUML supports reuse by means of *domain* (subsystem) definitions, and UML-RSDS supports reuse by definition of reusable components (Chapter 10).

UML-RSDS and xUML are based on modelling using the standard UML model notations, with some variations (action language in the case of xUML, use cases specified by constraints in UML-RSDS), and following a general MDA process (CIM to PIM to PSM to code). Platform modelling is explicitly carried out in xUML but not in UML-RSDS, which uses a single PSM (design) language. Sage uses variants of UML models oriented to reactive system definition using classes and agents. These include environmental, design, behavioural and runtime models. An executable system is produced by integration of these models. MDD-SLAP maps MDD process activities (requirements analysis and high-level design; detailed design and code generation; integration and testing) into three successive sprints used to produce a new model-based increment of a system. Hybrid MDD envisages three separate teams operating in parallel: an agile development team hand-crafting parts of each release; a business analyst team providing system requirements and working with a MDD team to produce domain models. The MDD team also develops synthesised code. MDD-SLAP and Hybrid MDD have the most elaborated development processes. The survey of [5] identifies that Scrum-based approaches such as MDD-SLAP are the most common in practical use of agile MBD (5 of the seven cases examined), with XP also often used (4 of 7 cases).

Most of the development approaches have been applied in a single main domain area. Apart from Sage, there seems no intrinsic reason why the approaches should be restricted in their domains of use, and UML-RSDS and Hybrid MDD are intended to be used widely for any small-medium sized system.

16.2.2 Comparison of xUML and UML-RSDS

These two approaches are both formally-oriented and UML-based MBD approaches. Executable UML (xUML) uses UML class diagrams, state machines and an action language to define explicit platform-independent specifications of systems. Class collaboration diagrams, domains and sequence diagrams are also used. In xUML, classes have state machines and objects interact by sending signals to each other. There is an underlying concurrent execution model for systems: objects synchronise by communication, but otherwise execute independently. xUML targets a wide range of implementation platforms, including C, VHDL, etc. It is a commercial product, marketed by Abstract Solutions Ltd.

In contrast, UML-RSDS uses UML class diagrams, OCL and use cases to define declarative PIM specifications. Individual systems are sequential, although these can interact via remote procedure calls in a distributed implementation. Translations to Java, C#, C++ are provided: it is oriented to this family of languages. It is open source. The system construction process supported by UML-RSDS is shown in Fig. 16.5.

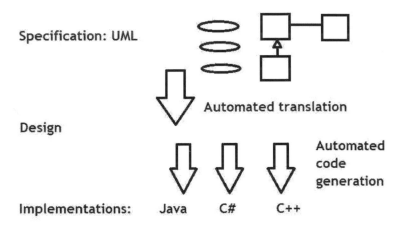

Figure 16.5: UML-RSDS software production process

The architecture of the implemented system in UML-RSDS has a standard structure (Fig. 16.6): a simple user interface component (GUI.java in a Java implementation) invokes operations of a Singleton class (Controller) which has operations corresponding to the use cases of the system, and which acts as a single point of access to the system functionality. Unlike in xUML, it is not possible to vary the design structure.

In the generated UML-RSDS code there are also classes corresponding to each specification class of the class diagram, and their operations are invoked by the controller class, which is the single point of entry (a Facade) for the functional tier of the generated system.

To summarise the differences between the two approaches:

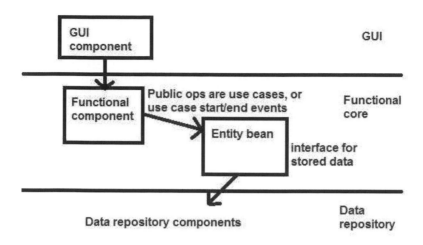

Figure 16.6: UML-RSDS application architecture

- UML-RSDS can be more abstract (tending to the CIM level): use cases are specified purely as logical pre/post predicates, with implicit algorithms. Pseudocode designs are synthesised automatically from these predicates (with some limited user intervention possible).

- UML-RSDS is more restrictive at the PSM level: only the Java-family of languages is supported, and the generated code is aligned class-by-class to the specification. A fixed architectural structure is generated.

- Executable UML requires more work in modelling the execution platform, but permits more variation in the platform and architecture.

- UML-RSDS provides verification capabilities via B AMN, SMV and Z3. xUML provides a specification simulator.

UML-RSDS may therefore be more appropriate for limited and lightweight use of MBD alongside traditional coding, as a first step to adopting MBD. xUML requires a more substantial committment to MBD, and a more substantial revision of development practices.

16.3 Agile MBD processes for UML-RSDS

We can adopt ideas from the Scrum, MDD-SLAP and Hybrid MDD processes to define a general procedure for using UML-RSDS with an agile development approach. The following guidelines for adoption and application of agile MBD are proposed, on the basis of our experiences in case studies:

- **Utilise lead developers**: When introducing MBD to a team inexperienced in its use, employ a small number of team members – especially those who are most positive about the approach and who have appropriate technical backgrounds – to take the lead in acquiring technical understanding and skill in the MBD approach. The lead developers can then train their colleagues.

- **Use paired or small team modelling**: Small teams working together on a task or use case can be very effective, particularly if each team contains a lead developer, who can act as the technical expert. It is suggested in [15] that such teams should also contain a customer representative.

- **Use a clearly defined process and management structure**: The development should be based on a well-defined process, such as XP, Scrum, or the MBD adaptions of these given in this chapter or by MDD-SLAP and Hybrid MDD. A team organiser, such as a Scrum master, who operates as a facilitator and co-ordinator is an important factor, the organiser should not try to dictate work at a fine-grained level but instead enable sub-teams to be effective, self-organised and to work together.

- **Refactor at the specification level**: Refactor application models, not code, to improve system quality and efficiency.

- **Extend the scope of MBD**: Encompassing more of the system into the automated MBD process reduces development costs and time.

- **Look for reuse opportunities**: If a product is part of a programme of development, with previous related systems, there may be existing components that can be reused to assist in the current product development. External libraries (e.g., QuantLib for financial applications) may be available for use. Also look for opportunities to create new reusable components, as discussed in Chapter 10.

A detailed agile MBD process for UML-RSDS can be based upon the MDD-SLAP process. Each development iteration is split into three phases (Fig. 16.7):

- **Requirements and specification:** Identify and refine the iteration requirements from the iteration backlog, and express new/modified functionalities as system use case definitions. Requirements engineering techniques such as exploratory prototyping and scenario analysis can be used, as described in Chapter 17. This phase corresponds to the Application requirements sprint in MDD-SLAP. Its outcome is an iteration backlog with clear and detailed requirements for each work item.

If the use of MBD is novel for the majority of developers in the project team, assign lead developers to take the lead in acquiring technical skills in MBD and UML-RSDS.

■ **Development, verification, code generation:** Subteams allocate developers to work items and write unit tests for their assigned use cases. Subteams work on their items in the development phase of an iteration, using techniques such as evolutionary prototyping, in collaboration with stakeholder representatives, to construct detailed use case specifications. Formal verification at the specification level can be used to check critical properties, as described in Chapter 18. Reuse opportunities should be regularly considered, along with specification refactoring.

Daily Scrum-style meetings can be held within subteams to monitor progress, update plans and address problems. Techniques such as a Scrum board and burndown chart can be used to manage work allocation and progress. The phase terminates with the generation of a complete code version incorporating all the required functionalities from the iteration backlog.

■ **Integration and testing:** Do regular full builds, testing and integration in a SIFT phase, including integration with other software and manually-coded parts of the system.

In parallel with these phases, a tooling team may be employed to provide necessary extensions or adaptions to UML-RSDS. For example, to write new data converters or code generators needed by the iteration. After each sprint, a sprint review is held, and planning for the next sprint is carried out, identifying the sprint backlog from the updated product backlog.

The options (ii) (correct-by-construction code generation) and (i) (models as code) from Tables 16.2 and 16.3 are selected for the UML-RSDS agile development process, to increase the automation of development. The explicit requirements phase, active reuse, and the use of models as code addresses the problems identified in Table 16.4.

In the UML-RSDS agile MBD process detailed development activities are organised on the basis of use cases:

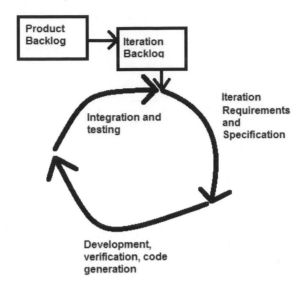

Figure 16.7: UML-RSDS agile MBD process

- Build a baseline class diagram (for a new development) or identify the relevant parts of an existing model (for an enhancement/maintenance development), identify and refine the system use case definitions based on the requirements.

- Developers write unit tests for their assigned use cases. All developers share the same system model (class diagram) but only need access to the use cases they are working on (update access) or that provide functionalities needed by these use cases (read-only access).

- Developers work on their tasks: they should only normally enhance or extend the class diagram, not delete elements or modify existing elements – if any change, including rationalisations, need to be performed, the developer should get the agreement of all the involved team members and team managers.

- The definitions of individual use cases should be stored in separate files where possible, and separate from the main system description.

Good communication within the team is needed. For larger systems the division into separate teams with parallel activities proposed by Hybrid MDD may be necessary. The recognition of reusable components within a product line may result in the establishment of a substantial library of components to support the development of related products. This could also be viewed as a *product line platform* for the domain of systems in the product line.

16.3.1 Examples of UML-RSDS agile MBD

As an example of development, consider that five use cases are to be implemented in a series of sprints for a new release of a system, according to Fig. 16.2. A base class diagram already exists, and is stored in file mm.txt. In each iteration, requirements for the iteration tasks are elicited and formalised in a requirements phase, which leads to their description in terms of textual and semi-formal rules based on the class diagram.

In the development phases, developer 1 takes responsibility for use cases f3 and f5 and writes tests for these. He works on the use cases, and keeps them in files f3.txt and f5.txt. Developer 2 works on the independent use case f2 and keeps its definition in f2.txt. All model and test files are stored in a version control system. At some point in the first sprint, developer 1 identifies necessary enhancements to the class diagram (e.g., that new identity attributes are needed in some classes) and gets the agreement of developer 2 and the team management to make this change.

On completion of the first sprint, f2.txt and f3.txt are passed to developer 3 who needs them (but cannot change them) for development of f1. The definition of f1 is maintained in file f1.txt, and this and f2.txt and f3.txt are passed to developer 2 for the final sprint.

Unit testing in the SIFT phases involves generating executable code for the use case to be tested, and applying the executable to the tests. Integration involves loading mm.txt into UML-RSDS, followed by the files of all use cases to be integrated: if a use case depends on other use cases then all files of (recursively) supplier use cases need to be loaded also. Name clashes in operations will be avoided if the use cases have distinct names, and if any user-defined operations have distinct names from each other and from any use case.

An alternative variant of this approach could assign to particular developers/subteams the responsibility for specific modules, where a module consists of a class diagram and set of use cases operating on that class diagram. In this case:

■ Each module has one developer (or a development subteam), who works on its use cases.

■ Modules should be maintained as far as possible as independent components, capable of reuse in different systems.

■ Developers must agree interfaces of modules, and any shared data.

The developer of one module should never need to see the generated code of another module. They may have read-only access to the class diagram and use case specifications of supplier modules to their module.

An example of such a development could be a financial system development, where there are three modules identified: (i) a main computation component which reads investment datasets and performs calculations on these; (ii) an input-output utility module, supporting data read and write to spreadsheets; (iii) a module containing low-level computation routines, such as combinatorial and statistical functions. Module (i) depends on (ii) and (iii). Alternatively, a module such as (ii) could be supplied by external hand-crafted code that needs to be integrated into the development, using the composition techniques described in Chapter 10.

Summary

This chapter has described agile and model-based software development approaches, and we have identified ways in which UML-RSDS can be used as a tool within such development approaches. The following chapter will consider in detail the requirements engineering and specification of systems in UML-RSDS.

References

[1] K. Beck et al., *Principles behind the Agile Manifesto*, Agile Alliance, 2001. http://agilemanifesto.org/principles.

[2] K. Beck and C. Andres, *Extreme Programming Explained: Embrace change*, 2nd edition, Addison Wesley, 2004.

[3] M. Fowler, K. Beck, J. Brant, W. Opdyke and D. Roberts, *Refactoring: improving the design of existing code*, Addison-Wesley, 1999.

[4] G. Guta, W. Schreiner and D. Draheim, *A lightweight MDSD process applied in small projects*, Proceedings 35th Euromicro conference on Software Engineering and Advanced Applications, IEEE, 2009.

[5] S. Hansson, Y. Zhao and H. Burden, *How MAD are we?: Empirical evidence for model-driven agile development*, 2014.

[6] J. Kirby, *Model-driven Agile Development of Reactive Multi-agent Systems*, COMPSAC '06, 2006.

[7] K. Lano, *The UML-RSDS Manual,* http://www.dcs.kcl.ac.uk/staff/kcl/uml2web, 2015.

[8] G. Larman and V. Basili, *Iterative and Incremental Development: A brief history,* IEEE Computer Society, pp. 47–56, 2003.

[9] I. Lazar, B. Parv, S. Monogna, I.-G. Czibula and C.-L. Lazar, *An agile MDA approach for executable UML structured activities,* Studia Univ. Babes-Bolyai, Informatica, Vol. LII, No. 2, 2007.

[10] R. Matinnejad, *Agile Model Driven Development: an intelligent compromise,* 9th International Conference on Software Engineering Research, Management and Applications, pp. 197–202, 2011.

[11] S. Mellor and M. Balcer, *Executable UML: A foundation for model-driven architectures,* Addison-Wesley, Boston, 2002.

[12] M.B. Nakicenovic, *An Agile Driven Architecture Modernization to a Model-Driven Development Solution,* International Journal on Advances in Software, Vol. 5, Nos. 3, 4, pp. 308–322, 2012.

[13] K. Schwaber and M. Beedble, *Agile software development with Scrum,* Pearson, 2012.

[14] Version One, 9th Annual State of Agile Survey, 2015.

[15] Y. Zhang and S. Patel, *Agile model-driven development in practice,* IEEE Software, Vol. 28, No. 2, pp. 84–91, 2011.

Chapter 17

Requirements Analysis and Specification

Requirements analysis aims to identify the actual requirements for a system, and to express these in a precise and systematic form. This is an essential process for any type of software development: errors or omissions in requirements can be very expensive to correct at later development stages, and they are a significant cause of project failure. Requirements specification defines a precise model which formalises the requirements – in UML-RSDS this model is also the system specification, which is used as the starting point for automated system synthesis.

17.1   Stages in the requirements engineering process

The following four phases have been identified as the main stages in requirements engineering [7]:

- Domain analysis and requirements elicitation: identify stakeholders and gather information on the system domain and the system requirements from users, customers and other stakeholders and sources.

- Evaluation and negotiation: identify conflicts, imprecision, omissions and redundancies in the requirements, and consult and negotiate with stakeholders to reach agreement on resolving these issues.

- Specification and documentation: systematically document the requirements as a system requirements specification, in a formal or precise notation, to serve as an agreement between developers and stakeholders on what will be delivered.

- Validation and verification: check the formalised requirements for consistency, completeness and ability to satisfy stakeholder requirements.

In the following sections we describe the specific techniques that we use for these stages, in UML-RSDS developments of model transformations.

17.2 Requirements engineering for model transformations

Requirements engineering for model transformations involves specialised techniques and approaches, because transformations (i) have highly complex behaviour, involving non-deterministic application of rules and inspection/construction of complex model data; (ii) are often high-integrity and business-critical systems, with strong requirements for reliability and correctness. Transformations do not usually involve much user interaction (they are usually batch-processing systems), but may have security requirements if they process secure data. Correctness requirements which are particularly significant for transformations, due to their characteristic execution as a series of rewrite rule applications, with the order of these applications not algorithmically-determined, are: (i) confluence (that the output models produced by the transformation from a given input model are equivalent, regardless of the rule application orders); (ii) termination (regardless of execution order); (iii) to achieve specified properties of the target model, regardless of execution order: this is referred to as *semantic correctness*.

A transformation is expected to produce models which conform to the target language (this is termed *syntactic correctness*). In addition, correctness of a transformation may include that the semantics of source models is preserved in their target models: this is referred to as *model-level semantic preservation*. For migration, refinement and bidirectional (bx) transformations in particular, *traceability* of the transformation is important: to be able to identify for each target model element which source element(s) it has been derived from. Conservativeness is important for high-integrity code generation and refinement transformations.

The source and target languages of a transformation may be precisely specified by metamodels, or aspects of these may need to be discovered or postulated (e.g., in the case of migration of legacy data where the original data schema has been lost). In addition, the requirements for its processing may initially be quite unclear. For a migration

transformation, analysis will be needed to identify how elements of the source language should be mapped to elements of the target: there may not be a clear relationship between parts of these languages, there may be ambiguities and choices in mapping, and there may be necessary assumptions on the input models for a given mapping strategy to be well-defined. There are specialist tools and languages for migrations, such as COPE and Epsilon Flock, which may be selected. The requirements specification should identify how each entity type and feature of the source language should be migrated to the target.

For refactorings, the additional complications arising from update-in-place processing need to be considered: the application of one rule to a model may enable further rule applications which were not originally enabled. Confluence may be difficult to enforce, and may be considered optional (for example, if a refactoring could produce one of a number of different restructurings of a model, of equal quality). The choice of transformation technology will need to consider the level of support for update-in-place processing. Some languages such as ATL and QVT have limited update-in-place support. The requirements specification should identify all the distinct situations which need to be processed by the transformation: the arrangements of model elements and their inter-relationships and significant feature values, and how these situations should be transformed.

Code-generation transformations may be very large, with hundreds of rules for the different cases of modelling language elements to be implemented in code. Effective organisation and modularisation of the transformation, and selection of appropriate processing strategies, are important aspects to consider. Template-based generation of program language text is a useful facility for code generators, and is provided by transformation technologies such as EGL and ATL templates. The requirements specification needs to identify how each source language construct should be translated to code.

The stakeholders of a transformation typically include not only the users of the transformation itself, but also users of the target models or products of the transformation process. For example, a code-generation transformation produces software code for various applications, whilst a refactoring or migration transformation produces refactored/migrated models for use by developers. In the case of a bx transformation both source and target models can be in active use.

Requirements may be functional or non-functional (e.g., concerned with the size of generated models, transformation efficiency or confluence). Another distinction which is useful for transformations is between *local* and *global* requirements:

■ Local requirements concern localised parts of one or more models. *Mapping* requirements define when and how a part of one model should be mapped to part of another. *Rewriting/refactoring* requirements concern when and how a part of a model should be refactored/transformed in-place.

■ Global requirements concern properties of an entire model. For example, that some global measure of complexity or redundancy is decreased by a refactoring transformation. Invariants, assumptions and postconditions of a transformation usually apply at the entire model level.

17.3   Requirements elicitation

A large number of requirements elicitation techniques have been devised. In the following sections we summarise some of these, and consider their relevance for the requirements analysis of transformations.

Observation

This involves the requirements engineer observing the current manual/semi-automated process used for the transformation.

It is relevant if a currently manual software development or transformation process is to be automated as a transformation. For example, if a procedure for constructing web applications or EIS of a particular architectural structure is to be automated. Observation can capture the operational steps of the manual process currently used by developers, as a basis for the specification of the automated process.

The technique is relevant for all kinds of transformations.

Unstructured interviews

In this technique the requirements engineer asks stakeholders open-ended questions about the domain and current process.

The technique is relevant in identifying the important issues which a transformation should have as goals. For refactorings, these could be what are the important goals for quality improvement of a model/system. For refinements, what are the important properties of the generated code (e.g., efficiency, conformance to a coding standard, readability, etc.). For general transformations, what is the scope of the mapping (which forms of input models are intended to be processed), what semantic/structural properties should be preserved, and what required restrictions there are on the output model structure.

Some possible questions which could be used in this technique are (for source models):

■ What size range of input models should the transformation be capable of processing? What are the required data formats/encodings for these models?

■ What logical assumptions can be made about the input model(s)? Are there constraints which they should satisfy, in addition to the source language structure constraints? If assumptions can be made, is it the responsibility of the transformation to check them, or will this be done prior to the transformation?

■ Should the source model be preserved, or can it be overwritten?

■ Are there security restrictions on source model data which should be observed?

Questions regarding the transformation processing could be:

■ What category of transformation is needed (refinement, migration, refactoring, bidirectional)?

■ Should the transformation be entirely automated, or should there be scope for interaction, e.g., if a choice of different possible refactorings needs to be made?

■ How will errors in processing be handled and reported? Should the transformation terminate on the occurrence of an error?

■ What are the timing/efficiency requirements for the transformation? What is the maximum permitted time for processing models of specific sizes?

■ Should the transformation processing include tracing?

■ Is there a requirement for the source and target models to be maintained consistently with each other, i.e., for model synchronisation and change propagation to be supported? What directions of change propagation are required (source to target, target to source or both)?

■ Is there a requirement for continuous input data processing, i.e., for a streaming transformation?

■ Are there environmental or organisational restrictions on the transformation languages/tools to be used, e.g., that they should operate within Eclipse?

■ Is confluence required?

■ Should the transformation preserve the source model semantics either in its entirety or partially? (Model-level semantic preservation).

Regarding the target model, possible questions could be:

■ What are the required data format(s)/encoding(s) of the target model(s)?

■ What logical properties should be ensured for the target models, in addition to conformance to the target metamodel?

This technique is relevant for all kinds of transformations, and for the requirements analysis of the product backlog in an agile development.

Structured interviews

In this technique the requirements engineer asks stakeholders prepared questions about the domain and system.

The requirements engineer needs to define appropriate questions which help to identify issues of scope and product (output model) requirements, as for unstructured interviews. This technique is relevant to all forms of transformation problem.

We have defined a catalogue of MT requirements for refactorings, bidirectional transformations, refinements and migrations, as an aid for structured interviews, and as a checklist to ensure that all forms of requirement appropriate for the transformation are considered (examples from the catalogue are shown in Table 17.1). Model-level semantic preservation and syntactic correctness are relevant global functional requirements for all categories of transformation.

This technique is suitable for all categories of transformations, and for iteration requirements analysis in agile development.

Document mining

This involves deriving information from documentation about an existing system or procedures, and from documentation on the required system.

For transformation problems this is particularly useful to obtain detailed information on the source and target metamodels and their constraints. These metamodels may be defined in standards (such as the OMG standards for UML and BPMN) or more localised documents such as the data schemas of particular enterprise repositories.

Table 17.1: Transformation requirements catalogue

	Refactoring	*Refinement, Migration*	*Bidirectional*
Local Functional	Rewrites/ refactorings	Mappings	Correspondence rules
Local Non-functional	Completeness (all cases considered)	Completeness (all source entities, features mapped)	Completeness (all entities, features considered)
Global Functional	Improvement in quality measure(s); Invariance of language constraints; Assumptions; Postconditions; Model-level semantic preservation; Syntactic correctness	Invariance (tracing target to source); Assumptions; Postconditions; Syntactic correctness; Model-level semantic preservation; Conservativeness	Bidirectionality; Model synchronisation; Assumptions; Postconditions; Hippocraticness; Syntactic correctness; Model-level semantic preservation
Global Non-functional	Termination; Efficiency; Genericity; Confluence; Extensibility; Fault tolerance; Security; Interoperability; Modularity	Termination; Efficiency; Traceability; Confluence; Extensibility Fault tolerance; Security; Interoperability; Modularity	Termination; Efficiency; Traceability; Confluence; Extensibility Fault tolerance; Security; Interoperability; Modularity

Reverse engineering

This involves extracting design and specification information from existing (usually legacy) software. This is useful for identifying data schema/metamodel structures, and as a first step in re-engineering/migration of applications from one programming language/environment to another.

Brainstorming

In this technique the requirements engineer asks a group of stakeholders to generate ideas about the system and problem.

This may be useful for very open-ended/new transformation problems where there is no clear understanding of how to carry out the transformation. For example, complex forms of migration where it is not yet understood how data in the source and target languages should correspond, likewise for complex refinements or merging transformations involving synthesis of information from multiple input models to produce a target model. Complex refactorings such as the introduction of design patterns could also use this approach.

Rapid prototyping

In this technique a stakeholder is asked to comment on a prototype solution.

This technique is relevant for all forms of transformation, where the transformation can be effectively prototyped. Rules could be expressed in a concrete grammar form and reviewed by stakeholders, along with visualisations of input and output models. This approach fits well with an Agile development process for transformations. Some transformation tools and environments are well-suited to rapid prototyping, such as GROOVE. For others, such as ETL or QVT, the complexity of rule semantics may produce misleading results. In UML-RSDS we usually produce simplified versions of the transformation rules, operating on full or simplified versions of the language metamodels. Rules may be considered in isolation before combining them with other rules.

Scenario analysis

In this approach the requirements engineer formulates detailed scenarios/use cases of the system for discussion with the stakeholders.

This is highly relevant for MT requirements elicitation, particularly for local functional requirements. Scenarios can be defined for the different required cases of transformation processing. The scenarios can be used as the basis of requirements formalisation. This technique is proposed for transformations in [2]. We typically use concrete grammar sketches in the notations of the source and target models, or informal rules, to describe scenarios.

A risk with scenario analysis is that this may fail to be complete and may not cover all cases of expected transformation processing. It is more suited to the identification of local rather than global requirements, and to functional rather than non-functional requirements.

Ethnographic methods

These involve systematic observation of actual practice in a workplace.

As for Observation, this may be useful to identify current work practices (such as coding strategies) which can be automated as transformations.

We do not mandate any particular requirements elicitation approach for UML-RSDS, however prototyping and scenario analysis fit in well with the UML-RSDS development approach, and have been used in most UML-RSDS developments. We have also used document mining in several development projects.

17.4   Evaluation and negotiation

Evaluation and negotiation techniques include: exploratory and evolutionary prototyping; viewpoint-based analysis; scenarios; goal-oriented analysis; state machines and other diagrammatic analysis modelling languages; formal modelling languages.

For UML-RSDS, prototyping techniques have been used for evaluating requirements, and for identifying deficiencies and areas where the intended behaviour of the system is not yet well understood. A goal-oriented analysis notation such as KAOS or SysML [1] can be used to document the decomposition of requirements into subgoals. A formal modelling notation such as OCL, temporal logic, or state machines/state charts can be used to expose the implications of requirements, such as inconsistencies, conflicts or incompleteness.

Scenario-based modelling is usually used with prototyping in UML-RSDS. Conflicts between scenarios are identified (cases where more than one scenario could be applicable), and any incompleteness (cases where no scenario applies). Conflicts may be resolved by strengthening application conditions (making the scenario more specialised), or by placing priority orders on scenarios so that one is always applied in preference to another if both are applicable to the same model situation. Incompleteness can be resolved by adding more cases, or by agreement with the customer that the uncovered situations are excluded from the inputs to be processed by the transformation. Scenarios can evolve into rule specifications, with more detail added, and they may be refined into more specialised cases of behaviour.

Global requirements may be refined to local requirements, e.g., by the decomposition of global requirements into a number of cases for different kinds of individual model elements. For update-in-place transformations (reactive or refactoring), syntactic correctness and model-level semantic preservation requirements can be refined to invariance requirements. Initial high-level requirements or goals for a transformation can be decomposed into more specific subgoals, in ways that are characteristic of transformations:

- Model-level semantic preservation for an update-in-place transformation can be refined into an invariance requirement (that the semantics of the model is equal to/equivalent to a constant), and then decomposed into requirements that this invariant is preserved by each rule application.

- Syntactic correctness of update-in-place transformations can be refined to an invariance property that the model satisfies (is conformant with) the metamodel, and then further decomposed into subgoals that each transformation step maintains this invariant.

- A goal to reduce a measure of poor quality in a model, for a refactoring transformation, can be decomposed into cases based on the different possibilities of poor structure in the model, and into subgoals that each transformation rule reduces the measure.

- For reactive systems, a requirement to maintain desired properties of the EUC can be decomposed into specific reactions to input events.

- For migration transformations, a general intended mapping of source to target can be refined into specific source entity-to-target entity mappings based on information elicited from stakeholders of the transformation, and hence decomposed into goals for specific mapping rules.

- Likewise for refinement transformation mapping goals. An example of such a decomposition, for the UML to relational database transformation, is given in [2].

For UML-RSDS we primarily use prototyping at the evaluation stage, with simplified versions of metamodels and rules used to investigate the intended transformation behaviour. This is focussed upon scenarios for local functional requirements, however global requirements could be expressed and evaluated in terms of particular measures (for quality improvements).

17.5   Requirements specification and documentation

Techniques for this stage include: UML and OCL; structured natural language; formal modelling languages.

At the initial stages of requirements elicitation and analysis, the intended effect of a transformation is often expressed by sketches or diagrams using the concrete grammar of the source and target languages concerned (if such grammars exist), or by node and line graphs if there is no concrete grammar. A benefit of concrete grammar rules is that they are directly understandable by stakeholders with knowledge of the source and target language notations. They are also independent of specific MT languages or technologies. Concrete grammar diagrams can be made more precise during requirements formalisation, or refined into abstract grammar rules. An informal mapping/refactoring requirement of the form

> "For each instance e of entity type E, that satisfies condition Cond, establish Pred"

can be formalised as a UML-RSDS use case postcondition

```
E::
  Cond' => Pred'
```

where *Cond'* formalises Cond, and *Pred'* formalises Pred.

An informal mapping/refactoring requirement of the form

> "For each pair of instances e1 of entity type E1, and e2 of entity type E2, that satisfy condition Cond, establish Pred"

can be formalised as a use case postcondition

```
E1::
  e2 : E2 & Cond' => Pred'
```

or as

```
E2::
  e1 : E1 & Cond' => Pred'
```

It is important to avoid explicit assumptions about rule execution orders at this stage, unless such orders are mandated in the requirements. Often it is the case that different rule execution orders are possible (for example, to map attributes to columns before mapping classes to tables, in a UML to relational database transformation; or the reverse order), and the choice between such orders is a design or implementation issue and depends in part upon the MT language chosen for implementation.

Mandated orders of rules can be expressed separately from the rules themselves, either in text, e.g.: "All applications of Class2Table should occur before any application of Attribute2Column" or more formally in temporal logic:

$$Attribute2Column(a) \Rightarrow \blacklozenge \forall c : Class \cdot Class2Table(c)$$

Abstract grammar *transformation cases* are used to formalise MT requirements in [2]. In UML-RSDS the specification of a transformation consists of one or more UML use cases, each consisting of one or more transformation rules, defined by the use case postcondition constraints in OCL. Each externally-required use case from the functional requirements should be expressed as a UML-RSDS use case, but these may be further decomposed into internal use cases which perform sub-steps or phases of the required functionalities. Defining one case for each constraint avoids premature commitment to particular execution orders, enables testing of constraints in isolation, gives the developer greater control over the form of the eventual design and implementation, and can increase the flexibility and reusability of the specification.

Rules should be specified in the simplest manner possible which achieves the required effect, following the principle:

> *Define rules which express the required behaviour in the simplest and clearest form possible.*

Specification patterns such as Phased Construction and Map Objects Before Links should be used to structure and organise rules. Measures of rule complexity are given by the UML-RSDS tools to help guide developers in the simplification of rules. One syntactic measure is the sum of the number of OCL operators plus the number of user identifiers in a rule: a reasonable upper bound on this measure could be 40, and rules exceeding this limit should be decomposed into simpler rules or called operations.

17.6   Requirements validation and verification

Techniques for this stage include: prototyping with testing; formal requirements inspection; requirements checklists; formal modelling and proof/model-checking.

The formalised rules produced by the previous stage can be checked for internal correctness properties such as definedness and determinacy, which should hold for meaningful rules. These checks are performed by the *Generate Design* option of the UML-RSDS tools, and the results are displayed on the console window. A prototype implementation can be generated, and its behaviour on a range of test case input models, covering all of the scenarios considered during requirements elicitation, can be checked.

Global properties of invariance can be checked by proof, using the B formalism (Chapter 18). Proof can also be used to show that model complexity/redundancy measures are decreased by rule applications, for refactoring transformations. Variant expressions can be defined to prove termination of a transformation: if each rule application can be proved to strictly decrease this non-negative integer-valued expression, then the transformation must terminate. Model checkers such as nuSMV [6] can be used to check if required temporal properties are enforced by the implementation.

17.7 Selection of requirements engineering techniques

The following recommendations can be made for the use of the requirements techniques described above:

Initial elicitation stage, with poorly understood/unclear/non-specific requirements: interviews; structured interviews; observation; brainstorming; document mining; reverse engineering.

The stakeholders of the system are identified. Information on the functional and non-functional requirements is elicited from stakeholders and obtained from documentation. Initially expressed general requirements are made more specific and definite, their scope and intent are clarified, and implicit unstated requirements are made explicit. For a migration or refinement transformation from language S to language T, it will be necessary to identify how language elements of S should be represented in terms of T elements. For a refactoring, it will be necessary to identify when and how a general requirement to improve model quality should be put into effect as model rewritings in particular model situations.

Advanced elicitation stage, with decomposed requirements: scenarios; prototyping.

The specific requirements obtained from the first stage are represented as scenarios described by concrete grammar sketches/outline rules. Their functional behaviour can be encoded in prototypes for validation by stakeholders.

Particular migration/refinement/refactoring scenarios can be expressed and validated in this manner.

Evaluation and negotiation: scenarios; prototyping; formal analysis (for high-integrity systems).

Both functional and non-functional requirements are decomposed into more specific goals. The functional scenarios are checked for completeness, consistency and correctness with regard to stakeholder expectations, and enhanced and refined as necessary. Negotiation on the requirements takes place, using the detailed scenarios.

Requirements formalisation (documentation): UML; OCL; formal modelling (for high-integrity systems).

The concrete grammar rules are formalised as abstract grammar rules in OCL. Assumptions, invariants and conformance conditions are also precisely defined as OCL expressions. Nonfunctional requirements are precisely documented in terms of appropriate measures.

Validation and verification: testing; inspection; formal proof and model-checking (for high-integrity systems).

The formalised specification is tested, inspected and analysed for correctness with respect to stakeholder expectations and for internal consistency. In UML-RSDS this specification will also serve as the basis of the implemented system. The use of optimisation or architectural design patterns (Chapter 9) may be necessary to achieve efficiency/capacity requirements.

17.8 Requirements engineering example: class diagram refactoring

This is an example of an in-place endogenous transformation which refactors class diagrams to improve their quality by removing redundant feature declarations. Figure 17.1 shows the metamodel of the source/target language of this transformation.

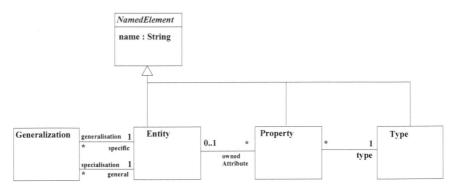

Figure 17.1: Basic class diagram metamodel

17.8.1 Requirements elicitation

The stakeholders of this system are: (i) the company using class diagrams in its development approach, which aims to improve the use of

UML in its development process; (ii) developers using the class diagrams for analysis and modelling; (iii) coders using the class diagrams as input for manual coding.

The initial requirements statement was:

> Refactor a UML class diagram to remove all cases of duplicated attribute declarations in sibling classes (classes which have a common parent).

This statement is concerned purely with the functional behaviour of the transformation. By means of structured interviews with the customer (and with the end users of the refactored diagrams, the development team) we can uncover further, non-functional, requirements:

- *Scope*: all valid input class diagrams with single inheritance and no concrete superclasses should be processed.

- *Efficiency*: the refactoring should be able to process diagrams with 1000 classes and 10,000 attributes in a practical time (less than 5 minutes).

- *Correctness*: the start and end models should have equivalent semantics (model-level semantic preservation/equivalence).

- *Minimality of the target model*: minimise the number of new classes introduced, to avoid introducing superfluous classes into the model.

- *Confluence* would be desirable, but is not mandatory.

The functional requirements can also be clarified and more precisely scoped by the interview process:

- A global functional requirement is the invariance of the class diagram language constraints: that there is no multiple inheritance, and no concrete class with a subclass (syntactic correctness/conformance).

- It is not proposed to refactor associations because of the additional complications this would cause to the developers. Only attributes are to be considered.

By scenario analysis using concrete grammar sketches (in class diagram notation) the main functional requirement is decomposed into three cases: (i) where all (2 or more) direct subclasses of one class have identical attribute declarations (Fig. 17.2); (ii) where 2 or more direct subclasses have identical attribute declarations (Fig. 17.3); (iii) where 2 or more root classes have identical attribute declarations (Fig. 17.4).

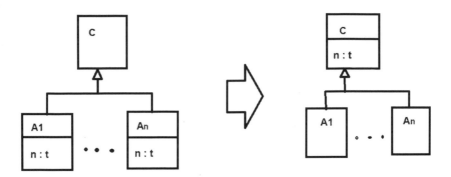

Figure 17.2: Scenario 1

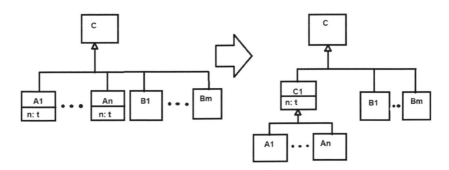

Figure 17.3: Scenario 2

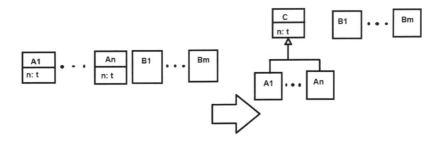

Figure 17.4: Scenario 3

17.8.2 Evaluation and negotiation

At this point we should ask if these scenarios are complete: if they cover all intended cases of the required refactorings. By analysis of the possible structures of class diagrams, and taking into account the invariant of single inheritance, it can be deduced that they are complete. The scenarios are consistent since there is no overlap between their assumptions, however two or more cases may be applicable to the same class diagram, so that a priority order needs to be assigned to them. By exploratory prototyping and testing using particular examples of class diagrams, such as Fig. 2.9, we can identify that the requirement for minimality means that rule 1 "Pull up attributes" should be prioritised over rules 2 "Create subclass" or 3 "Create root class". In addition, the largest sets of duplicated attributes in sibling classes should be removed before smaller sets, for rules 2 and 3.

17.8.3 Requirements formalisation

To formalise the functional requirements, we express the three scenarios as OCL constraints using the abstract grammar of the language of Fig. 17.1.

Rule 1: If the set $g = c.specialisation.specific$ of all direct subclasses of a class c has two or more elements, and all classes in g have an owned attribute with the same name n and type t, add an attribute of this name and type to c, and remove the copies from each element of g (Fig. 17.2).

Rule 2: If a class c has two or more direct subclasses $g = c.specialisation.specific$, and there is a subset $g1$ of g, of size at least 2, all the elements of $g1$ have an owned attribute with the same name n and type t, but there are elements of $g - g1$ without such an attribute, introduce a new class $c1$ as a subclass of c. $c1$ should also be set as a direct superclass of all those classes in g which own a copy of the cloned attribute. Add an attribute of name n and type t to $c1$ and remove the copies from each of its direct subclasses (Fig. 17.3).

Rule 3: If there are two or more root classes all of which have an owned attribute with the same name n and type t, create a new root class c. Make c the direct superclass of all root classes with such an attribute, and add an attribute of name n and type t to c and remove the copies from each of the direct subclasses (Fig. 17.4).

These can then be encoded as three rules in the UML-RSDS constraint language: Each of these operates on instances of *Entity*:

$(C1)$:
$a : specialisation.specific.ownedAttribute$ &
$specialisation.size > 1$ &
$specialisation.specific {\rightarrow} forAll($
$\quad\quad ownedAttribute {\rightarrow} exists(b \mid b.name = a.name$ & $b.type = a.type)) \Rightarrow$
$\quad\quad\quad a : ownedAttribute$ &
$\quad\quad\quad specialisation.specific.ownedAttribute {\rightarrow} select($
$\quad\quad\quad\quad\quad\quad\quad\quad\quad name = a.name) {\rightarrow} isDeleted()$

$(C2)$:
$a : specialisation.specific.ownedAttribute$ &
$v = specialisation {\rightarrow} select($
$\quad\quad specific.ownedAttribute {\rightarrow} exists(b \mid b.name = a.name$ & $b.type = a.type))$
$\quad\quad\quad$ & $v.size > 1 \Rightarrow$
$\quad\quad Entity {\rightarrow} exists(e \mid e.name = name + \text{``\_2\_''} + a.name$ &
$\quad\quad\quad a : e.ownedAttribute$ &
$\quad\quad\quad e.specialisation = v$ &
$\quad\quad\quad Generalization {\rightarrow} exists(g \mid g : specialisation$ & $g.specific = e))$ &
$\quad\quad\quad v.specific.ownedAttribute {\rightarrow} select(name = a.name) {\rightarrow} isDeleted()$

$(C3)$:
$a : ownedAttribute$ &
$generalisation.size = 0$ &
$v = Entity {\rightarrow} select(generalisation.size = 0$ &
$\quad\quad ownedAttribute {\rightarrow} exists(b \mid b.name = a.name$ & $b.type = a.type))$ &
$v.size > 1 \Rightarrow$
$\quad\quad Entity {\rightarrow} exists(e \mid e.name = name + \text{``\_3\_''} + a.name$ &
$\quad\quad\quad a : e.ownedAttribute$ &
$\quad\quad\quad v.ownedAttribute {\rightarrow} select(name = a.name) {\rightarrow} isDeleted()$ &
$\quad\quad\quad v {\rightarrow} forAll(c \mid Generalization {\rightarrow} exists(g \mid$
$\quad\quad\quad\quad\quad\quad\quad\quad g : e.specialisation$ & $g.specific = c)))$

The assumptions/invariants can likewise be formalised as OCL constraints in UML-RSDS:

$Entity {\rightarrow} isUnique(name)$
$Type {\rightarrow} isUnique(name)$
$Entity {\rightarrow} forAll(e \mid e.allAttributes {\rightarrow} isUnique(name))$

where *allAttributes* is the collection of declared and inherited attributes of an entity. The condition of single inheritance is expressed by the constraint:

$generalisation.size \leq 1$

on *Entity*.

A suitable variant expression is *Property.size*, this is decreased by each rule termination. It is related to the quality measure, which is the number of duplicate attributes in the diagram.

Model-level semantic equivalence can be defined in terms of the semantics $Sem(d)$ which for a class diagram d returns the collection of leaf entities with their complete (owned and inherited) set of attribute descriptors (attribute name and type). This collection should be constant throughout the transformation.

17.8.4   Validation and verification

The functional requirements can be checked by executing the prototype transformation on test cases. In addition, informal reasoning can be used to check that each rule application preserves the invariants. For example, no rule introduces new types, or modifies existing types, so the invariant that type names are unique is clearly preserved by rule applications. Likewise, the model-level semantics is also preserved. Formal proof could be carried out using B.

Termination follows by establishing that each rule application decreases the number of attributes in the diagram, i.e., *Property.size*. The efficiency requirements can be verified by executing the prototype transformation on realistic test cases of increasing size. The Java implementation generated by the UML-RSDS tools shows an above-linear growth of execution time when constructing large sets of elements. Table 17.2 shows the results of the tests on multiple copies of a basic test case with four classes and two attributes with two duplicates for each attribute.

Table 17.2: Execution test results for UML-RSDS

Test case	Number of classes	Number of attributes	Execution time
2*100	400	400	90ms
2*200	800	800	330ms
2*500	2000	2000	2363ms
2*1000	4000	4000	13s
2*5000	20000	20000	156s
2*10000	40000	40000	1137s

It can be observed that confluence fails, by executing the transformation on semantically-equivalent but distinct input models and identifying that the results may not be equivalent. The constraints C2 and C3 do not necessarily select the largest collections of attributes to rationalise at each step, and hence may not satisfy the minimality requirement. This could be corrected by more complex constraint conditions, or by using an Auxiliary Metamodel strategy to explicitly represent alternative families of attributes which are candidates for merging.

Summary

In this chapter we have identified requirements engineering techniques for model transformations. We have also described a requirements engineering process for UML-RSDS, and requirements engineering techniques that can be used in this process.

References

[1] S. Friedenthal, A. Moore and R. Steiner, *A Practical Guide to SysML: The systems modelling language*, Morgan Kaufmann, 2009.

[2] E. Guerra, J. de Lara, D. Kolovos, R. Paige and O. Marchi dos Santos, *Engineering Model Transformations with transML*, SoSyM, Vol. 13, No. 3, July 2013, pp. 555–577.

[3] S. Kolahdouz-Rahimi, K. Lano, S. Pillay, J. Troya and P. Van Gorp, *Evaluation of model transformation approaches for model refactoring*, Science of Computer Programming, 2013, http://dx.doi.org/10.1016/j.scico.2013.07.013.

[4] K. Lano, *The UML-RSDS Manual*, http://www.dcs.kcl.ac.uk/staff/kcl/uml2web, 2015.

[5] N. Maiden and G. Rugg, *ACRE: selecting methods for requirements acquisition*, Software Engineering Journal, May 1996, pp. 183–192.

[6] NuSMV, http://nusmv.fbk.eu, 2015.

[7] I. Sommerville and G. Kotonya, *Requirements Engineering: Processes and Techniques*, J. Wiley, 1998.

Chapter 18

System Verification

Validation and verification of a system are essential activities through-out the development process: validation checks that we are "building the right system": that requirements are correctly expressed in a specification, whilst verification checks that we are "building the system right", that a specification is consistent and internally correct, and that the design meets necessary conditions for termination, confluence and correctness with respect to the specification. In this chapter we describe the validation and verification techniques which are supported by UML-RSDS.

The main emphasis of UML-RSDS is to ensure that code synthesised from models is *correct by construction*: that provided the models satisfy some (relatively easy to check) conditions, the generated implementation will be correct with respect to these models, will terminate, be confluent, etc. This reduces the verification effort compared to post-hoc testing and proof of the implementation. This approach places restrictions on the form of specifications, however (that use cases should only have type 0 or type 1 postconditions, and should satisfy syntactic non-interference, etc.), so verification techniques are still needed for situations (such as refactoring transformations) which fail to meet these restrictions.

18.1 Class diagram correctness

Several checks are made during the construction of a class diagram, to avoid the creation of invalid diagrams:

■ Creation of a class with the same name as an existing class: not permitted.

■ Creation of an attribute or rolename for a class which already has (or inherits) a data feature of this name: not permitted.

■ Creation of cycles of inheritance: not permitted.

■ Definition of multiple inheritance: permitted with a warning that the design would be invalid if used for a language other than C++.

■ Creation of an inheritance with a concrete class as the superclass: not permitted. Such diagrams should be refactored to use an abstract superclass instead.

18.2 State machine correctness

The following checks are made during the construction of a state machine diagram:

■ Creation of a state with the same name as an existing state: not permitted.

■ Creation of two transitions triggered by the same event from the same state: permitted with a warning that the developer must ensure the transitions have disjoint (logically conflicting) guards.

The option *Check Structure* can be used to identify potential problems with operation behaviour defined by state machines: cases of unstructured code are identified. States coloured red on the diagram are those states involved in a loop.

18.3 Use case correctness

The correctness of use cases is checked by analysing the definedness, determinacy and data dependencies of the use case postcondition constraints, and by only permitting include/extend relationships which satisfy normal structural restrictions, as described in Chapter 5. Use cases should have distinct names. Their constraints should only refer to classes and features within the same system (or external classes represented via placeholder/proxy classes in the system class diagram). The postconditions should satisfy the data-dependency conditions of syntactic non-interference (Chapter 5), and warnings are issued if these do not hold. Confluence checks are also carried out on type 0 and type 1 constraints, and warnings are given if these fail to be confluent.

Specifiers should also ensure that calls of update operations do not occur in use case invariants, assumptions, postcondition constraint conditions or in other contexts where pure values are expected. It is bad practice to use update operations in postcondition succedents, but this may be necessary in some cases.

18.3.1 *Definedness and determinacy of expressions*

Usually, constraints in operation or use case postconditions should have well-defined and determinate values. This means that errors such as possible division by zero, attempts to access sequence, set or qualified role values outside the range of their index domain, operation call or feature application to possibly undefined objects, and other internal semantic errors of a specification must be detected. Such errors may also indicate incorrect or incomplete formalisation of requirements, ie., validation errors.

Errors of definedness include:

■ Possible division by zero: an expression of the form $e1/e2$ or $e1$ *mod* $e2$ where $e2$ may be 0.

■ Reference to an out-of-range index:

$$sq[i]$$

for a sequence or string sq where $i \leq 0$ or $sq.size < i$ is possible.

■ Application of an operator that requires a non-empty collection, to a possibly empty collection:

$$col{\rightarrow}max()$$

and likewise for *min*, *any*, *last*, *first*, *front*, *tail*.

Definedness is analysed in UML-RSDS by calculating a *definedness condition* $def(E)$ for each expression E, which gives the conditions under which E is well-defined.

For each postcondition, precondition and invariant constraint Cn of a use case, the definedness condition $def(Cn)$ is a necessary assumption which should hold before the constraint is applied or evaluated, in order that its evaluation is well-defined. For example, if an expression $e{\rightarrow}any()$ occurs in a constraint succedent, there should be an antecedent condition such as $e.size > 0$ to enforce that the collection e is non-empty. Likewise for $e{\rightarrow}min()$, $e{\rightarrow}max()$, etc. Postcondition constraints should normally also satisfy the condition of determinacy. Examples of the clauses for the definedness function $def : Exp(L) \to Exp(L)$ are given in Table 18.1.

Table 18.1: Definedness conditions for expressions

Constraint expression e	Definedness condition def(e)
e.f Data feature application	$def(e)$ & $E.allInstances() \to includes(e)$ where E is the declared classifier of e
Operation call $e.op(p)$	$def(e)$ & $E.allInstances() \to includes(e)$ & $def(p)$ & $def(e.Post_{op}(p))$ where E is the declared classifier of e, $Post_{op}$ the postcondition of op
a/b $a \bmod b$	$b \neq 0$ & $def(a)$ & $def(b)$
$s[ind]$ sequence, string s	$ind > 0$ & $ind \leq s \to size()$ & $def(s)$ & $def(ind)$
$E[v]$ entity type E with identity attribute id, v single-valued	$E.id \to includes(v)$ & $def(v)$
$s \to last()$ $s \to first()$ $s \to max()$ $s \to min()$	$s \to size() > 0$ & $def(s)$
$s \to any(P)$	$s \to exists(P)$ & $def(s)$ & $def(P)$
$v.sqrt$	$v \geq 0$ & $def(v)$
$v.log$, $v.log10$	$v > 0$ & $def(v)$
$v.asin$, $v.acos$	$(v.abs \leq 1)$ & $def(v)$
$v.pow(x)$	$(v < 0 \Rightarrow x : int)$ & $(v = 0 \Rightarrow x > 0)$ & $def(v)$ & $def(x)$
A & B A or B $A \Rightarrow B$	$def(A)$ & $def(B)$ $def(A)$ & $def(B)$ $def(A)$ & $(A \Rightarrow def(B))$
$E \to exists(x \mid A)$ $E \to forAll(x \mid A)$	$def(E)$ & $E \to forAll(x \mid def(A))$

Definedness of an operation call requires proof of termination of the call. Definedness of *or*, & requires definedness of both arguments because different implementation/evaluation strategies could be used in different formalisms or programming languages: it cannot be assumed that short-cut evaluation will be used (in ATL, for example, strict evaluation of logical operators is used [1]). Only in the case of implication is the left hand side used as a 'guard' to ensure the definedness of the succedent. We treat $A \Rightarrow B$ equivalently to OCL *if A then B else true*. Failure of determinacy, where an expression might evaluate to different values, is also usually a sign of an internal error in a specification. As for definedness, an expression $det(E)$ gives conditions under which E is ensured to be determinate. Examples of the clauses for the determinacy condition $det : Exp(L) \to Exp(L)$ are given in Table 18.2.

Table 18.2: Determinacy conditions for expressions

Constraint expression e	*Determinacy condition det(e)*
$s \to any(P)$	$s \to select(P) \to size() = 1$ & $det(s)$ & $det(P)$
$s \to asSequence()$	$s \to size() \leq 1$ & $det(s)$
	for set-valued s
Case-conjunction $(E1 \Rightarrow P1)$ & ... & $(En \Rightarrow Pn)$	Conjunction of $not(Ei$ & $Ej)$ for $i \neq j$, and each $(det(Ei)$ & $(Ei \Rightarrow det(Pi)))$
A & B	$det(A)$ & $det(B)$
$A \Rightarrow B$	$det(A)$ & $(A \Rightarrow det(B))$
$E \to exists(x \mid A)$ $E \to exists1(x \mid A)$	$det(E)$ & $E \to forAll(x \mid det(A))$
$E \to forAll(x \mid A)$	$det(E)$ & $E \to forAll(x \mid det(A))$ Additionally, order-independence of A for $x : E$.

The determinacy and definedness conditions for operation and use case postconditions are displayed in the console window when the *Generate Design* option is selected for a UML-RSDS specification. As discussed above, the antecedent of a constraint should imply the definedness of the succedent:

$$Ante \Rightarrow def(Succ)$$

The overall definedness condition $def(Cn)$ of a postcondition constraint should be incorporated into the preconditions (assumptions) of the use case: if the postconditions are $C_1, ..., C_n$, then the definedness of C_j for $1 \leq j \leq n$ is ensured by the assumption

$$C_1 \& ... \& C_{j-1} \Rightarrow def(C_j)$$

because the implementation $stat(C_1, ..., C_{j-1})$ of the preceding constraints establishes their conjunction, and hence, under the above assumption, also the definedness of C_j. An example of this approach to ensure definedness is the correlation calculator problem of Chapter 2.

18.3.2 *Confluence checks*

The UML-RSDS tools use syntactic checking to check the confluence of type 0 or type 1 constraints (other forms of constraint need confluence proof using variants, as described in Section 18.5). A constraint Cn on class E, of the form

$$Ante \Rightarrow Succ$$

is checked as follows:

1. *self* of type E is added to a set *iterated*, as is each implicitly universally quantified variable $c : C$ of class type occurring in *Ante*. Each distinct combination of bindings to these variables is iterated over exactly once by a bounded-loop implementation of the constraint. (Type 2 constraints may reapply the constraint to particular combinations more than once, and type 3 constraints may also introduce new combinations to be iterated over). Type 0 constraints do not have a context class or implicit *self* variable.

2. A list *created* of the existentially-quantified variables t in $T \rightarrow exists(t \mid pred)$ formulae in *Succ* is maintained. These are the objects which are newly created in each application of the constraint (not looked-up and modified). t is only added to *created* if:

   (a) T is a concrete entity type and not of pre-form,

   (b) either T has no unique/primary key, or its key is assigned by a top-level equation $t.key = c.ckey$ to the primary key of the only element c of *iterated*.

   These conditions ensure that t is genuinely new.

3. Assignments $t.f = e$ for a direct feature f of $t \in$ *created* are confluent, if $rd(e)$ is disjoint from $wr(Cn)$, as are assignments $self.f = val$ or $c.f = val$ for a value val (with no variables, including *self*) and $c \in$ *iterated*. Assignments $c.f = c.g$ for direct features of $c \in$ *iterated* are also confluent.

4. Assignments $T_j[sId].g = e$ are confluent if sId is the primary key of the only *iterated* entity type S_j, and if there is a preceding confluent constraint which maps S_j to T_j (so that there is a 1-to-0..1 relation between these entity types based on the primary key values).

5. A formula $t : e.r$ is confluent if $t \in$ *created*, and r is an unordered role. $e : t.r$ and $e <: t.r$ are confluent if $t \in$ *created* and r is unordered, or if e is an *iterated* variable which has an ordered iteration range (not an entity type). $rd(e)$ must also be disjoint from $wr(Cn)$ in both cases.

6. $e1 \rightarrow includes(e2)$ is treated as for $e2 : e1$, and $e1 \rightarrow includesAll(e2)$ is treated as for $e2 <: e1$.

7. In the case of bidirectional associations, the explicit update to one end, and the corresponding implicit update to the other end must both be confluent.

8. A conjunction $e1$ & $e2$ is confluent if $e1$ and $e2$ are.

9. $e1 \Rightarrow e2$ is confluent if $e2$ is.

10. $T \rightarrow exists(t \mid pred)$ is confluent if *pred* is confluent under the addition of t to *created*, if it is eligible to be added.

11. $T \rightarrow forAll(t \mid pred)$ is confluent if *pred* is confluent under the addition of t to *iterated*.

12. $e \rightarrow display()$ is confluent if there is at most one variable in e, from *iterated*, and with an ordered iteration range.

These rules ensure that data written on previous iterations of Cn cannot affect the execution of the current application of Cn. Set-valued collections, such as the set $E.allInstances$ of objects of a class E, should not be used directly to produce a sequence-valued collection, because the order of the latter will be arbitrary. The sorting operators can instead be used to make the order of the source domain expression determinate.

As an example, the classic UML to RDB transformation is confluent if written as:

```
UMLClass::
  Table->exists( t | t.name = name &
    attributes->forAll( a |
        Column->exists( c | c.name = a.name & c : t.columns &
          c.typename = a.type.name ) ) )
```

If *name* is a primary key for *UMLClass* and *Table*, but not for *Column*, and *attributes* and *columns* are unordered, then t and c are added to *created*, and all updates are confluent.

18.4 Correctness by construction

It is a key principle of UML-RSDS that logical constraints have a dual interpretation both as specifications of required behaviour, and as inputs for code generators which produce programs that are guaranteed to correctly implement this behaviour.

For use cases, this principle means that the use case postconditions both describe the logical contract of the use case: the postconditions can be assumed to be true at termination of the use case, and they also define the code implementation which ensures that this contract is carried out:

If a use case uc has postconditions C_1 to C_n which are all of type 0 or type 1, satisfy syntactic non-interference, confluence and definedness and determinacy conditions, then the implementation code $stat(C_1)$; ...; $stat(C_n)$ of uc is terminating, confluent and correct with respect to its specification [4]. That is, this code establishes the conjunction C_1 & ... & C_n.

The restrictions on the C_i can be relaxed slightly by using semantic non-interference instead of syntactic non-interference: there may be cases where two constraints C_i and C_j both write to the same data, but do so in ways that do not invalidate the other constraint. For example, if both add objects to the same unordered collection.

18.5   Synthesis of B AMN

B is a formal language with powerful analysis capabilities for checking the correctness of specifications [2]. Several commercial or free tools exist for B:

- BToolkit

- Atelier B

- B4Free

The following restrictions on UML-RSDS specifications are necessary before they can be translated to B:

- Attributes of different classes must have different names.

- Update operations cannot have return values or be recursively defined.

- Feature, variable and class names should have more than one letter. Underscore cannot be used in class, variable or feature names.

- Real values cannot be used, only integers, strings and booleans, and enumerated types. Some B implementations only support natural numbers: non-negative integers.

The UML-RSDS type `int` corresponds to `INT` in B, i.e., 32-bit signed integers.

Two options for generating B are provided: (i) separate B machines for each root entity of the class diagram; (ii) one B machine for the entire system. The first can be used if there are not invocations in both directions between two entities (in different inheritance hierarchies), and no bidirectional associations between such entities. In addition, if no entity in one hierarchy contains code creating entity instances in another hierarchy. Otherwise, in the case of such mutual dependencies, option (ii) must be used.

The following verification properties of a UML-RSDS transformation specification τ from source language S to target language T can be checked using B:

1. Syntactic correctness: if a source model m of S satisfies all the assumptions Asm of τ, then the transformation will produce valid target models n of T from m which satisfy the language constraints Γ_T of T.

2. Model-level semantic preservation: if τ maps a source model m to target model n, then these have equivalent semantics under semantics-assigning maps Sem_S and Sem_T:

$$Sem_S(m) \equiv Sem_T(n)$$

3. Semantic preservation: if a predicate φ holds in m, then any target model n produced from m satisfies an interpretation $\chi(\varphi)$ of the formula. χ depends upon τ.

4. Semantic correctness: that a given implementation for τ satisfies its specification.

5. Confluence: that all result models n produced from a given source model m must be isomorphic.

6. Termination: that τ is guaranteed to terminate if applied to valid source models which satisfy Asm.

Proof-based techniques for verifying transformation correctness properties have two main advantages: (i) they can prove the properties for all cases of a transformation, that is, for arbitrary input models and for a range of different implementations; (ii) a record of the proof can be produced, and subjected to further checking, if certification is required. However, proof techniques invariably involve substantial human expertise and resources, due to the interactive nature of the most general forms of proof techniques, and the necessity to work both in the notation of the proof tool and in the transformation notation.

We have selected B AMN as a suitable formalism for proof-based verification, B is a mature formalism, with good tool support, which automates the majority of simple proof obligations. We provide an automated mapping from transformation specifications into B, and this mapping is designed to facilitate the comprehension of the B AMN proof obligations in terms of the transformation being verified. The entity types and features of the languages involved in a transformation τ are mapped into mathematical sets and functions in B. OCL expressions are systematically mapped into set-theory expressions.

A B AMN specification consists of a linked collection of modules, termed *machines*. Each machine encapsulates data and operations on that data. Each transformation τ is represented in a single main B machine M_τ, together with an auxiliary *SystemTypes* machine containing type definitions.

The mapping from UML-RSDS to B performs the following translations:

- Each source and target language (class diagram) L is represented by sets es for each entity type E of the language, with $es \subseteq objects$, and maps $f : es \to Typ$ for each feature f of E, together with B encodings of the constraints Γ_L of L for unmodified L. In cases where a language entity type or feature g is both read and written by the transformation, a syntactically distinct copy g_pre is used to represent the initial value of g at the start of the transformation. A supertype F of entity type E has B invariant $es \subseteq fs$. Abstract entity types E have a B invariant $es = f1s \cup \ldots \cup fls$ where the Fi are the direct subtypes of E.

  For each concrete entity type E of a source language, there is an operation $create\_E$ which creates a new instance of E and adds this to es. For each data feature f of an entity type E there is an operation $setf(ex, fx)$ which sets $f(ex)$ to fx.

- The assumptions Asm of the transformation can be included in the machine invariant (using g_pre in place of g for data which is written by the transformation). Asm is also included in the preconditions of the source language operations $create\_E$ and $setf$.

- Each use case postcondition *rule* is encoded as an operation with input parameters the objects which are read by *rule* (including additional quantified variables), and with its effect derived from the rule succedent or from the *behavior* of a design of *rule*. The operation represents transformation computation steps δ_i of the *rule* design.

- Orderings of the steps for particular use case designs can be encoded by preconditions of the operations, expressing that the effect of one or more other *rule'* has been already established for all applicable elements.

■ Invariant predicates *Inv* are added as B invariants, using *g_pre* to express pre-state values *g*@pre.

The mapping to B is suitable to support the proof of invariance properties, syntactic correctness, model-level semantic preservation, semantic preservation and semantic correctness by using internal consistency proof in B. A more complex mapping is necessary for the proof of confluence and termination, using refinement proof [3].

The general form of a B machine M_τ representing a separate-models transformation τ with source language S and target language T is:

```
MACHINE Mt SEES SystemTypes
VARIABLES
  /* variables for each entity type and feature of S */
  /* variables for each entity type and feature of T */
INVARIANT
  /* typing definitions for each entity type and feature of S and T */
  GammaS &
  Asm0 & Inv
INITIALISATION
  /* var := {} for each variable */
OPERATIONS
  /* creation operations for entity types of S, restricted by Asm */
  /* update operations for features of S, restricted by Asm */
  /* operations representing transformation steps */
END
```

The machine represents the transformation at any point in its execution. *Asm*0 is the part of *Asm* which refers only to source model data. *SystemTypes* defines the type *Object_OBJ* of all objects, and any other type definitions required, e.g., of enumerated types.

The operations to create and update S elements are used to set up the source model data of the transformation. Subsequently, the operations representing transformation steps are performed. If *Asm*0 consists of universally quantified formulae $\forall s : S_i \cdot \psi$, then the instantiated formulae $\psi[sx/s]$ are used as restrictions on operations creating $sx : S_i$ (or subclasses of S_i). Likewise, operation $setf(sx, fx)$ modifying feature f of S_i has a precondition $\psi[sx/s, fx/s.f]$. All these operations will include the preconditions *Asm*1 from *Asm* which concern only the target model.

As an example, the transformation of Fig. 7.2 can be defined by the following partial machine:

```
MACHINE Mt SEES SystemTypes
VARIABLES objects, as, xx, bs, yy
INVARIANT
  objects <: Object_OBJ &
  as <: objects & bs <: objects &
```

```
xx : as --> INT & yy : bs --> INT &
!bb.(bb : bs => #aa.(aa : as & yy(bb) = xx(aa)*xx(aa)))
INITIALISATION
  objects, as, xx, bs, yy := {}, {}, {}, {}, {}
```

The invariant expresses Γ_S and the *Inv* property

$$B \rightarrow forAll(b \mid A \rightarrow exists(a \mid b.y = a.x * a.x))$$

of the transformation. $\#b.P$ is B syntax for $\exists b \cdot P$, $!a.P$ is B syntax for $\forall a \cdot P$. & denotes conjunction, $<:$ denotes $\subseteq$ and $-->$ is $\rightarrow$ (the total function type constructor). A universal set *objects* of existing objects is maintained, this is a subset of the static type *Object_OBJ* declared in *SystemTypes*. The operations representing computation steps are derived from the rule designs $stat(Cn)$ of the constraints Cn. This modelling approach facilitates verification using weakest precondition calculation, compared to more abstract encodings. If Cn has the form

$$SCond \;\Rightarrow\; Succ$$

on context entity S_i then the operation representing a computation step δ_i of Ci is:

```
delta_i(si) =
  PRE si : sis & SCond & not(si.Succ) &
    C1 & ... & Ci-1 & def(si.Succ)
  THEN
    stat'(si.Succ)
  END
```

where $stat'(P)$ encodes the procedural interpretation $stat(P)$ of P in B program-like statements, AMN generalised substitutions. These have a similar syntax to the programming language described in Appendix A.2, and use the same weakest-precondition semantics. B has an additional statement form $v := e1 \| w := e2$ of *parallel assignment*: the assignments are performed order-independently, with the values of $e1$, $e2$ being simultaneously assigned to v, w. The ANY WHERE THEN statement of B corresponds to a UML-RSDS creation statement, and to let definitions.

If the design of τ defines a non-standard rule design of Ci, this design could be encoded in B in place of the above definition of *delta_i*. If τ's design requires that all constraints $C1$, ..., $Ci - 1$ are established before Ci, this ordering can be encoded by including $C1$, ..., $Ci - 1$ in the preconditions of *delta_i*. $not(Succ)$ can be omitted if negative application conditions are not checked by the design of Ci, as is the case for type 1 constraints. For the mapping to B, $def(Succ)$ includes checks that numeric expressions in *Succ* are within the size bounds of the finite numeric types *NAT* and *INT* of B, and that *objects* $\neq$ *Object_OBJ* prior to any creation of a new object.

The computational model of a transformation τ expressed in M_τ therefore coincides with the definition of transformation computation described in [4]: a computation of τ is a sequence of transformation steps executed in an indeterminate order, constrained only by the need to maintain *Inv*, and, if a specific design *I* is defined, to satisfy the ordering restrictions of *I*'s behaviour.

For the example of Fig. 7.2 the resulting completed B machine M_τ has:

```
OPERATIONS
  create_A(xxxx) =
    PRE xxxx : INT & objects /= Object_OBJ & bs = {}
    THEN
        ANY ax WHERE ax : Object_OBJ - objects
        THEN
            as := as \/ { ax } || objects := objects \/ { ax } ||
            xx(ax) := xxxx
        END
    END;

  setx(ax,xxxx) =
    PRE ax : as & xxxx : INT & bs = {}
    THEN
       xx(ax) := xxxx
    END;

  r1(ax) =
    PRE ax : as & not( #bb.(bb : bs & yy(bb) = xx(ax)*xx(ax)) ) &
        objects /= Object_OBJ & xx(ax)*xx(ax) : INT
    THEN
      ANY bb WHERE bb : Object_OBJ - objects
      THEN
        bs := bs \/ { bb } || objects := objects \/ { bb } ||
        yy(bb) := xx(ax)*xx(ax)
      END
    END
END
```

The assumption *Asm* is $B = Set\{\}$, which is expressed as $bs = \{\}$. $r1$ defines the transformation step of the postcondition constraint. The machine is generated automatically by the UML-RSDS tools from the UML specification of the transformation.[1] UML-RSDS encodes into B

---

[1] In practice, single-letter feature, variable and entity type names should be avoided in the specification, since these have a special meaning in B AMN.

the semantics of all cases of updates to associations, including situations with mutually inverse association ends.

Using these machines we can verify syntactic correctness and semantic preservation properties of a model transformation, by means of *internal consistency* proof of the B machine representing the transformation and its metamodels. Internal consistency of a B machine consists of the following logical conditions:

■ That the state space of the machine is non-empty: $\exists\, v.I$ where v is the tuple of variables of the machine, and I its invariant.

■ That the initialisation establishes the invariant: $[Init]I$

■ That each operation maintains the invariant:

$$Pre \wedge I \;\Rightarrow\; [Code]I$$

where *Pre* is the precondition of the operation, and *Code* its effect.

B machines implicitly satisfy the *frame axiom* for state changes: variables v which are not explicitly updated by an operation are assumed not to be modified by the operation. This corresponds to the assumption made in UML-RSDS that v is unmodified by activity *act* if $v \notin wr(act)$.

Proof of verification properties can be carried out using B, as follows (for separate models transformations):

1. Internal consistency proof of M_τ establishes that *Inv* is an invariant of the transformation.

2. By adding the axioms of Γ_T to the INVARIANT clause, the validity of these during the transformation and in the final state of the transformation can be proved by internal consistency proof, establishing syntactic correctness.

3. Model-level semantic preservation can be verified by encoding the model semantics $Sem(m)$ in M_τ, and proving that this is invariant over transformation steps (for refactoring transformations).

4. By adding φ and $\chi(\varphi)$ to the INVARIANT of M_τ, semantic preservation of φ can be proved by internal consistency proof. Creation and update operations to set up the source model must be suitably restricted by φ.

Termination, confluence and semantic correctness proof needs to use suitable Q variants for each constraint.

Using Atelier B version 4.0, 13 proof obligations for internal consistency of the above machine M_τ are generated, of which 10 are automatically proved, and the remainder can be interactively proved using the provided proof assistant tool.

The three unproved obligations are:

```
"'Local hypotheses'" &
ax: A_OBJ &
not(ax: as) &
bb: bs &
"'Check that the invariant (!bb.(bb: bs => #aa.(aa: as &
yy(bb) = xx(aa)*xx(aa))))
is preserved by the operation - ref 3.4'"
```
=>
```
#aa.(aa: as\/{ax} & yy(bb) = (xx <+ { ax |-> xxx })(aa)*(xx <+
{ ax |-> xxx })(aa))
```


```
"'Local hypotheses'" &
bb: bs &
"'Check that the invariant (!bb.(bb: bs => #aa.(aa: as &
yy(bb) = xx(aa)*xx(aa))))
is preserved by the operation - ref 3.4'"
```
=>
```
#aa.(aa: as & yy(bb) = (xx <+ { ax |-> xxxx })(aa)*(xx <+
{ ax |-> xxxx })(aa))
```


```
"'Local hypotheses'" &
bb: B_OBJ &
not(bb: bs) &
bb$0: bs\/{bb} &
"'Check that the invariant (!bb.(bb: bs => #aa.(aa: as &
yy(bb) = xx(aa)*xx(aa))))
is preserved by the operation - ref 3.4'"
```
=>
```
#aa.(aa: as & (yy <+ { bb |-> xx(ax)*xx(ax) })(bb$0) =
xx(aa)*xx(aa))
```

Each of these can be proved by adding additional logical inferences to express why they hold. In the first case, the assumption $bb : bs$ means that

```
#aa.(aa: as & yy(bb) = xx(aa)*xx(aa))
```

holds, from the invariant. From $aa : as$ we can deduce $aa : aa \cup \{ax\}$, and from the assumption $not(ax : as)$ we can deduce $ax \neq aa$ and therefore that

```
(xx <+ { ax |-> xxx })(aa) = xx(aa)
```

and therefore that the required conclusion of the first proof obligation holds.

18.6 Synthesis of SMV

We utilise the SMV/nuSMV language and model checker [5] to analyse temporal properties of systems. We select SMV because it is an established industrial-strength tool which supports linear temporal logic (LTL). LTL defines properties over sequences of states using the operators $\bigcirc$ (in the next state), $\diamond$ (in the current or some future state), $\square$ (in the current and all future states), $\blacklozenge$ (strictly in the past).

SMV models systems in *modules*, which may contain variables ranging over finite domains such as subranges a..b of natural numbers and enumerated sets. The initial values of variables are set by initialisation statements $init(v) := e$. A $next(v) := e$ statement identifies how the value of variable v changes in execution steps of the module. In the UML to SMV encoding objects are modelled by positive integer object identities, attributes and associations are represented as variables, and classes are represented by modules parameterised by the object identity values (so that separate copies of the variables exist for each object of the class). A specific numeric upper bound must be given for the number of possible objects of each class (the bound is specified in the class definition dialog, Fig. 3.2).

A UML-RSDS system is modelled in SMV by modelling system execution steps as module execution steps. The structure of an SMV specification of a class diagram is as follows:

```
MODULE main
VAR
  C : Controller;
  MEntity1 : Entity(C,1);
  .... object instances ....

MODULE Controller
VAR
  Entityid : 1..n;
  event : { createEntity, killEntity, event1, ..., eventm, none };

MODULE Entity(C, id)
VAR
  alive : boolean;
  ... attributes ...
DEFINE
  TcreateEntity := C.event = createEntity & C.Entityid = id;
  TkillEntity := C.event = killEntity & C.Entityid = id;
  Tevent1 := C.event = event1 & C.Entityid = id & alive = TRUE;
```

```
...
ASSIGN
  init(alive) := FALSE;

  next(alive) :=
    case
      TcreateEntity : TRUE;
      TkillEntity : FALSE;
      TRUE : alive;
    esac;
```

Each class *Entity* is represented in a separate module, and each instance is listed as a module instance in the main module. System events are listed in the Controller, and the effect of these events on specific objects are defined in the module specific to the class of that object. The value of the *Controller* variable *event* in each execution step identifies which event occurs, and the value of the appropriate *Eid* variable indicates which object of class E the event occurs on.

Associations $r : A \to B$ of 1-multiplicity are represented as attributes

```
r : 1..bcard
```

where *bcard* is the maximum permitted number of objects of B. Events to set and unset this role are included. The lower bound 0 is used for 0..1-multiplicity roles to represent an absent B object. For *-multiplicity unordered roles $r : A \to Set(B)$, an array representation is used instead:

```
r : array 1..bcard of 0..1
```

with the presence/absence of a B element with identity value i being indicated by $r[i] = 1$ or $r[i] = 0$. Operations to add and remove elements are provided. The Controller Aid and Bid variables identify which links are being added/removed. The restrictions of SMV/nuSMV imply that only attributes and expressions of the following kinds can be represented in SMV:

- Booleans and boolean operations.

- Enumerated types.

- Integers and operations on integers within a bounded range.

- Strings represented as elements of an enumerated type. String operations cannot be represented.

SMV keywords must be avoided in specifications to be translated to SMV. These include the temporal operators A, F, O, G, H, X, Y, Z, U, S, V, T, EX, AX, EF, AF, EG, AG, etc. [5]. Classical logic is used in SMV, as in B. The semantics of integer division in nuSMV is now (since version 2.4.0) the standard one used in Java, C#, C++, B and OCL. The temporal logic operators are denoted in SMV by **G** (for □), **F** (for ◇), **X** (for ◯) and **O** (for ◆).

For separate-models transformations, the UML to SMV mapping needs to be modified as follows. Source entities are represented by modules with frozen variables and no assignments: the source model data is fixed at the initial time point. There are no *createE* or *killE* events for any entity. If a type 1 transformation rule r iterates over $s : S_i$ and has the form

$$Ante \implies T_j \rightarrow exists(t \mid TCond \ \& \ P)$$

then the SMV module for T_j has a parameter of module type S_i, and r is an event of the *Controller*, and $S_i id$ is a Controller variable. The T_j module has a transition defined as

```
Tr := C.event = r & C.Siid = id
```

identifying that the event for r takes place on the S_i object with id equal to the current T_j object, and that the S_i object (statically assigned to parameter S) exists. The updates to features f of t defined in *TCond*, P are then specified by $next(f)$ statements, using Tr as a condition, and $next(alive)$ is set to *TRUE* under condition Tr. An assumption of the main module expresses that the event r can only take place if *Ante* is true for the $C.Siid = id$ instance. We assume that source objects are mapped to target objects with the same object identifier number.

The *a2b* transformation can be encoded as follows, in the case of a model with two A objects and two B objects:

```
MODULE main
VAR
  C : Controller;
  MA1 : AA(C,1);
  MA2 : AA(C,2);
  MB1 : B(C,MA1,1);
  MB2 : B(C,MA2,2);

MODULE Controller
VAR
  Aid : 1..2;
  Bid : 1..2;
  event : { a2b1 };
```

```
MODULE AA(C, id)
FROZENVAR
  x : 0..10;

MODULE B(C, AA, id)
VAR
  alive : boolean;
  y : 0..100;
DEFINE
  Ta2b1 := C.event = a2b1 & C.Bid = id;
ASSIGN
  init(alive) := FALSE;

  next(alive) :=
    case
      Ta2b1 : TRUE;
      TRUE : alive;
    esac;

  init(y) := 0;

  next(y) :=
    case
      Ta2b1 : AA.x*AA.x;
      TRUE : y;
    esac;
```

The possible histories of this SMV system are executions of $a2b1$ on the two B module instances, corresponding to the B instances created from the two A instances. The A instances are initialised with arbitrary integer values x in 0..10.

The invariant property of the transformation can be checked as:

```
LTLSPEC
  G(MB1.alive = TRUE ->  MB1.y = MA1.x*MA1.x) &
  G(MB2.alive = TRUE ->  MB2.y = MA2.x*MA2.x)
```

Counter-examples can also be generated, and are expressed as execution histories, for example:

```
NuSMV > check_ltlspec
-- specification  G (MB1.y < 10 & MB2.y < 10)  is false
-- as demonstrated by the following execution sequence
Trace Description: LTL Counterexample
Trace Type: Counterexample
-> State: 1.1 <-
  MA1.x = 7
  MA2.x = 0
  C.Aid = 1
```

```
  C.Bid = 1
  MB1.alive = FALSE
  MB1.y = 0
  MB2.alive = FALSE
  MB2.y = 0
  C.event = a2b1
  MB1.Ta2b1 = TRUE
  MB2.Ta2b1 = FALSE
-- Loop starts here
-> State: 1.2 <-
  MB1.alive = TRUE
  MB1.y = 49
```

Summary

In this chapter we have described the validation and verification techniques which are supported by UML-RSDS, and which help to provide assurance of system correctness. Syntactic checks of diagram correctness, and of expression definedness and determinacy are provided within the tools. Semantic mathematical analysis via external tools (B, SMV, Z3) is facilitated by automated translations from UML-RSDS to the notations of these tools.

References

[1] F. Jouault, F. Allilaire, J. Bézivin and I. Kurtev, *ATL: A model transformation tool*, Sci. Comput. Program. 72(1-2) (2008) 31–39.

[2] K. Lano, *The B Language and Method*, Springer-Verlag, 1996.

[3] K. Lano, S. Kolahdouz-Rahimi and T. Clark, *Comparing verification techniques for model transformations*, Modevva workshop, MODELS 2012.

[4] K. Lano and S. Kolahdouz-Rahimi, *Constraint-based specification of model transformations*, Journal of Systems and Software, February 2013.

[5] NuSMV, http://nusmv.fbk.eu, 2015.

Chapter 19

Reactive System Development with UML-RSDS

Reactive systems are software systems which have the responsibility to control the state of some equipment under control (EUC): some external devices or other elements which can respond to commands from the reactive system, and whose state can be monitored by the reactive system.

UML-RSDS supports the specification of reactive systems via the use of (i) constraint-based specification of reactive system behaviour; (ii) explicit specification of behaviour via state machines; (iii) specification of temporal properties via interactions; (iv) transformations defining reactions as transformation rules.

19.1 Constraint-based specification of reactive systems

Reactive systems can be modelled abstractly by class diagrams, and their state specified by attributes representing the values of sensors and actuators for the EUC: the sensors provide information about the state of the EUC to the control system, whilst the actuators provide a means for the control system to affect the EUC state. Thus the sensor data is an input to the control system, and the actuator settings are outputs.

The most abstract and declarative means of defining the control system functionality is via constraints

$$Condition \implies Response$$

which relate the sensor attribute values (usually given on the LHS) to the actuator attribute values (usually given on the RHS). These constraints are *invariants* of the control system: the system is required to maintain them as true. The invariants of a system not only have a logical interpretation as conditions which should be maintained, but also can be interpreted as procedural instructions for how the invariants should be maintained. For example, if a tank in a chemical processing plant (Fig. 19.1) has a high level sensor *highsensor* and an inlet value *invalve*, an invariant could be:

$$highsensor = true \implies invalve = false$$

to express that if the fluid level is high, then the inlet value should be closed.

This could be procedurally interpreted as:

$$sethighsensor(true) \ \& \ highsensor = false \implies setinvalve(false)$$

That is, when the event of the high level sensor going on occurs (is detected by the reactive system), the inlet valve is switched off (the reactive system should command the valve to close).

Likewise, a constraint

$$lowsensor = false \implies invalve = true \ \& \ outvalve = false$$

has a procedural interpretation to open the inlet valve and close the outlet valve if the fluid level is below the low sensor.

Generally, any event which makes the LHS of a constraint Cn true should also trigger the actions $stat(RHS)$ of the procedural interpretation of the RHS.

Figure 19.1 shows the class diagram of this system. The attributes representing sensor states have the annotation ?, whilst those representing actuators have the annotation !. These are the visual indicators of *sensor* and *actuator* stereotypes for attributes (these stereotypes are entered via the attribute dialog, Fig. 3.3). These stereotypes are used in code generation and in formal analysis (e.g., for translation to SMV). Syntactic completeness and consistency analysis can be performed. Completeness checks that all combinations of sensor values are considered in the constraints:

1. Does each sensor attribute appear in at least one constraint assumption?

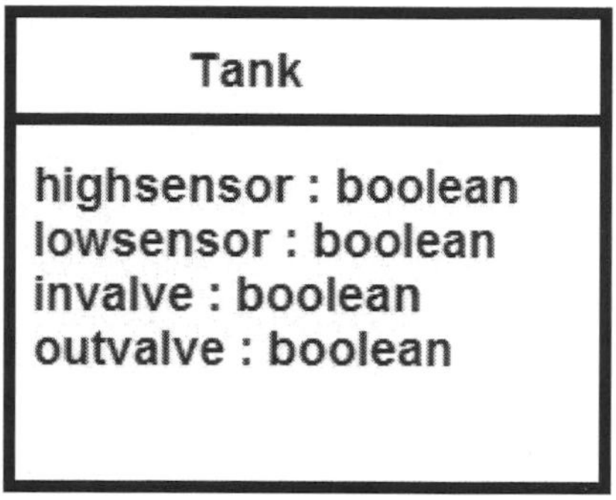

```
┌─────────────────────────────────┐
│                                 │
│              Tank               │
│                                 │
├─────────────────────────────────┤
│ highsensor : boolean            │
│ lowsensor : boolean             │
│ invalve : boolean               │
│ outvalve : boolean              │
│                                 │
│                                 │
└─────────────────────────────────┘
```

Figure 19.1: Tank class diagram

2. For each sensor s, and each possible value v of the sensor, does a formula $s = v$ occur in at least one constraint assumption?

For the tank system these checks fail, because no constraint compares either *highsensor* to *false*, or *lowsensor* to *true*. This can be corrected by adding additional constraints.

Consistency checking identifies if two antecedents can both be true at the same time, while both their succedents involve different settings to the same actuator. For the tank there is the inconsistency that if *lowsensor* = *false* and *highsensor* = *true* then *invalve* has conflicting settings. This can be corrected by making the constraint assumptions more specific, e.g.:

$$highsensor = true \ \& \ lowsensor = true \ \Rightarrow \ invalve = false$$

and

$$lowsensor = false \ \& \ highsensor = false \ \Rightarrow \ invalve = true \ \&$$
$$outvalve = false$$

Part of the generated Java code for Tank is:

```
class Tank
  implements SystemTypes
{
  private boolean highsensor = false; // sensor
  private boolean lowsensor = false; // sensor
  private boolean invalve = false; // actuator
  private boolean outvalve = false; // actuator

  public void sethighsensor(boolean highsensor_x) { highsensor =
    highsensor_x;
```

```
    if (highsensor == true) { invalve = false; }
  }

  public void setlowsensor(boolean lowsensor_x) { lowsensor =
   lowsensor_x;
    if (lowsensor == false) { invalve = true;
    outvalve = false; }
  }

  ....

}
```

B could be used to prove properties of the specification, as described in Chapter 18. Alternatively, SMV could be used to check if required properties hold. The SMV modules generated from this specification are:

```
MODULE main
VAR
  C : Controller;
  MTank1 : Tank(C,1);
LTLSPEC
  G(((MTank1.highsensor = TRUE -> MTank1.invalve = FALSE) &
     (MTank1.lowsensor = FALSE -> MTank1.invalve = TRUE &
      MTank1.outvalve = FALSE)) ->
     (MTank1.lowsensor = TRUE -> MTank1.outvalve = TRUE));

MODULE Controller
VAR
  Tankid : 1..1;
  event : { createTank, killTank, highsensorFALSE, highsensorTRUE,
            lowsensorFALSE, lowsensorTRUE, none };

MODULE Tank(C, id)
VAR
  alive : boolean;
  highsensor : boolean;
  lowsensor : boolean;
  invalve : boolean;
  outvalve : boolean;
DEFINE
  TcreateTank := C.event = createTank & C.Tankid = id;
  TkillTank := C.event = killTank & C.Tankid = id;
  ThighsensorFALSE := C.event = highsensorFALSE & C.Tankid = id &
   alive = TRUE;
  ThighsensorTRUE := C.event = highsensorTRUE & C.Tankid = id &
   alive = TRUE;
  TlowsensorFALSE := C.event = lowsensorFALSE & C.Tankid = id &
   alive = TRUE;
```

```
  TlowsensorTRUE := C.event = lowsensorTRUE & C.Tankid = id &
    alive = TRUE;
ASSIGN
  init(alive) := FALSE;

  init(highsensor) := FALSE;

  init(lowsensor) := FALSE;

  init(invalve) := FALSE;

  next(invalve) :=
    case
      ThighsensorTRUE : FALSE;
      TlowsensorFALSE : TRUE;
      TRUE : invalve;
    esac;

  init(outvalve) := FALSE;

  next(outvalve) :=
    case
      TlowsensorFALSE : FALSE;
      TRUE : outvalve;
    esac;

  next(alive) :=
    case
      TcreateTank : TRUE;
      TkillTank : FALSE;
      TRUE : alive;
    esac;

  next(highsensor) :=
    case
      ThighsensorFALSE : FALSE;
      ThighsensorTRUE : TRUE;
      TRUE : highsensor;
    esac;

  next(lowsensor) :=
    case
      TlowsensorFALSE : FALSE;
      TlowsensorTRUE : TRUE;
      TRUE : lowsensor;
    esac;
```

Events (changes in attribute values) are only included for the sensor attributes. The invariants of the system are encoded as assumptions in the main module LTLSPEC. To check that other properties are valid, given these assumptions, these can be added as conclusions of the LTLSPEC. In this example, a counterexample to the property *lowsensor = true ⇒ outvalve = true* is generated by SMV to show that this property fails, indicating that it does not follow from the invariants:

```
NuSMV > read_model -i tank.smv
NuSMV > go
WARNING: single-value variable 'C.Tankid' has been stored as a constant
NuSMV > check_ltlspec
-- specification  G (((MTank1.highsensor = TRUE -> MTank1.invalve =
FALSE) & (MTank1.lowsensor = FALSE -> (MTank1.invalve = TRUE &
MTank1.outvalve = FALSE))) ->
(MTank1.lowsensor = TRUE -> MTank1.outvalve = TRUE))  is false
-- as demonstrated by the following execution sequence
Trace Description: LTL Counterexample
Trace Type: Counterexample
-> State: 1.1 <-
  C.event = createTank
  MTank1.alive = FALSE
  MTank1.highsensor = FALSE
  MTank1.lowsensor = FALSE
  MTank1.invalve = FALSE
  MTank1.outvalve = FALSE
  C.Tankid = 1
  MTank1.TlowsensorTRUE = FALSE
  MTank1.TlowsensorFALSE = FALSE
  MTank1.ThighsensorTRUE = FALSE
  MTank1.ThighsensorFALSE = FALSE
  MTank1.TkillTank = FALSE
  MTank1.TcreateTank = TRUE
-> State: 1.2 <-
  C.event = lowsensorTRUE
  MTank1.alive = TRUE
  MTank1.TlowsensorTRUE = TRUE
  MTank1.TcreateTank = FALSE
-> State: 1.3 <-
  C.event = createTank
  MTank1.lowsensor = TRUE
  MTank1.TlowsensorTRUE = FALSE
  MTank1.TcreateTank = TRUE
-- Loop starts here
-> State: 1.4 <-
```

In the final state *lowsensor = TRUE* but *outvalve = FALSE*, invalidating the conclusion of the LTLSPEC whilst validating its assumption, so the LTLSPEC is false in this state.

19.2 State machines

State machines define the dynamic behaviour of objects and operations. They can be used to give operation definitions (instead of pre and postconditions), and to express the life cycle of objects. For example, a student object could have a linear lifecycle of successive states *Year*1, *Year*2, *Year*3 and *Graduated*.

An editor for state machines is provided, Fig. 19.2 shows the interface for this editor.

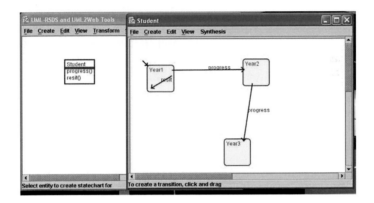

Figure 19.2: State machine editor

There are the following options:

File menu – options to save, load and print the state machine, and options to instantiate a class state machine for a particular object, and to take the product of two state machines. State machine data for model element *m* is saved and retrieved from the file *output/m.dat*.

Create menu – options to create states and transitions.

Edit menu – options to edit the state machine states and transitions and to resize the diagram.

View menu – options to view the lists of all states, transitions, events and attributes of the model.

Synthesis menu – options to analyse the state machine structure, to generate B and to carry out slicing of the state machine.

On the class diagram editor, the *Transformation* menu option *Express state machine in class diagram* adds variables and expressions to the class diagram to express the meaning of a state machine for an entity.

When an operation state machine is specified, the option *Check structure* on the state machine editor Synthesis menu should be applied before code is generated for the operation (on either the class diagram or state machine editor tool). This option identifies terminal, loop and decision states (displayed as green, red and blue, respectively), and warns the user if the state machine is not in the form of structured code. This analysis is then used to map the state machine into Java, C# or C++ code by the Generate code options on the class diagram Synthesis menu. Currently, only the subset of UML state machine notation with basic states is supported by UML-RSDS, although in principle larger subsets could be encoded [2].

Reactive systems can be specified explicitly by state machines which define the system response to input events, represented as operations. The behaviour of the tank control system of Section 19.1 can be explicitly specified by a state machine which has transitions for the sensor operations *sethighsensor* and *setlowsensor*, and these transitions can invoke actuator operations such as *setinvalve*, *setoutvalve*. Alternatively, each sensor and actuator can be modelled by separate components, each with its own state machine – a more refined specification closer to the actual physical implementation of the system. Figure 19.3 shows the class diagram and sensor state machine for this form of specification of the tank control system. The *TankControl* receives sensor event notifications from the two sensors, maintains its own internal representation of the sensor states, and issues commands to the valves dependent on the sensor states and events.

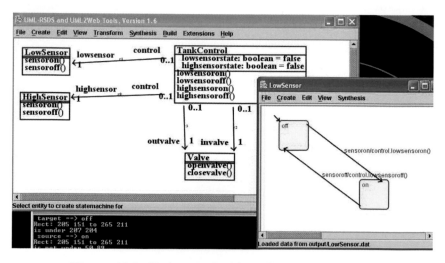

Figure 19.3: Tank control with explicit state machines

The notation *sensoron/control.lowsensoron()* on the state machine transitions indicates that the sensor event *sensoron* leads to an invocation of the tank control operation *lowsensoron()* when this transition is triggered. In general, a transition can have the annotation $e[G]/action$, indicating that if e occurs when the state machine is in the source state of the transition, and condition G is true, then the *action* is executed. The default for G is *true*. The *action* may be any statement (activity) valid in the context of the class or operation of the state machine.

An example of an operation state machine is the definition of *TankControl :: lowsensoroff* (Fig. 19.4).

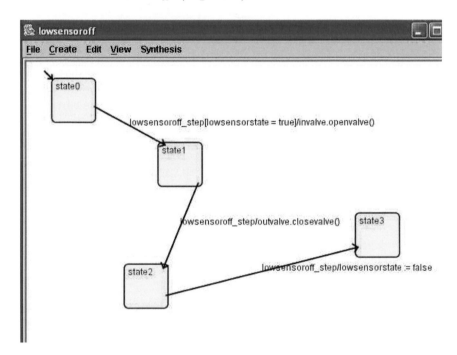

Figure 19.4: Operation state machine

This state machine is then used to generate Java code using the Generate Design and Generate Java 4 options on the Synthesis menu, resulting in the following code in the TankControl class:

```
public void lowsensoroff()
{ TankControl tankcontrolx = this;
  invalve.openvalve();
  outvalve.closevalve();
  lowsensorstate = false;
  return;
}
```

19.3   Interactions

Interactions can be created as UML sequence diagrams, these give examples of system behaviour in terms of object communications. They do not have a formal semantics, and are not used in code generation for systems, but can help to illustrate the processing of specific use cases and to describe expected scenarios of system behaviour, and to agree the details of use cases with customers, during requirements engineering.

The editor for interactions is shown in Fig. 19.5. The vertical lines are object lifelines, showing the time lines of individual objects (time increases from the top to the bottom of the screen). Messages are shown as arrows from sender object to receiver object: the operation invoked is shown on the arrow and must be an operation of the class of the receiver. Operation executions are shown as grey rectangles on the object lifeline, indicating that the object is executing an operation during an interval. A cross at the end of a lifeline indicates destruction of the object.

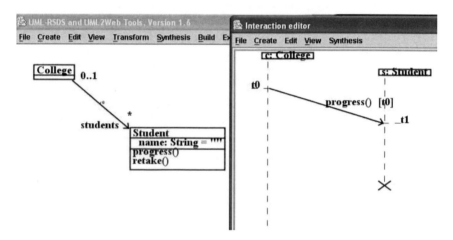

Figure 19.5: Interactions editor

The main interaction editor options are:

File menu – options to save, load and print models.

Create menu – options to create lifelines, messages, states, execution instances, and annotations.

Edit menu – options to edit an interaction.

View menu – options to view lifelines, messages, etc.

Synthesis menu – options to generate the formal real-time logic meaning of the diagram.

19.4 Reactive transformations

Model transformations can be used to define reactive systems: the transformation use case represents the reaction cycle of the reactive controller, and its rules define the responses of the system to given situations in the source model data, which can represent the state of a monitored system (sensor data and an internal representation of the environment). The target model can represent the actuators which the reactive system controls to affect the system under control.

For the tank control system we could write a use case *cycle* to represent the control system reaction cycle: reading all sensor inputs and producing corresponding actuator outputs according to the control invariants. The use case therefore has the control invariants as its postconditions:

> *Tank* ::
>   *highsensor* = *true* ⇒ *invalve* = *false*
> *Tank* ::
>   *lowsensor* = *false* ⇒ *invalve* = *true* & *outvalve* = *false*

As in Section 19.1, the consistency and completeness of these constraints should be checked as part of their validation.

19.4.1 *Case study: football player*

This case study was the TTC 2014 live case problem [1]: to write a transformation which controls the positions and actions of a football team, and responds to the actions of the opposing team and the position of the ball. The global functional requirement of the system is to score more goals than the opposing team. The transformation communicates with a server via sockets, the server maintains the state of the game, which is effectively the system to be controlled (the EUC). Actions of the teams are sent to the server, and it sends out to each participant (blue team and red team) the updated pitch data with player and ball positions. Data is transmitted as text files in XML format, specifically as EMF XMIResource files. The problem is an example of a reactive transformation: a transformation which is intended to operate repeatedly to monitor an external system (in this case, the football pitch) and to take actions to affect this system. Figure 19.6 shows the class diagram of this system.

The *Update* and *Action* classes describe the responses of the control system (the transformation) to the current state of the *SoccerPitch* (player positions for both teams, and the ball position). Each response may consist of a number of actions for the players of the responding

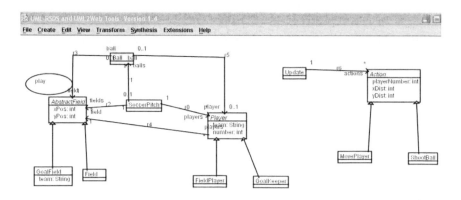

Figure 19.6: Class diagram of football game

team, and can either be an instruction to move a player, or for a player (with the ball) to shoot the ball. Attributes *xDist* and *yDist* are the horizontal and vertical distances for the player to move or for the ball to be kicked.

Figure 19.7 shows the visual interface of the football pitch, which is the equipment/system under control for this reactive system. Numbers denote players, and there are two teams, red and blue, which would normally be controlled by distinct versions of the reactive control system.

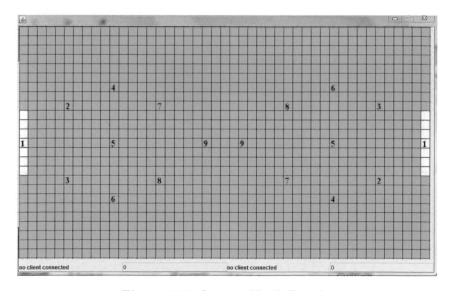

Figure 19.7: Layout of football pitch

There are several restrictions on the allowed moves:

- Each player can only perform at most one action in each turn.

- A player owning the ball can move at most 2 places in x and y directions. A player without the ball can move at most 3 places in x and y directions.

- A goalkeeper can move only on his own team's goal fields.

- Players cannot be moved off the pitch. Nor can the ball be shot off the pitch.

- A shot can move the ball at most 7 places in x and y directions.

- No more than 4 shoot ball actions can take place in each update.

The penalty in each of these cases is a red card – the player involved in the action is removed from the game.

The case study is quite open-ended, in that the global requirement can be refined in many different ways. A wide range of different strategies could be used to play the game, such as defensive or offensive styles of play. There is scope also to build in artificial intelligence techniques to compute suitable moves. One approach is to define specific tactics for each category of player (goalkeeper, defender, midfielder, forward). For example, the goalkeeper specific behaviour is expressed by the operation:

```
Player::
goalkeeperaction(u : Update)
pre: true
post:
  ( ball.size > 0 =>
        ShootBall->exists( a |
              a.playerNumber = number &
              a.xDist = 7 & a.yDist = -3 &
              a : u.actions ) &
        MovePlayer->exists( m |
              m.playerNumber = 5 &
              m.xDist = -3 & m.yDist = -3 &
              m : u.actions )
  )
```

This expresses that if the goalkeeper (of the blue team) has the ball, he should shoot it to the central midfielder number 5, and direct this player to move to the ball. The two actions are added to the update u supplied as a parameter.

The blue team central midfielder behaviour is expressed by:

```
Player::
cmaction(u : Update, theball : Ball)
pre: true
post:
  ( ball.size > 0 & field.xPos < 39 =>
      MovePlayer->exists( m |
          m.playerNumber = number &
          m.xDist = 2 & m.yDist = 0 &
          m : u.actions ) ) &
  ( ball.size > 0 & field.xPos >= 39 =>
      ShootBall->exists( m |
          m.playerNumber = number &
          m.xDist = 44 - field.xPos &
          m.yDist = 0 & m : u.actions ) ) &
  ( theball.blueTeamhasBall() = false =>
                                      moveToBall(u,theball) )
```

If the player has the ball and is not within shooting distance of the red goal, then he should move forward. If he is within shooting distance and has the ball, then he should shoot, otherwise if the blue team does not have the ball, he should move towards the ball.

The reactive behaviour of the blue team controller is expressed by a use case *play*, which has the postcondition:

```
theball = Ball->any() & goalkeeper = GoalKeeper->select(team /= "RED")->any() &
player5 = FieldPlayer->select(team /= "RED" & number = 5)->any() &
player2 = FieldPlayer->select(team /= "RED" & number = 2)->any() &
player3 = FieldPlayer->select(team /= "RED" & number = 3)->any() &
player4 = FieldPlayer->select(team /= "RED" & number = 4)->any() &
player6 = FieldPlayer->select(team /= "RED" & number = 6)->any() &
player7 = FieldPlayer->select(team /= "RED" & number = 7)->any() &
player8 = FieldPlayer->select(team /= "RED" & number = 8)->any() &
player9 = FieldPlayer->select(team /= "RED" & number = 9)->any()   =>
    Update->exists( u | goalkeeper.goalkeeperaction(u) & player5.cmaction(u,theball) &
            player2.defenderaction(u,theball) & player3.defenderaction(u,theball) &
            player4.midfielderaction(u,theball) & player6.midfielderaction(u,theball) &
            player7.midfielderaction(u,theball) & player8.midfielderaction(u,theball) &
            player9.midfielderaction(u,theball) )
```

The antecedent simply defines let-variables to hold the ball and individual players. In the succedent each player adds their own actions to the update. Verification of this use case should check that it generates updates which respect the rules on allowed actions listed above. According to extensive testing this is the case, but no formal proof was carried out.

The implementation of the *play* use case is invoked by a SoccerClient class (manually written), which executes a loop which reads the socket from the soccer server, extracts the SoccerPitch model as an XML-encoded string, and supplies this to a Controller operation *cycle* which constructs the input model from the XML data. The Controller *play* use case is then invoked and the Update data which it produces is then returned to the SoccerClient as an XML file and sent to the soccer server:

```
int turns = 0;
while (turns < 400)
{ StringBuffer xmlstring = new StringBuffer();
  s = in.readLine();  // get new pitch model from server

  while (s != null && !(s.equals(END_MARKER)))
  { s = in.readLine();
    xmlstring.append(s);
  }
  String resp = Controller.cycle(xmlstring.toString());

  out.println(START_MARKER);
  out.println(resp);
  out.println(END_MARKER);
  out.flush();  // send updates to server
}
in.close();
out.close();
client.close();
} catch (Exception e) { e.printStackTrace(); }
```

The efficiency and response time were satisfactory. The basic playing strategy defined by *play* could be improved by better co-ordination between players and increased use of multi-player moves. Greater use of abstraction in the specification would be beneficial, instead of rules being expressed in terms of specific numeric positions and distances.

Summary

In this chapter we have identified techniques for specifying reactive systems in UML-RSDS, using constraints, state machines, interactions and transformations.

References

[1] T. Horn, *TTC 2014 Live case problem: Transformation tool contest world cup*, TTC 2014.

[2] K. Lano and D. Clark, *Direct semantics of extended state machines*, Journal of Object Technology, Vol. 6, No. 9, 2007.

Chapter 20

Enterprise Systems Development with UML-RSDS

Enterprise information systems hold and manage business-critical data for a company or organisation. They usually implement the core business operations of an enterprise. Examples include accounts data and accounts management operations for a bank. EIS typically involve distributed processing and large-scale secure data storage. The structures and components of an EIS are often of a standard form, independent of the specific application, and EIS platforms such as Java Enterprise Edition (Java EE) and Microsoft .Net provide much of the machinery of data management, data persistence, transaction management and distributed processing which is needed by any EIS. Using UML-RSDS, many of the components of an EIS can be automatically generated from a specification class diagram of the application data, and from identified use cases operating on this data.

20.1 EIS synthesis

An enterprise information system (EIS) implemented with Java technologies typically consists of five tiers of components (Fig. 20.1):

Client tier This contains web pages or other interfaces by which clients use the system. Typical components are HTML files, applets, etc.

Presentation tier Components which construct the GUI of the system and handle requests from the client tier. For example, Java servlets and JSPs.

Business tier Components which represent the business operations (services) offered by the system, and the business entities of the system. These typically include Session Beans and Entity Beans, and Value Objects, which are used to transfer data between the business tier and other tiers.

Integration tier This contains components which serve as a mediating interface between the business and resource tiers: abstracting the resource components. It typically consists of database interfaces and web service interfaces.

Resource tier This tier contains databases and other resources used by the system. Web services provided by external organisations are also included here.

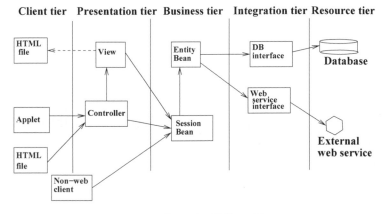

Figure 20.1: Five-tier EIS architecture

Such systems can be defined using many different technologies and techniques. In UML-RSDS we use Java technologies, and three alternative system styles:

- Servlet style: presentation tier is coded using only servlets and auxiliary classes to generate web pages.

- JSP style: presentation tier is coded only using JSPs to handle web requests and to generate web pages.

- J2EE style: Java Entity beans and Session beans are constructed to define the business tier of an application, together with value objects and a database interface class.

In each case, the system specification is given as a class diagram and set of use cases defining the user operations to be provided by the system. These are defined using the first field of the use case dialog (Fig. 5.1) to name the operation, the second field to name the entity, and the third (if needed) to name a specific feature.

EIS use cases can be:

- create E: create an instance of entity E (initializing its attribute values)

- delete E: delete an instance of E

- edit E: edit an instance of entity E (setting its attribute values)

- add E r: add an element to the role set r of an instance of E

- remove E r: remove an element from the role set r of an instance of E

- list E: list all instances of E

- searchBy E a: find instances of E with a given value for attribute a.

These operations are the standard CRUD (create, read, update, delete) actions provided by most data management systems. Any invariant constraints that are defined for a persistent entity are used to generate validation checks on the web pages and in server side functional components. The use cases and class diagram elements map to EIS code components as follows (Table 20.1).

Table 20.1: Mapping of UML-RSDS to web code

Element	*Servlet style*	*JSP style*	*J2EE style*
Class E	Database table	Session/Entity bean Value object	Session bean, Entity bean, Value object
Attribute	Table column form field	as Servlet style as Servlet style	as Servlet style as Servlet style
Use case *op*	CommandPage.java (view) opPage.java (form generator) op.html (form) opResultPage.java (view) Dbi.java (data access object)	commands.html op.jsp (view + controller) op.html (form) Dbi.java	 as JSP style

In the following section we give an example of the JSP-style EIS architecture.

20.2 Example EIS application: bank accounts system

This example is a simple but typical case of an EIS. The system maintains details of the bank customers, their accounts, and transactions on these accounts (Fig. 20.2).

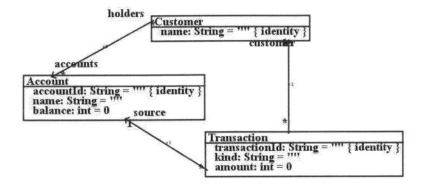

Figure 20.2: Bank account EIS class diagram

The use cases considered are:

- create Account;

- create Customer;

- create Transaction;

- add Customer accounts;

- list Account;

- searchBy Customer name.

An invariant of Account is that *balance* ≥ 0.

The *Web system/JSP* option on the *Synthesis* menu then produces a set of files for the client, presentation, business and integration tier of this EIS, according to Table 20.1. The overall architecture of the JSP style of generated web system is shown in Fig. 20.3.

A standard physical organisation of a Java-based web application consists of a subdirectory *app* named after the application, in a directory *webapps* of the web server. Within *app* there are directories (i) *servlets* containing HTML and JSP files (in the case of a JSP-based architecture) and servlets, and (ii) *WEB-INF* containing business-tier Java components in a subdirectory *classes*.

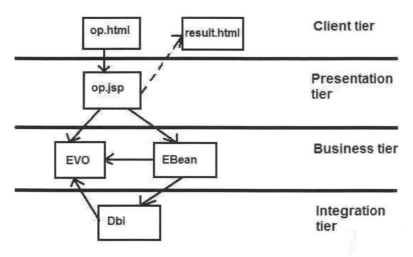

Figure 20.3: JSP style EIS architecture

20.2.1 Client tier

Web pages *op.html* for each use case *op* are synthesised for the client tier. These contain fields for all the input parameters of *op*, and a submit button. They invoke the corresponding *op.jsp* in the presentation tier. The *op.html* web pages should be placed in *webapps/app/servlets*. In our case study we have, for example, *addCustomeraccounts.html* (Fig. 20.4) and *searchBycustomername.html* (Fig. 20.5).

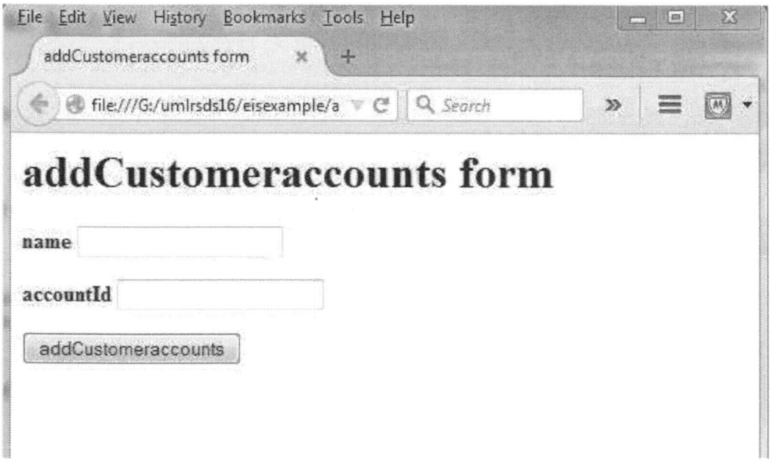

Figure 20.4: Add customer accounts form

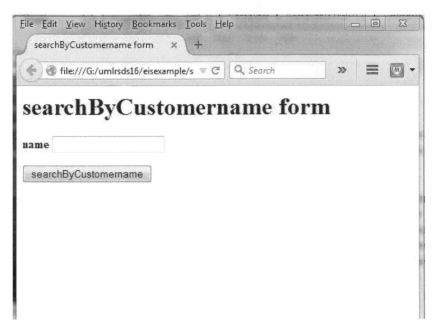

Figure 20.5: Search by customer name form

20.2.2 Presentation tier

In the presentation tier, a JSP *op.jsp* is defined for each use case *op*. This JSP receives the data from *op.html*, calls the session/entity bean responsible for *op*, and then generates a result *opresult.html* page to display the outcome of the operation. An example is the JSP to create an account:

```
<jsp:useBean id="account" scope="session" class="beans.AccountBean"/>
<jsp:setProperty name="account"  property="accountId"  param="accountId"/>
<jsp:setProperty name="account"  property="name"  param="name"/>
<jsp:setProperty name="account"  property="balance"  param="balance"/>

<html>

<head><title>createAccount</title></head>

<body>

<h1>createAccount</h1>

<% if (account.iscreateAccounterror())
{ %> <h2>Error in data: <%= account.errors() %></h2>
<h2>Press Back to re-enter</h2> <% }
else { account.createAccount(); %>
```

```
<h2>createAccount performed</h2>
<% } %>

<hr>

<% include file="commands.html" %>

</body>
</html>
```

The *jsp*:*useBean* directive links the JSP to the AccountBean instance *account*, the *jsp* : *setProperty* lines copy the form data to this instance, and the body of the JSP tests if there is an error in this data, and calls *createAccount* on *account* to create the new account (ultimately by adding a new row to the *Account* table in the database) if there is no error. The JSP files should be placed in *webapps/app/servlets*.

20.2.3 Business tier

Entity/session bean classes *EBean* are synthesised for each persistent entity type (class). These beans interact with the Dbi component in the integration tier to store and extract instances of the entity, and to perform data validation checks on instance data based on the attribute types and entity invariants. They have operations for each use case that involves the entity, and error-checking operations for each use case on the entity. For example, *AccountBean* in our case study is:

```
package beans;

import java.util.*;
import java.sql.*;

public class AccountBean
{ Dbi dbi = new Dbi();
  private String accountId = "";
  private String name = "";
  private String balance = "";
  private int ibalance = 0;
  private Vector errors = new Vector();

  public AccountBean() {}

  public void setaccountId(String accountIdx)
  { accountId = accountIdx; }

  public void setname(String namex)
  { name = namex; }

  public void setbalance(String balancex)
```

```
{ balance = balancex; }

public void resetData()
{ accountId = "";
  name = "";
  balance = "";
}

public boolean iscreateAccounterror()
{ errors.clear();
  try { ibalance = Integer.parseInt(balance); }
  catch (Exception e)
  { errors.add(balance + " is not an integer"); }
  if (ibalance >= 0) { }
  else
  { errors.add("Constraint: ibalance >= 0 failed"); }
  return errors.size() > 0; }

public boolean islistAccounterror()
{ errors.clear();
  return errors.size() > 0; }

public String errors() { return errors.toString(); }

public void createAccount()
{ dbi.createAccount(accountId, name, ibalance);
  resetData(); }

public Iterator listAccount()
{ ResultSet rs = dbi.listAccount();
 List rs_list = new ArrayList();
 try
 { while (rs.next())
   { rs_list.add(new AccountVO(rs.getString("accountId"),
        rs.getString("name"),rs.getInt("balance")));      }
 } catch (Exception e) { }
 resetData();
 return rs_list.iterator();
 }
}
```

Value object classes are generated for each entity, to provide a technology-neutral means of passing data between tiers of the EIS, as in the operation *listAccount* above. In the bank system there are value objects for *Customer*, *Account* and *Transaction*, e.g.:

```
package beans;

public class CustomerVO
```

```
{
 private String name;

  public CustomerVO(String namex)
  {    name = namex;
  }

  public String getname()
  { return name; }

}
```

All of these classes should be placed in the *beans* subdirectory of *webapps/app/WEB-INF/classes* and compiled there.

20.2.4 Integration tier

The integration tier contains the Dbi.java class, which uses Java JDBC to update and read a relational database using SQL commands. This class should also be placed in *webapps/app/WEB-INF/classes/beans*. In the bank system, the Dbi class is as follows:

```
package beans;

import java.sql.*;

public class Dbi
{ private Connection connection;
  private static String defaultDriver = "";
  private static String defaultDb = "";
  private PreparedStatement createAccountStatement;
  private PreparedStatement createCustomerStatement;
  private PreparedStatement createTransactionStatement;
  private PreparedStatement listAccountStatement;
  private PreparedStatement addCustomeraccountsStatement;
  private PreparedStatement searchByCustomernameStatement;
  public Dbi() { this(defaultDriver,defaultDb); }

  public Dbi(String driver, String db)
  { try
    { Class.forName(driver);
      connection = DriverManager.getConnection(db);
      createAccountStatement =
        connection.prepareStatement(
        "INSERT INTO Account (accountId,name,balance) VALUES (?,?,?)");
      createCustomerStatement =
        connection.prepareStatement(
          "INSERT INTO Customer (name) VALUES (?)");
```

```
    createTransactionStatement =
      connection.prepareStatement(
        "INSERT INTO Transaction (transactionId,kind,amount)
          VALUES (?,?,?)");
    listAccountStatement =
      connection.prepareStatement(
        "SELECT accountId,name,balance FROM Account");
    addCustomeraccountsStatement =
      connection.prepareStatement(
        "UPDATE Account SET Account.name = ? WHERE Account.
          accountId = ?");
    searchByCustomernameStatement =
      connection.prepareStatement(
        "SELECT name FROM Customer WHERE name = ?");
  } catch (Exception e) { }
}

public synchronized void createAccount(String accountId,
 String name,int balance)
{ try
  { createAccountStatement.setString(1, accountId);
    createAccountStatement.setString(2, name);
    createAccountStatement.setInt(3, balance);
    createAccountStatement.executeUpdate();
    connection.commit();
  } catch (Exception e) { e.printStackTrace(); }
}

public synchronized void createCustomer(String name)
{ try
  { createCustomerStatement.setString(1, name);
    createCustomerStatement.executeUpdate();
    connection.commit();
  } catch (Exception e) { e.printStackTrace(); }
}

public synchronized void createTransaction(String transactionId,
 String kind,int amount)
{ try
  { createTransactionStatement.setString(1, transactionId);
    createTransactionStatement.setString(2, kind);
    createTransactionStatement.setInt(3, amount);
    createTransactionStatement.executeUpdate();
    connection.commit();
  } catch (Exception e) { e.printStackTrace(); }
}

public synchronized ResultSet listAccount()
{ try
```

```
    { return listAccountStatement.executeQuery();
  } catch (Exception e) { e.printStackTrace(); }
  return null; }

  public synchronized void addCustomeraccounts(String name,
   String accountId)
  { try
    {   addCustomeraccountsStatement.setString(1, name);
      addCustomeraccountsStatement.setString(2, accountId);
      addCustomeraccountsStatement.executeUpdate();
    connection.commit();
  } catch (Exception e) { e.printStackTrace(); }
  }

  public synchronized ResultSet searchByCustomername(String name)
  { try
    {   searchByCustomernameStatement.setString(1, name);
      return searchByCustomernameStatement.executeQuery();
  } catch (Exception e) { e.printStackTrace(); }
  return null; }

  public synchronized void logoff()
  { try { connection.close(); }
    catch (Exception e) { e.printStackTrace(); }
  }
}
```

For the final production code, the debugging calls of *printStackTrace* would be removed.

Summary

In this chapter we have described how EIS applications can be synthesised using UML-RSDS, and we have given a detailed example of EIS synthesis.

Chapter 21

Applications of UML-RSDS in Education and Industry

In this chapter we discuss the teaching of UML and model-based development using UML-RSDS. We describe three case studies of UML-RSDS, including two which are suitable for educational use (case studies 1 and 2). An industrial application of a complex financial system is also presented.

21.1 Teaching using UML-RSDS

UML-RSDS has been used for teaching software specification and design using UML, and for practical student projects using model-based and agile development. This has mainly been at the second year level of undergraduate courses. Only a small subset of UML-RSDS features need to be considered for such teaching:

- Introducing UML and the relationship between UML and object-oriented programming languages: the core class diagram notations of classes, attributes, associations, operations and inheritance are needed. More elaborate notations such as association classes, composition, and qualified associations need not be considered. The class diagram editor and code generation facilities of UML-RSDS are used.

- Dynamic modelling: the state machine editor and code generation facilities can be used, together with the interactions editor.

- Model-based development: class diagrams, use cases and constraints are needed, to specify systems and model transformations. The code generators are used to generate executable implementations.

As discussed below, students may find problems using UML-RSDS or other MBD tools, because of the conceptual novelty of writing executable specifications, and because of the tool complexity. We recommend using a clearly defined specification and development procedure which students should follow with the tool, and restricting the notations considered to a sufficient subset. For example, the most often used OCL operators in UML-RSDS specifications are : and →*includes*, →*exists*, conjunction and implication, object lookup by identity, numeric operators and comparisons, →*select*, →*size*, and →*forAll*. To solve a particular problem, students can be given a set of operators and language elements to use, which will be *sufficient* for the problem.

21.2   Case study 1: FIXML code generation

This case study was based on the problem described in [18]. Financial transactions can be electronically expressed using formats such as the FIX (Financial Information eXchange) format. New variants/extensions of such message formats can be introduced, which leads to problems in the maintenance of end-user software: the user software, written in various programming languages, which generates and processes financial transaction messages will need to be updated to the latest version of the format each time it changes. In [18] the authors proposed to address this problem by automatically synthesising program code representing the transaction messages from a single XML definition of the message format, so that users would always have the latest code definitions available. For this case study we restricted attention to generating Java, C# and C++ class declarations from messages in FIXML 4.4 format, as defined at http://fixwiki.org/fixwiki/FPL:FIXML_Syntax, and http://www.fixtradingcommunity.org.

The solution transformation should take as input a text file of a message in XML FIXML 4.4 Schema format, and produce as output corresponding Java, C# and C++ text files representing this data.

The problem is divided into the following use cases:

1. Map data represented in an XML text file to an instance model of the XML metamodel (Fig. 21.1).

2. Map a model of the XML metamodel to a model of a suitable metamodel for the programming language/languages under consideration. This has subtasks: 2a. Map XML nodes to classes; 2b. Map XML attributes to attributes; 2c. Map subnodes to object instances.

3. Generate program text from the program model.

In principle these use cases could be developed independently, although the subteams or developers responsible for use cases 2 and 3 need to agree on the programming language metamodel(s) to be used.

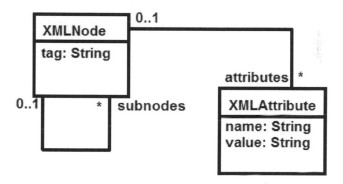

Figure 21.1: XML metamodel

The problem was set as the assessed coursework (counting for 15% of the course marks) for the second year undergraduate course "Object-oriented Specification and Design" (OSD) at King's College in 2013. It was scheduled in the last four weeks at the end of the course. OSD covers UML and MBD and agile development at an introductory level. Students also have experience of team working on the concurrent Software Engineering Group project (SEG). Approximately 120 students were on the course, and these were divided into 12 teams of 10 students each.

The case study involves research into FIXML, XML, UML-RSDS and C# and C++, and definition of use cases in UML-RSDS using OCL. None of these topics had been taught to the students. Scrum, XP, and an outline agile development approach using UML-RSDS had been taught, and the teams were recommended to appoint a team leader. A short (5 page) requirements document was provided, and links to the UML-RSDS tools and manual. Each week there was a one hour timetabled lab session where teams could meet and ask for help from postgraduate students who had some UML-RSDS knowledge.

21.2.1 Solution

The class diagram of a possible solution (specific to Java code output) is shown in Fig. 21.2.

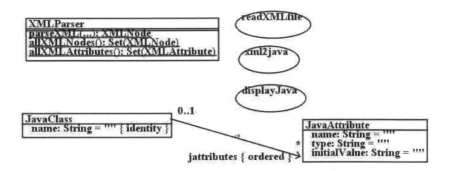

Figure 21.2: FIXML system specification

The class *XMLParser* is an external class (its code is provided by handwritten Java) with the operations

```
query static parseXML(f : String) : XMLNode
```

```
query static allXMLNodes() : Set(XMLNode)
```

```
query static allXMLAttributes() : Set(XMLAttribute)
```

These parse a given XML document and return the sets of all XML nodes and attributes defined in the document. These operations are used to carry out the first use case, *readXMLfile*, which has the postconditions:

```
XMLParser.parseXML("test1.xml")
```

```
XMLParser.allXMLNodes() <: XMLNode &
XMLParser.allXMLAttributes() <: XMLAttribute
```

The second postcondition adds all the parsed XML nodes and attributes from `test1.xml` to the sets of instances of *XMLNode* and *XMLAttribute*, respectively.

The *xml2java* use case has the postcondition constraints:

```
XMLNode::
  JavaClass->exists( jc | jc.name = tag )
```

which creates a Java class for each XMLNode (task 2a). Since *name* is an identity attribute for *JavaClass*, multiple XMLNodes with the same tag will be represented by a *single* JavaClass.

For task 2b there is the postcondition:

```
XMLNode::
  att : attributes & jc = JavaClass[tag] &
  att.name /: jc.jattributes@pre.name@pre  =>
      JavaAttribute->exists( ja |
              ja.name = att.name & ja.type = "String" &
              ja.initialValue = att.value & ja : jc.jattributes )
```

This maps all XML attributes of a given XML node *self* to program attributes of the program class *JavaClass[tag]* corresponding to *self*. For each pair of an XML node *self* and attribute *att* : *attributes* a new JavaAttribute is created and added to *JavaClass[tag]*. This double iteration is needed because attribute names are not unique: two different XML nodes could both have attributes with a particular name. Thus a pure Phased Construction approach, with attributes mapped first and then looked-up by their key, is not possible. The condition `att.name /: jc.jattributes@pre.name@pre` is needed to check that no program attribute with name *att.name* is already in the program class: an invalid class would result if two attributes with the same name were present. The constraint is of type 1 because pre-forms of *jattributes* and *JavaAttribute::name* are used in the antecedent, so that the read frame of the constraint is disjoint from the write frame (a case of the Replace Fixed-point by Bounded Iteration pattern, Chapter 9). It is not confluent, because the unordered association *XMLNode::attributes* may be iterated over in an arbitrary order, so that two different attributes with the same name but different initialisations could be processed in either order, resulting in two different *jattribute* collections – because only the first XML attribute to be processed will produce a Java attribute.

For task 2c a similar constraint is used to map subnodes to program attributes:

```
XMLNode::
sn : subnodes  =>
    JavaAttribute->exists( ja |
        ja.name = sn.tag + "_object" + JavaClass[tag].jattributes
         @pre->size() &
        ja.type = sn.tag &
        ja.initialValue = "new " + sn.tag + "()" &
        ja : JavaClass[tag].jattributes )
```

There may be multiple subnodes with the same tag, and each must be separately represented in the code output, so we append the number *JavaClass[tag].jattributes@pre→size()* to the Java attribute name to distinguish these. This number increments each time an attribute is added to the class *JavaClass*[*tag*]. Since *subnodes* is unordered, this constraint is not confluent: different orders of iteration through *subnodes* may produce different variable names in the Java class.

The third use case is carried out by the *displayJava* use case:

```
JavaClass::
( "class " + name + " {" )->display() &
jattributes->forAll( ja |
    ( "    " + ja.type + " " + ja.name + " = " + ja.initialValue + ";"
    )->display() ) & "}\n"->display()
```

The same metamodel for Java programs can be used also for C# and C++, and only the *displayX* use case needs to be adapted to print out programs in the syntax of these languages.

21.2.2 Outcome

The outcome of the case study is summarised in Table 21.1.

Table 21.1: Case 1 results

Teams	Mark range	Result
5, 8, 9, 10	80+	Comprehensive solution and testing, well-organised team
12	80+	Good solution, but used manual coding, not UML-RSDS
4, 7, 11	70–80	Some errors/incompleteness
2, 3, 6	50–60	Failed to complete some tasks
1	Below 40	Failed all tasks, group split into two.

Examples of good practices included:

■ Division of a team into sub-teams with sub-team leaders, and separation of team roles into researchers and developers (teams 8, 11).

■ Test-driven development (teams 8, 9).

■ Metamodel refactoring, to merge different versions of program metamodels for Java, C# and C++ into a single program metamodel.

Because of the difficulty of the problem, teams tended to work together as a unit on each use case, rather than divide into subteams with separate responsibilities. In retrospect the complexity of the task was too high for second year undergraduates, and all the teams struggled both to understand the task and to apply UML-RSDS. With intensive effort, the best teams did manage to master the technical problems and to carry out all the mandated tests on example FIX XML files. The most difficult part of the problem was use case 2, which involved using a particular form of constraint quantification to avoid creating duplicate program features in cases where an XML node has multiple direct subnodes with the same tag name. All teams used UML-RSDS to try to solve the problem, except for team 12, which produced a hand-coded Java solution. The effort expended by this team seemed comparable to that of the successful UML-RSDS teams, but their coding effort was higher whilst their research effort was lower.

Conclusions that can be drawn from this case study are that an excessively complex task is a bad choice as a first project in MBD, and that developers should instead build their expertise using less challenging applications. Only four teams managed to master the development approach, others either reverted to manual coding or produced incomplete solutions. The total effort expended by successful MBD teams was not in excess of that expended by the successful manual coding team, which suggests that the approach can be feasible even in adverse circumstances.

21.3   Case study 2: Electronic health records (EHR) analysis and migration

This case study was the OSD assessed coursework for 2014. It was intended to be somewhat easier than the 2013 coursework. Approximately 140 second year undergraduate students participated, divided into 14 teams of 9 or 10 members.

There were three top level use cases: (1) to analyse a dataset of GP patient data conforming to the language of Fig. 21.3 for cases of missing names, address, etc., feature values; (2) to display information on referrals and consultations in date-sorted order; (3) to integrate the GP patient data with hospital patient data conforming to the EHR language of Fig. 21.4 to produce an integrated dataset conforming to a third model (Fig. 21.5).

Table 21.2 summarises the use cases and their subtasks.

Students were allocated randomly to teams. Teams were advised to select a leader, and to apply an agile development process, although a specific process was not mandated. A short (2 page) requirements document was provided, and links to the UML-RSDS tools and manual. Each week there was a one hour timetabled lab session where teams could meet and ask for help from postgraduate students who had some UML-RSDS knowledge.

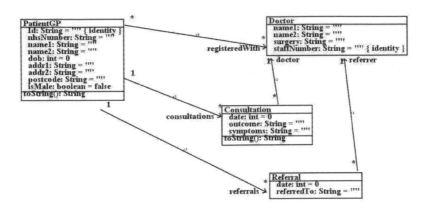

Figure 21.3: GP patient EHR structure gpmm1

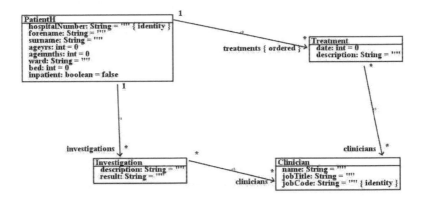

Figure 21.4: Hospital patient EHR structure gpmm2

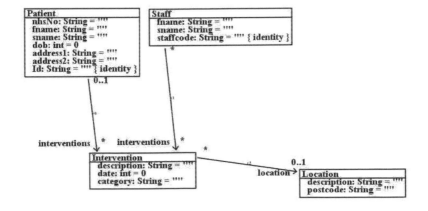

Figure 21.5: Integrated patient EHR structure gpmm3

Table 21.2: Use cases for EHR analysis/migration application

Use case	Subtasks	Models
1. Analyse data	1a. Detect missing dob, names, addresses in GP dataset	gpmm1
	1b. Detect duplicate patient records	gpmm1
2. View data	2a. Display consultations of each GP patient, in date order	gpmm1
	2b. Display referrals of each GP patient, in date order	gpmm1
3. Integrate data	Combine gpmm1, gpmm2 data into gpmm3	gpmm1, gpmm2, gpmm3

21.3.1 Solution

A possible solution for use case 1 could be the following postconditions of a use case *check*:

```
dob <= 0   =>   ("Patient " + self + " has no valid date of birth")
->display()


name1 = ""   =>   ("Patient " + self + " has no valid first name")
->display()


name2 = ""   =>   ("Patient " + self + " has no valid second name")
->display()


addr1 + addr2 = ""   =>   ("Patient " + self + " has no valid address")
->display()
```

All of these constraints are on the entity context *PatientGP*.

To check for duplicated patients, the following *check* postcondition on entity context *PatientGP* could be used:

```
p : PatientGP & Id < p.Id &
name1 = p.name1 & name2 = p.name2 & dob = p.dob & isMale = p.isMale   =>
            ("Patients " + self + " and " + p + " seem to be duplicates")
            ->display()
```

This performs a double iteration over *PatientGP*, comparing *self* and *p*. The condition *Id* < *p.Id* is used, instead of *Id* ≠ *p.Id*, because we only want to consider each distinct pair once.

For the second use case, *viewData*, to display all consultation data for a given GP patient, sorted by date (most recent last), we can use the →*sortedBy* operator:

```
cons = consultations->sortedBy(date)   =>
                        cons->forAll( c | c->display() )
```

iterated on *PatientGP*, where a suitable *toString()* operation has been added to *Consultation*. Likewise for referrals.

For the third use case to integrate corresponding GP and hospital datasets, we need to convert from integer date of births in the format yearMonthDay (e.g., 19561130) to age in years and months. The age in years is

$$currentYear - (dob/10000)$$

with integer division used on the dob to extract the year. The age in months is

$$currentMonth - ((dob \; mod \; 10000)/100)$$

A solution is then, for December 2014:

```
p : PatientH & name1 = p.forename & name2 = p.surname &
(2014 - (dob/10000)) = p.ageyrs &
(12 - (dob mod 10000)/100) = p.agemnths  =>
    Patient->exists( q | q.Id = Id & q.nhsNo = nhsNumber & q.fname =
    name1 &
            q.sname = name2 & q.dob = dob & q.address1 = addr1 &
            q.address2 = addr2 )
```

on context *PatientGP*.

21.3.2 Outcome

Of the 14 teams, 13 successfully applied the tools and an agile methodology to produce a working solution. Table 21.3 shows the characteristics of the different team solutions. Training time refers to the time needed to learn MBD using UML-RSDS.

Typically the teams divided into subteams, with each subteam given a particular task to develop, so that a degree of parallel development could occur, taking advantage of the independence of the three use cases. Most groups had a defined leader role (this had been advised in the coursework description), and the lack of a leader generally resulted in a poor outcome (as in teams 1, 4, 9, 12, 14).

The key difficulties encountered by most teams were:

■ Lack of prior experience in using UML.

■ The unfamiliar style of UML-RSDS compared to tools such as Visual Studio, Net Beans and other IDEs.

■ Conceptual difficulty with the idea of MBD.

Table 21.3: Outcomes of EHR case study

Team	Training time	Problems, issues	Technical outcome	Agile process	Activities, issues in agile process
1	> 1 week	Usability problems	8/10	8/10	Disorganised and individual working
2	1 week	None	9/10	8/10	No experience of large teams
3	> 1 week	Lack of tool documentation	8/10	9/10	Used pair modelling, proactive time planning
4	1 week	Inadequate requirements	7/10	8/10	No leader. Parallel working
5	1 week	Usability problems	9/10	8/10	Lead developers
6	1 week	Used model refactoring	8/10	9/10	Used Scrum, sub-team modelling
7	1 week	Started modelling without sufficient tool knowledge	8/10	9/10	Risk analysis, paired modelling
8	1 week	Lead developers trained team	9/10	9/10	Small team modelling
9	> 1 week	Specification difficulties	7/10	7/10	No leader, disorganised
10	1 week	Lead developers trained team	8/10	8/10	Detailed planning, scheduling
11	1 week	Unfamiliar style of tool	9/10	9/10	Used XP
12	> 1 week	Lacked UML knowledge	7/10	5/10	Team split into 2
13	2 weeks	Difficulties using MBD/tools	8/10	8/10	Strong leadership
14	2 weeks	–	0/10	0/10	Failed to work as a team

■ Inadequate user documentation for the tools – in particular students struggled to understand how the tools were supposed to be used, and the connection between the specifications written in the tool and the code produced.

■ Team management and communication problems due to the size of the teams and variation in skill levels and commitment within a team.

Nonetheless, in 12 of 14 cases the student teams overcame these problems. Two teams (12 and 14) had severe management problems, resulting in failure in the case of team 14.

Particular issues can be seen in the following quotes from the team reports:

> "As with all software there was a learning curve involved in its use, and once we had progressed along this curve and gained some familiarity we found that the software was much easier to use, and every increase in our fluency with the software empowered us to produce higher quality solutions with increasing ease." (Team 8)

> "We found however, that becoming more familiar with UML-RSDS was more of a priority in order to be able to solve further tasks, as it is quite different to anything we had used before." (Team 10)

> "Many group members did not know UML and had to learn it." (Team 12)

The teams were almost unanimous in identifying that they should have committed more time at the start of the project to understand the tools and the MBD approach. This is a case where the agile principle of starting development as soon as possible needs to be tempered by the need for adequate understanding of a new tool and development technique.

Although all students had just attended 8 weeks of an introductory course on UML, some teams had problems with members who had not yet understood UML, which is fundamental to applying MBD with UML-RSDS.

Factors which seemed particularly important in overcoming problems with UML-RSDS and MBD were:

■ The use of 'lead developers': a few team members who take the lead in mastering the tool/MBD concepts and who then train their colleagues. This spreads knowledge faster and more effectively than all team individuals trying to learn the material independently. Teams that used this approach had a low training time of 1 week, and achieved an average technical score of 8.66, versus 7.18 for other teams. This difference is statistically significant at the 4% level (removing team 14 from the data).

■ Pair-based or small team modelling, with subteams of 2 to 4 people working around one machine. This seems to help to identify errors in modelling which individual developers may make, and additionally, if there is a lead developer in each sub-team, to propagate tool and MBD expertise. Teams using this approach achieved an average technical score of 8.25, compared to 7.2 for other teams. This difference is however not statistically significant if team 14 is excluded.

Teams using both approaches achieved an average technical score of 9, compared to those using just one (8.2) or none (6.9).

Another good practice was the use of model refactoring to improve an initial solution with too complex or too finely-divided use cases into a solution with more appropriate use cases.

The impact of poor team management and the lack of a defined process seems more significant for the outcome of a team, compared to technical problems. The Pearson correlation coefficient of the management/process mark of the project teams with their overall mark is 0.91, suggesting a strong positive relation between team management quality and overall project quality. Groups with a well-defined process and team organisation were able to overcome technical problems more effectively than those with poor management. Groups 3, 5, 7, 11 and 13 are the instances of the first category, and these groups achieved an average of 8.4/10 in the technical score, whilst groups 1, 4, 9, 12 and 14 are the instances of the second category, and these groups achieved an average of 5.8/10 in the technical score. An agile process seems to be helpful in achieving a good technical outcome: the correlation of the agile process and technical outcome scores in Table 21.3 is 0.93.

The outcomes of this case study were better than for the first case study: the average mark was 79% in case study 2, compared to 67.5% for case study 1. This appears to be due to three main factors: (i) a simpler case study involving reduced domain research and technical requirements compared to case study 1; (ii) improvements to the UML-RSDS tools; (iii) stronger advice to follow an agile development approach.

In conclusion, this case study illustrated the problems which may occur when industrial development teams are introduced to MBD and MBD tools for the first time. The positive conclusions which can be drawn are that UML-RSDS appears to be an approach which quite inexperienced developers can use successfully for a range of tasks, even with limited access to tool experts, and that the difficulties involved in learning the tools and development approach are not significantly greater than those that could be encountered with any new SE environment or tools.

21.4 Case study 3: Financial risk evaluation

This case study concerns the risk evaluation of multiple-share financial investments known as *Collateralized Debt Obligations* (CDO), where a portfolio of investments is partitioned into a collection of sectors, and there is the possibility of contagion of defaults between different companies in the same sector [2, 16]. Risk analysis of a CDO contract involves computing the overall probability $P(S = s)$ of a financial loss s based upon the probability of individual company defaults and the probability of default infection within sectors.

The loss estimation function $P(S = s)$ and risk estimation function $P(S \geq s)$ are required. The case study was carried out in conjunction with a financial risk analyst, who was also the customer of the development. Implementations in Java, C# and C++ were required. The required use cases and subtasks are given in Table 21.4. Use case 3 depends upon use case 2.

Table 21.4: Use cases for CDO risk analysis application

Use case	Subtasks	Description
1. Load data		Read sector data from a .csv spreadsheet
2. Calculate Poisson approximation of loss function	2a Calculate probability of no contagion	
	2b. Calculate probability of contagion	
	2c. Combine 2a, 2b	
3. Calculate risk function		
4. Write data		Write data from 2 or 3 to a .csv spreadsheet

First a phase of research was needed to understand the problem and to clarify the actual computations required. Then tasks 2a, 2b and 2c were carried out in a first development iteration, as these were considered more critical than use cases 1 or 4. Then use case 3 was performed in development iteration 2, and finally use cases 1 and 4 – which both involved use of manual coding – were scheduled to be completed in a third development iteration. A further external requirement was introduced prior to this iteration: to handle the case of cross-sector contagion. This requirement was then scheduled prior to tasks 1 and 4 in a new iteration.

Figure 21.6 shows the system specification of the solution produced at the end of the first development iteration. L is the credit loss per default, in each sector. p is the probability of each default in the sector,

q is the probability of infection in the sector, and n is the number of companies in the sector. mu is the Poisson approximation parameter. $test$ is the prototype version of use case 2.

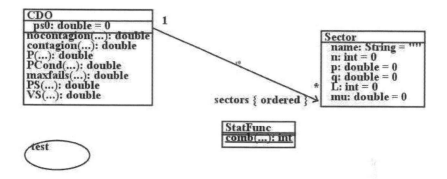

Figure 21.6: CDO version 1 system specification

The following model-based agile development techniques were employed:

■ Refactoring: the solutions of 2a and 2b were initially expressed as operations *nocontagion*, *contagion* of the CDO class (Fig. 21.6). It was then realised that they would be simpler and more efficient if defined as Sector operations. The refactoring Move Operation was used. This refactoring did not affect the external interface of the system.

■ Customer collaboration in development: the risk analyst gave detailed feedback on the generated code as it was produced, and carried out their own tests using data such as the realistic dataset of [16].

■ Replanning and revision of the release plan due to new requirements: the scheduled third iteration was postponed due to a new more urgent requirement being introduced.

■ Creation of a library component (*StatFunc*) for potentially reusable general functionalities.

Figure 21.7 shows the refactored system specification.

It was originally intended to use external hand-coded and optimised implementations of critical functions such as the combinatorial function $comb(int\ n, int\ m)$. However this would have resulted in the need for multiple versions of these functions to be coded, one for each target implementation language, and would also increase the time needed

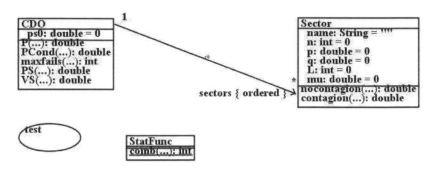

Figure 21.7: CDO version 2 system specification

for system integration. It was found instead that platform-independent specifications could be given in UML-RSDS which were of acceptable efficiency.

The initial efficiency of the loss computation was too low, with calculation of $P(S = s)$ for all values of $s \leq 20$ on the test data of [16] taking over 2 minutes on a standard Windows 7 laptop. To address this problem, the recursive operations and other operations with high usage were given the stereotype ≪ *cached* ≫ to avoid unnecessary recomputation. This stereotype means that operations are implemented using the *memoisation* technique of [17] to store previously-computed results. Table 21.5 shows the improvements in efficiency which this provides, and the results for generated code in other language versions.

Table 21.5: Execution times for CDO versions

Version	Execution time for first 20 $P(S = s)$ calls	Execution time for first 50 $P(S = s)$ calls
Unoptimised Java	121s	–
Optimised Java	32ms	93ms
C#	10ms	20ms
C++	62ms	100ms

The specification of use case 2 has the following postconditions:

```
CDO::
  s : sectors  =>  s.mu = 1 - ( ( 1 - s.p )->pow(s.n) )

CDO::
  ps0 = -sectors.mu.sum->exp()

CDO::
```

```
Integer.subrange(0,20)->forAll( s | PS(s)->display() )
```

The first constraint initialises the *mu* attribute value for each sector. The second then initialises *ps0* using these values. The third constraint calculates and displays $PS(s)$ for integer values s from 0 to 20. The operation $PS(s)$ computes the Poisson approximation of the loss function, and is itself decomposed into computations of losses based on the possible combinations of failures in individual companies. $P(k, m)$ is the probability of m defaults in sector k, $PCond(k, m)$ is the conditional probability of m defaults in sector k, given that there is at least one default:

```
CDO::
query P(k : int, m : int) : double
pre: true
post:
   result = StatFunc.comb(sectors[k].n,m) *
      ( sectors[k].nocontagion(m) + Integer.Sum(1,m - 1,i,sectors[k].
      contagion(i,m)) )
```

```
CDO::
query PCond(k : int, m : int) : double
pre: true
post:
   ( m >= 1 =>
      result = P(k,m) / ( 1 - ( ( 1 - sectors[k].p )->pow
      (sectors[k].n) ) ) ) &
   ( m < 1 => result = 0 )
```

The operation definitions are directly based upon the mathematical specifications of [16]. *Integer.Sum*(a, b, i, e) represents the mathematical sum $\Sigma_{i=a}^{b} e$.

maxfails(k, s) is the maximum number of defaults in sector k which can contribute to a total loss amount s. $PS(s)$ sums over the sectors the loss function $VS(k, s)$, which sums the probability-weighted loss amounts resulting from each of the possible non-zero numbers of defaults in sector k.

```
CDO::
query  maxfails(k : int, s : int) : int
pre: true
post:
   ( sectors[k].n <= ( s / sectors[k].L ) => result = sectors[k].n ) &
   ( sectors[k].n > ( s / sectors[k].L ) => result = s / sectors[k].L )
```

```
CDO::
query cached PS(s : int) : double
pre: true
post:
```

```
( s < 0 => result = 0 ) &
( s = 0 => result = ps0 ) &
( s > 0 => result = Integer.Sum(1,sectors.size,k,VS(k,s)) / s )

CDO::
query VS(k : int, s : int) : double
pre: true
post:
  result = Integer.Sum(1,maxfails(k,s),mk,
      ( sectors[k].mu * mk * sectors[k].L * PCond(k,mk) * PS(s - mk *
      sectors[k].L) ))
```

PS depends upon *VS*, which in turn depends upon *PS*. This mutual recursion in the definition of the *PS* operation is a strong indicator that optimisation using caching/memoisation is necessary for *PS*.

The following functions of *Sector* implement tasks 2a and 2b:

```
Sector::
query cached nocontagion(m : int) : double
pre: true
post:
  result = ( ( 1 - p )->pow(n - m) ) * ( p->pow(m) ) * ( ( 1 - q )
  ->pow(m * ( n - m )) )

Sector::
query contagion(i : int, m : int): double
pre : true
post:
  result = ( ( 1 - p )->pow(n - i) ) * ( p->pow(i) ) *
      ( ( 1 - q )->pow(i * ( n - m )) ) * ( ( 1 - ( ( 1 - q )
      ->pow(i) ) )->pow(m - i) ) *
      StatFunc.comb(m,i)
```

Finally, the combinatorial operator $comb(n, m)$ is defined in the utility class *StatFunc*:

```
StatFunc::
query static cached comb(n : int, m : int) : int
pre: n >= m & m >= 0 & n <= 25
post:
  ( n - m < m => result = Integer.Prd(m + 1,n,i,i) / Integer.
  Prd(1,n - m,j,j) ) &
  ( n - m >= m => result = Integer.Prd(n - m + 1,n,i,i) / Integer.
  Prd(1,m,j,j) )
```

This is also cached because it is called very frequently during the computation of *PS*.

The risk calculation function for task 3 is:

```
PLim(v : int) : double
```

```
pre: true
post:
    (v < 0   =>   result = 0) &
    (v >= 0  =>   result = 1 - Integer.Sum(0,v-1,k, PS(k)))
```

The new requirement to handle cross-sector contagion entails a revision to the system class diagram: it is necessary to represent companies (borrowers) which have a presence in several sectors, with a degree of weighting in each sector: the loss amount per sector is a weighted average of the loss due to each borrower (company in the sector):

$$L = sectorborrowers \rightarrow collect(omega * L) \rightarrow sum() \rightarrow round()$$

where *omega* is the weighting factor of the company in the sector. The functionality for tasks 2 and 3 also need to consider this case. Analysis of the requirement identifies that the class diagram should be extended as shown in Fig. 21.8. In addition, the existing versions of computations can be retained, with the loss per sector calculated prior to these computations using the constraint:

> *Sector* ::
> $L = sectorborrowers \rightarrow collect(borrower.L * omega * theta) \rightarrow$
> $sum() \rightarrow round()$

where *theta* is the fraction of the company participating in this sector.

A preliminary use case, *deriveSectorLoss* computes *Sector::L* from the provided *Borrower::L* and *BorrowerInSector::omega*, *Borrower In Sector::theta* values, using the above constraint. A further extension could calculate in a similar way the sector probability of default *p* from the individual probabilities of default of companies in the sector.

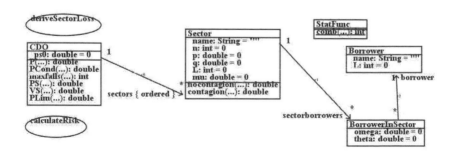

Figure 21.8: CDO version 3 system specification

Our experiences on this case study illustrate the UML-RSDS principles:

- Optimisation and refactoring should be carried out at the specification level in a platform-independent manner where possible, not at the code level.

- The scope of MBD should be extended as far as possible across the system development, reducing the extent of manual coding and integration wherever possible.

In conclusion, this case study showed that a successful outcome is possible for agile MBD in the highly demanding domain of computationally-intensive financial applications. A generic MBD tool, UML-RSDS, was able to produce code of comparable efficiency to existing hand-coded and highly optimised solutions.

21.5 Published case studies

Further examples of the application of UML-RSDS may be found in these publications:

- Migration transformations: UML version 1.4 to version 2.2 migration [9]; GMF migration [11].

- Refinement/enhancement transformations: Large-scale data analysis [15]; graph analysis [10]; UML to relational database [12].

- Refactoring transformations: Class diagram refactoring [7, 14]; State machine refactoring/analysis [8]; Petri-net to statechart mapping [13].

The specifications and executable code of some of these case studies may be found at: `www.dcs.kcl.ac.uk/staff/kcl/uml2web`.

Summary

In this chapter we have described how UML-RSDS can be used to support teaching of UML and MBD. We have also presented several different case studies of UML-RSDS development to illustrate the applications of the approach in education and in industry.

References

[1] K. Beck et al., *Principles behind the Agile Manifesto*, Agile Alliance, 2001. http://agilemanifesto.org/principles

[2] M. Davis and V. Lo, *Infectious Defaults*, Quantitative Finance, Vol. 1, No. 4, pp. 382–387, 2001.

[3] EGL, www.eclipse.org/epsilon/doc/egl, 2014.

[4] M. Fowler, K. Beck, J. Brant, W. Opdyke and D. Roberts, *Refactoring: improving the design of existing code*, Addison-Wesley, 1999.

[5] G. Guta, W. Schreiner and D. Draheim, *A lightweight MDSD process applied in small projects*, Proceedings 35th Euromicro conference on Software Engineering and Advanced Applications, IEEE, 2009.

[6] S. Hansson, Y. Zhao and H. Burden, *How MAD are we?: Empirical evidence for model-driven agile development*, 2014.

[7] S. Kolahdouz-Rahimi, K. Lano, S. Pillay, J. Troya and P. Van Gorp, *Evaluation of model transformation approaches for model refactoring*, Science of Computer Programming, 2013, http://dx.doi.org/10.1016/j.scico.2013.07.013.

[8] K. Lano and S. Kolahdouz-Rahimi, *Slicing of UML models using Model Transformations*, MODELS 2010, LNCS vol. 6395, pp. 228–242, 2010.

[9] K. Lano and S. Kolahdouz-Rahimi, *Migration case study using UML-RSDS*, TTC 2010, Malaga, Spain, July 2010. http://is.ieis.tue.nl/staff/pvgorp/events/TTC2010/submissions/final/uml-rsds.pdf.

[10] K. Lano and S. Kolahdouz-Rahimi, *Specification of the "Hello World" case study*, TTC 2011.

[11] K. Lano and S. Kolahdouz-Rahimi, *Solving the TTC 2011 migration case study with UML-RSDS*, TTC 2011, EPTCS vol. 74, pp. 36–41, 2011.

[12] K. Lano and S. Kolahdouz-Rahimi, *Constraint-based specification of Model Transformations*, Journal of Systems and Software, vol. 86, issue 2, February 2013, pp. 412–436.

[13] K. Lano, S. Kolahdouz-Rahimi and K. Maroukian, *Solving the Petri-Nets to Statecharts Transformation Case with UML-RSDS*, TTC 2013, EPTCS, 2013.

[14] K. Lano and S. Kolahdouz-Rahimi, *Case study: Class diagram restructuring*, www.planet-sl.org/community/_/ttc/ttc2013/cases/ClassDiagramRestructuring, 2013.

[15] K. Lano and S. Yassipour-Tehrani, *Solving the Movie Database Case with UML-RSDS*, TTC 2014.

[16] O. Hammarlid, *Aggregating sectors in the infectious defaults model*, Quantitative Finance, vol. 4, no. 1, pp. 64–69, 2004.

[17] D. Michie, *Memo functions and machine learning*, Nature, vol. 218, pp. 19–22, 1968.

[18] M.B. Nakicenovic, *An Agile Driven Architecture Modernization to a Model-Driven Development Solution*, International Journal on Advances in Software, vol. 5, nos. 3, 4, pp. 308–322, 2012.

Appendix A

UML-RSDS Syntax

A.1 OCL expression syntax

UML-RSDS uses both classical set theory expressions and OCL. It only uses sets and sequences, and not bags or ordered sets, unlike OCL. Symmetric binary operators such as $\cup$ and $\cap$ can be written in the classical style, rather than as operators on collections. Likewise for the binary logical operators. There are no null or undefined elements. Table A.1 shows the BNF concrete grammar of UML-RSDS OCL.

A < *unary_operator* > is one of: *any*, *size*, *isDeleted*, *display*, *min*, *max*, *sum*, *prd*, *sort*, *asSet*, *asSequence*, *sqrt*, *sqr*, *last*, *first*, *front*, *tail*, *closure*, *characters*, *subcollections*, *reverse*, *isEmpty*, *notEmpty*, *toUpperCase*, *toLowerCase*, *isInteger*, *isReal*, *toInteger*, *toReal*. The mathematical functions *ceil*, *round*, *floor*, *exp*, etc., can also be written as unary expressions, which is convenient if their argument is a function call or a complex bracketed expression.

Other unary and binary operators may be used in a *factor2_expression*, as described in Tables 4.3, 4.4, 4.5, 4.6 and 4.7. Other binary operators are *includes*, *including*, *excludes*, *excluding*, *union*, *intersection*, *selectMaximals*, *selectMinimals*, *includesAll*, *excludesAll*, *append*, *prepend*, *count*, *hasPrefix*, *hasSuffix*, *indexOf*, *sortedBy*. *oclIsKindOf* and *oclAsType* are unusual because the second argument is the name of a UML-RSDS type such as *int*, an entity class name, or *Set* or *Sequence*. Ternary operators are expressed as operation calls, e.g., *s.subrange*(i,j), *s.insertAt*(i,x). Likewise for the operators *Integer.Sum*(a,b,i,e) and *Integer.Prd*(a,b,i,e).

Table A.1: BNF grammar of UML-RSDS OCL

$<$ *expression* $>$	::=	$<$ *bracketed_expression* $>$ | $<$ *equality_expression* $>$ | $<$ *logical_expression* $>$ | $<$ *factor_expression* $>$
$<$ *bracketed_expression* $>$	::=	"(" $<$ *expression* $>$ ")"
$<$ *logical_expression* $>$	::=	$<$ *expression* $>$ $<$ *logical_op* $>$ $<$ *expression* $>$
$<$ *equality_expression* $>$	::=	$<$ *factor_expression* $>$ $<$ *equality_op* $>$ $<$ *factor_expression* $>$
$<$ *factor_expression* $>$	::=	$<$ *basic_expression* $>$ $<$ *factor_op* $>$ $<$ *factor_expression* $>$ | $<$ *factor2_expression* $>$
$<$ *factor2_expression* $>$	::=	$<$ *expression* $>$ "->" $<$ *unary_operator* $>$ "()" | $<$ *expression* $>$ "->exists(" $<$ *identifier* $>$ "|" $<$ *expression* $>$ ")" | $<$ *expression* $>$ "->exists1(" $<$ *identifier* $>$ "|" $<$ *expression* $>$ ")" | $<$ *expression* $>$ "->forAll(" $<$ *identifier* $>$ "|" $<$ *expression* $>$ ")" | $<$ *expression* $>$ "->exists(" $<$ *expression* $>$ ")" | $<$ *expression* $>$ "->exists1(" $<$ *expression* $>$ ")" | $<$ *expression* $>$ "->forAll(" $<$ *expression* $>$ ")" | $<$ *expression* $>$ "->select(" $<$ *expression* $>$ ")" | $<$ *expression* $>$ "->select(" $<$ *identifier* $>$ "|" $<$ *expression* $>$ ")" | $<$ *expression* $>$ "->reject(" $<$ *expression* $>$ ")" | $<$ *expression* $>$ "->reject(" $<$ *identifier* $>$ "|" $<$ *expression* $>$ ")" | $<$ *expression* $>$ "->collect(" $<$ *expression* $>$ ")" | $<$ *expression* $>$ "->collect(" $<$ *identifier* $>$ "|" $<$ *expression* $>$ ")" | $<$ *expression* $>$ "->unionAll(" $<$ *expression* $>$ ")" | $<$ *expression* $>$ "->intersectAll(" $<$ *expression* $>$ ")" | $<$ *expression* $>$ "->" $<$ *binary_operator* $>$ "(" $<$ *expression* $>$ ")" | $<$ *basic_expression* $>$
$<$ *basic_expression* $>$	::=	$<$ *set_expression* $>$ | $<$ *sequence_expression* $>$ | $<$ *call_expression* $>$ | $<$ *array_expression* $>$ | $<$ *identifier* $>$ | $<$ *value* $>$
$<$ *set_expression* $>$	::=	"Set{" $<$ *fe_sequence* $>$ "}"
$<$ *sequence_expression* $>$	::=	"Sequence{" $<$ *fe_sequence* $>$ "}"
$<$ *call_expression* $>$	::=	$<$ *identifier* $>$ "(" $<$ *fe_sequence* $>$ ")"
$<$ *array_expression* $>$	::=	$<$ *identifier* $>$ "[" $<$ *factor_expression* $>$ "]" | $<$ *identifier* $>$ "[" $<$ *factor_expression* $>$ "]." | $<$ *identifier* $>$

A *logical_op* is one of =>, &, or. An *equality_op* is one of =, / =, >, <, <: (subset-or-equal), <=, >=, :, / : (not-in). A *factor_op* is one of +, /, *, −, \/ (union), ⌢ (concatenation of sequences), /\ (intersection). An *fe_sequence* is a comma-separated sequence of factor expressions. Identifiers can contain "." (to denote reference to a feature of an object), but not as the first or last character, and occurrences must be separated by at least one other character. Identifiers can also contain "$". Spaces, underscores, hyphens, or other whitespace characters should not occur within operators or identifiers.

Valid function symbols are the numeric functions such as *sqrt*, *floor*, *abs*, and OCL operators such as *isReal*, *isInteger*, *toReal*, *toInteger*.

Figure A.1 shows the metamodel for UML-RSDS expressions, which defines the abstract syntax of the OCL expression language used in UML-RSDS. *BinaryExpression*, *BasicExpression*, *UnaryExpression* and

CollectionExpression all inherit from *Expression*. Basic expressions have self-associations *arrayIndex* and *objectRef* to link to their array arguments and object reference (if present), corresponding to the concrete syntax *objectRef.data[arrayIndex]* for navigations to sequence elements or navigations of qualified associations.

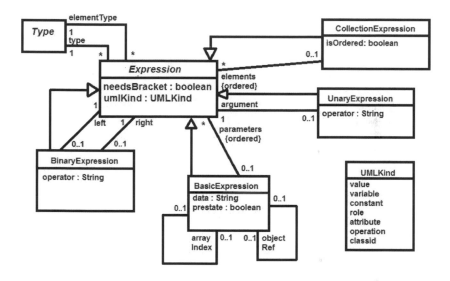

Figure A.1: UML-RSDS constraint language

For example, $x + 5$ is a BinaryExpression with operator $+$, and left and right BasicExpressions x and 5, of kind variable (or role or attribute) and value, respectively. $sq \rightarrow select(f = 5)$ is a BinaryExpression with operator $\rightarrow select$, whilst $E[x.id]$ is a BasicExpression of kind classid (if E is the name of a class), and with *arrayIndex* the BasicExpression $x.id$, whose *objectRef* is x and data is *id*.

Each expression has both a type and an element type. The element type identifies the type of the elements of a set-valued or sequence-valued expression.

A.2 Activity language syntax

Table A.2 shows the concrete syntax used in UML-RSDS to express UML structured activities.

Table A.2: Activity language syntax

< statement >	::=	< loop_statement > | < creation_statement > | < conditional_statement > | < sequence_statement > | < basic_statement >
< loop_statement >	::=	"while" < expression > "do" < statement > | "for" < expression > "do" < statement >
< conditional_statement >	::=	"if" < expression > "then" < statement > "else" < basic_statement >
< sequence_statement >	::=	< statement > ";" < statement >
< creation_statement >	::=	< identifier > ":" < identifier >
< basic_statement >	::=	< basic_expression > ":=" < expression > | "skip" | < identifier > ":" < identifier > ":=" < expression > | "execute" < expression > | "return" < expression > | "(" < statement > ")" | < call_expression >

Spaces are needed around statement keywords and around symbols such as ';' and ')', '(' when entering activities as text. The abstract syntax of UML-RSDS activities is defined by the metamodel of Fig. A.2. Implicit call statements represent calls of expressions as statements: *execute exp*. These have the effect of *stat(exp)*, which must be defined.

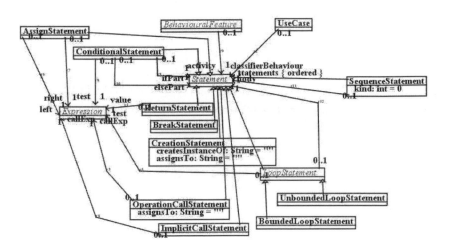

Figure A.2: Statement (activity) metamodel

Appendix B

UML-RSDS tool architecture and components

The UML-RSDS tool architecture is closely based upon the inter-relationships between the different UML languages which are supported by the tool: with OCL expressions as a fundamental notation used by all other UML-RSDS languages (class diagrams, activities, state machines, use cases and interactions), and class diagrams as the central notation which the other visual languages and activities depend upon. Figure B.1 shows the tool architecture of UML-RSDS version 1.5. Arrows indicate dependencies between modules.

Users interact primarily with the tools via the class diagram editor, which also manages the creation, deletion and editing of use cases and activities. Auxiliary editors for state machines and interactions are also provided. The *Class diagram* module is likewise the central functional component, dealing with the management, analysis and transformation of class diagrams. A large part of the UML 2 class diagram language is supported. Figure B.2 shows the supported parts of the UML class diagram metamodel.

The *linkedClass* of an association is the class of an association class. *memberEnd* always has exactly 2 elements in UML-RSDS. A use case is a subclass of *Classifier* but is actually considered as an *Entity*, and has *ownedAttribute*, *ownedOperation* and *constraint* links to its attributes, operations and invariants.

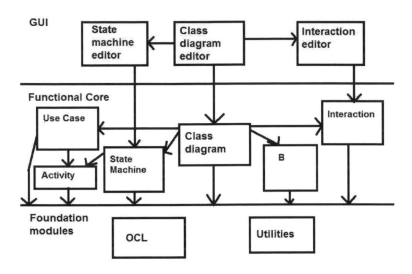

Figure B.1: UML-RSDS tool architecture

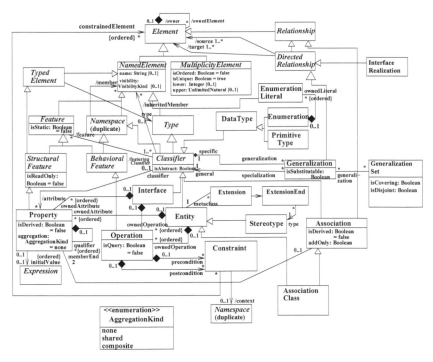

Figure B.2: UML-RSDS class diagram metamodel

Smaller modules deal with state machines, interactions, activities, use cases and the B notation. Finally, the foundational module *OCL* supports the management, analysis and transformation of OCL expressions, and *Utilities* provides general utility classes and operations. The activity language supported by the tools is defined by Fig. A.2. The UML-RSDS tool set is implemented in Java, and the tool classes themselves follow closely the structure of the UML metamodels, in order to facilitate reflexive use of the tools. Some example classes from each module are as follows:

Class diagram editor: UmlTool.java, UCDArea.java, LineData.java

State machine editor: StateWin.java, StatechartArea.java

Interaction editor: InteractionWin.java, InteractionArea.java

Class diagram: ModelElement.java, Entity.java, Association.java, Attribute.java, Generalisation.java, Type.java, BehaviouralFeature.java, Behaviour.java

State Machine: Statemachine.java, State.java, Transition.java, Event.java, StatemachineSlice.java

Use Case: UseCase.java, Extend.java, Include.java

Activity: Statement.java, AssignStatement.java, IfStatement.java

Interaction: InteractionElement.java, LifelineState.java, ExecutionInstance.java, Message.java

B: BComponent.java, BOp.java, BExpression.java

OCL: Expression.java, Constraint.java, BinaryExpression.java, BasicExpression.java, SetExpression.java, UnaryExpression.java

Utilities: Compiler.java, Compiler2.java, VectorUtil.java

Approximately 5000 person hours of development effort have been spent on the tools, about 50% of this on testing and verification.

Appendix C

Key principles of UML-RSDS

We summarise here the central principles of specification and development using UML-RSDS.

The specification is *the system.*

A logical constraint P can be interpreted both as a specification of system behaviour, and as a description of how P will be established in the system implementation.

These mean that a declarative high-level specification can be used for multiple purposes: (i) to express system functionality in a concise form, independent of code; (ii) to support verification at the specification level; (iii) as input for design and code synthesis to produce implementations in multiple target languages, which satisfy the specification by construction.

A post-condition constraint P means "Make P true" when interpreted as a specification of system behaviour.

Post-conditions of operations and of use cases can be interpreted in this way.

In particular, for use cases:

If a use case uc has post-conditions C_1 to C_n which are all of type 1, satisfy syntactic non-interference, confluence and

> *definedness and determinacy conditions, then the implementation code stat(C_1); ...; stat(C_n) of uc is terminating, confluent and correct with respect to its specification. That is, this code establishes the conjunction C_1 & ... & C_n.*

> *Improve the efficiency of a system at the specification level where possible, whilst keeping a clear and platform-independent specification style.*

Because a specification has a dual purpose as a description aimed at human readers, and as an input for automated code generation, it must both be clear and concise, and should avoid computationally inefficient formulations such as the use of duplicated complex expressions.

As for other software systems, patterns can provide systematic solutions for specification and design problems. In UML-RSDS patterns can be applied at the specification level, instead of design or code levels:

> *Use specification patterns where possible to improve the clarity, compositionality and efficiency of UML-RSDS systems.*

> *Model transformations can be specified as use cases, with use case post-conditions expressing the transformation rules.*

A large number of different MT languages exist, but we consider that it is preferable in the long term for transformations to be specified in a single standard language (UML) where possible, making use of the same facilities available for the specification, verification, design and implementation of general software systems. After careful consideration of alternative representations, we came to the conclusion that use cases, with a formalised specification of their behaviour, were the most suitable UML element to serve as descriptions of system functionalities and services, including model transformations.

For transformations, we have the principle:

> *Define rules which express the required behaviour in the simplest and clearest form possible.*

Regarding reuse of components, there is the principle:

> *When a functionality or set of related functionalities have been developed, and which seem to be of potential utility in other systems, make a reusable component consisting of these functionalities as use cases, supported by the local data. This component can be an externalApp in other UML-RSDS systems.*

For agile development, we have the principles:

Models as code: A UML-RSDS specification is both the documentation of a system and a description of its implementation.

UML-RSDS specifications should be used to support communication and collaboration between developers and stakeholders.

Principles which apply to the development process using UML-RSDS are:

Optimisation and refactoring should be carried out at the specification level in a platform-independent manner where possible, not at the code level.

The scope of MBD should be extended as far as possible across the system development, reducing the extent of manual coding and integration wherever possible.

Index